'Picking up where I left off with the Cutsforths in Cuzance, I was immediately whisked back to rural France and life in a small village. What a blissful read! In this second book, Cutsforth has perfected her ability to evoke the smells, tastes and simple pleasures of her "other" life in France. There is certainly plenty of hard work to balance it out as the couple renovate their investment — but what lingers is the sense of enjoyment and wonder.'

'Susan gives us an amazing glimpse of small town country life and wonderful sense of the personal histories of the town. The little snippets of small town gossip are utterly charming. From more dramas with the plumbing, hidden rodents that you can only hear (and I would pretend they weren't there as well) to the food ... food and more food.

'One cannot help but fall in love with the friends Susan makes and the neighbours who offer such kindness and hospitality to this Australian couple who have landed in their midst. Anyone reading this book will be inspired to dream and to follow their dreams. Not to mention being inspired to immerse oneself into the richness of a small French village. This book is charming!'

'I was enchanted by the fascinating insights into life in a small French village. Meeting up with the "cast of characters" again was like meeting up with old friends. There are heartfelt, poignant moments; there are evocative accounts of the French way of life; there is humour, but most of all, there is a strong sense of joining the writer and her husband as they tackle a project that most could not conceive of.'

Published by Melbourne Books
Level 9, 100 Collins Street,
Melbourne, VIC 3000
Australia
www.melbournebooks.com.au
info@melbournebooks.com.au

Copyright ©Susan Cutsforth 2013
All rights reserved. No part of this publication may be reproduced,
stored in a retrieval system, or transmitted in any form or
any means electronic, mechanical, photocopying, recording or
otherwise without the prior permission of the publishers.

Author: Cutsforth, Susan.
Title: Our House is Certainly Not in Paris.
ISBN: 9781922129482 (paperback)
Subjects: Cutsforth, Susan.
Cutsforth, Stuart.
Families--Australia--Biography.
Families--Travel--France--Cuzance.
Vacation homes--France--Cuzance.
Buildings--Repair and reconstruction--France--Cuzance.
Dewey Number: 306.85092

Book 1: Our House is Not in Paris (December 2012)
Book 2: Our House is Certainly Not in Paris (October 2014)

Our House is Certainly Not in Paris

Susan Cutsforth

M
MELBOURNE BOOKS

The Third Year in Le Lot

Pied de la Croix

'Set wide the window. Let me drink the day.'
— Edith Wharton

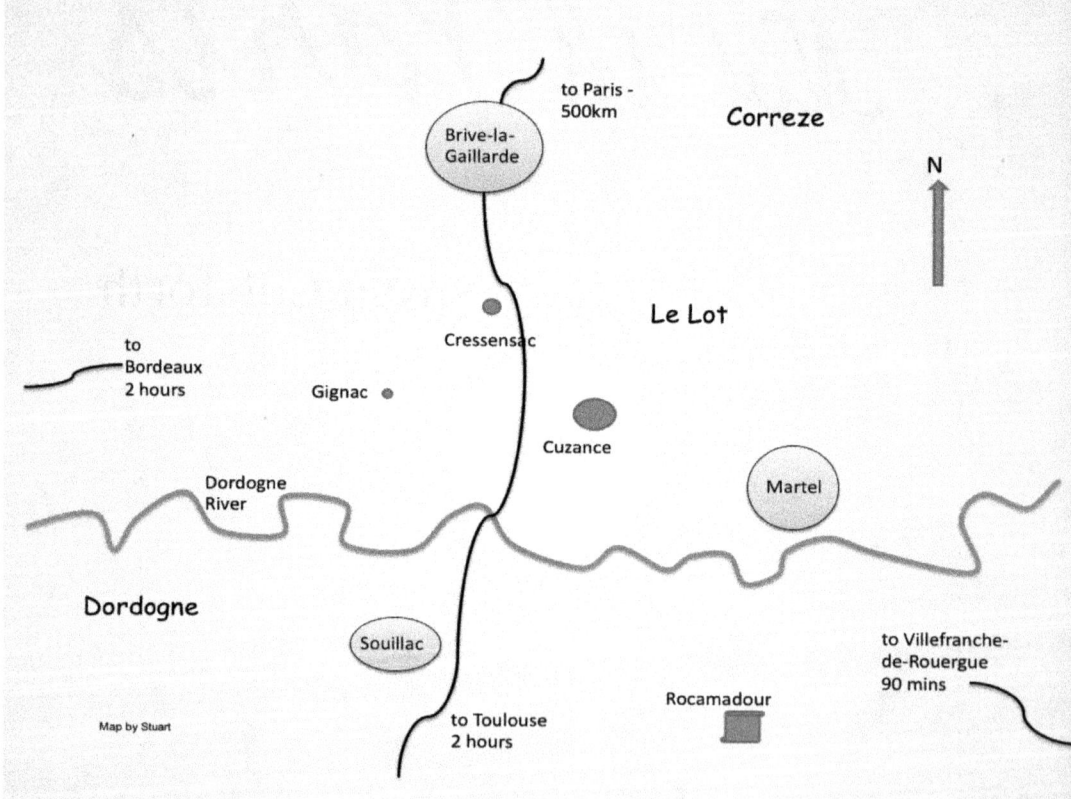

A glossary can be found at the end of this memoir

Prologue

Bonjour Pied de la Croix

This is our continuing story about renovating our petite maison in le Lot in south-west France. It traces the gentle unfolding of the days in the French countryside, for after the first two years on frenetic working vacances, when beaucoup travail — sheer hard work — was the order of the day, life has at last taken on a slightly slower rhythm in our petite village, Cuzance. We meet again our cast of French friends and make some new amis. Our efforts turn from restoring Pied de la Croix, to a sustained onslaught on the rambling, rustique jardin. Weeks are consumed by the madness of crazy paving while rare days of relaxation are overlaid by the somnolence of a French summer. The past and present merge as life in a rural village resonates with the braying of donkeys, the squealing of pigs and the daily promenade of villagers, some nearing a century, who have spent their entire life in Cuzance, witnesses to war and the rapid changes of the years.

As our return to Cuzance rushes towards us, I always have a vivid picture in my mind of our much-anticipated arrival. Despite the weariness of travel, and eagerness to rush inside to embrace our *petite maison*, I always pause on the threshold, to prolong my reunion with our beloved

French home. I glance up above the door, to see the date — 1882 — encased in a stone-carved heart. The simply etched heart is a symbol of all that our beloved French home means to us: our love of France, and this year, the eve of the celebration of our wedding in Istanbul, twenty-one years ago. The little heart represents all that is warm and loving within the walls of Pied de la Croix. There is no way possible that the truffle farmers who once lived here could have ever imagined that, one day, Australians from afar would reunite each year with their old farmhouse.

Finally, after just a couple of years, our hearts changed from sinking to soaring at our first sight of Pied de la Croix on our return. At last, the reunion with our little stone house was all that it should be. This year, there was no flapping tarpaulin covering the naked beams of the barn, no dead pigeon on the doorstep to greet us, and the grass was all beautifully mown. Inside, it was like a scene from a film: dust covers shrouding everything, ready to be whisked off and let life once again be breathed into our *petite maison* and begin another summer chapter in Cuzance. Once again, despite the inherent history of living in 100-year-old terraces in Sydney, this little house has a presence, a warmth — a strong beating heart that reaches out to enfold us.

What I especially love about our *petite maison* is that it never gives off an air of sad neglect when we arrive and unlock the door. It never feels reproachful or abandoned. Instead, it has just been simply hibernating, waiting to wake up and share our happiness at being in France again.

Before we return for our third year, Gérard and Dominique Murat, the new friends we made last year from the village, again share the unfolding seasons with us. This time we are joyous when we open their email photos to see the soft pink blossoms of our orchard in bloom. Just like the enchanting photos of Pied de la Croix wrapped in sparkling white, pristine snow that they had sent the previous Christmas, it is a season that we will probably never see ourselves. This time it is a season of renewal and, to my astonishment and delight, the lush grass beneath the budding apricots and pears, is already starting to resemble a meadow. It is less than a year since it has started to be regularly mown and yet the transformation is already well underway. Another source of pleasure and relief. Jean-Claude Chanel, the first friend we made in our village, tells us in March, before their return to Cuzance, that it is getting warmer at last in Lyon. Nevertheless, a farmer friend in Cuzance has told him that it still freezes there in the early morning. Finally though people are now taking off their coats and layers of clothes after a long, harsh winter, so now in the streets of Lyon you can see their heads and faces. I love the images that I share from afar of the changing seasons.

While it is our third summer in Cuzance, it is in fact only the second year that we have gone directly to our *petite maison* and yet it feels much longer. There is definitely a sense of true homecoming. Once again, it feels extraordinary to feel such a strong tug on the heart and such a palpable connection with a place, which in fact, we have only known such a short time. I think a sense of place and belonging is in the heart, as well as the bricks and mortar of Pied de la Croix. Yet this sense of belonging is baffling at times, for I can still barely speak a word of French.

I am determined at the outset of our third stay in our *petite maison*, that this time will not be a litany of lists. I am determined that our stay of a glorious two months will not be an endless account of days consumed by renovating. As I find myself getting older, I find myself slowing down. I find myself with an ever-growing desire not to spend my holiday working through the light-filled, long French summer days. I want to spend more time relaxing in the convivial company of our French friends, I want to explore the Lot more fully, I want to simply soak up the ambience and the pleasure of a summer spent in France. Time will tell.

In many ways, it is like returning to two homes. When we gather each year for the first time, on Jean-Claude and Françoise's terrace for an *apéritif*, and gaze at their glorious *jardin*, there is also a real sense of homecoming. Both Jean-Claude and Françoise will soon turn seventy, so we toast their forthcoming *anniversaire* and celebrate serendipitous friendship. We soak up the warmth, both of the summer evening and renewed camaraderie. And so, we are back again in our beloved Cuzance.

* * *

Some of you may be just joining us on our French adventure, so here's how it all started. For those of you continuing to share our Cuzance story, I hope you enjoy being reunited with our *petite maison*, Pied de la Croix, so named for the 'foot of the cross' in our village, and coincidentally, also the name of the previous owners of our French farmhouse.

Not many people in Australia can say they live in a village. Nor are many fortunate enough to own *une petite maison* on the other side of the world. Owning a farmhouse in France is the stuff dreams are made of. Well, most of the time.

Stuart and I live in a small town, Wombarra — one in a string of tiny towns dotted along the coastline of southern NSW. It is perched between the escarpment and the sea, and every day we see the ocean in all its wild and varying moods.

At night, there are often huge oil tankers on the horizon — their glistening lights like small islands — and trains flash across the bottom of the escarpment, their carriages shining like a string of jewels as they carry tired workers home from Sydney. We live in a coastal paradise.

But despite the peace and rugged beauty that surrounds us, there is a lure that grows stronger every year, taking us across the ocean to a place far removed.

For years, owning a house in France fell into the category of idle fantasy. But in 2010, the dream drew a little closer to reality when the Australian dollar suddenly soared. Suddenly, it became an affordable reality, and curious internet browsing, segued into booking a plane ticket.

Renovating has been the pattern of our married life, and we felt ready to embark on a project to buy a French farmhouse and bring it back to life — even if it meant working every hour under the sun on our annual *vacances*. And keep in mind, French summers mean very long hours of daylight.

Armed with a shortlist of properties and a strict set of criteria, Stuart left Sydney for France, determined to find our piece of paradise on the other side of the world. I went to school each day and remained anxiously on standby, waiting for news of the unfolding adventure.

Two of our main criteria were that the house was not to be a on a road or near a farm, largely to avoid the invasion of *les mouches* and also because peace and quiet are things we cherish. This was based in fact from my notebook for a future holiday house, after renting one in the Dordogne the previous year. There was no way we could have possibly imagined at the time that it would become, a mere six months later, the template for buying our own *petite maison*.

On our previous trip to France, we had stayed with a friend in the Pyrenees. But our hearts didn't resonate with the harsh landscape and atypical architecture. We felt we were in a foreign land and longed to return to the *département* with which we had both instantly connected — the hamlets, golden stone, towering limestone cliffs and walnut orchards of the Lot.

With just ten day's leave and a real estate agent who couldn't drive (surely the only one in the world!), Stuart traversed icy, treacherous roads to inspect ten houses in seven days. Many options were eliminated at a glance, and others just didn't fit the bill: right in the middle of town, too *grande*, too *petite*, too isolated, too dilapidated. The decision was huge, the responsibility was huge; Stuart had to get it right.

When he found Pied de la Croix in the village of Cuzance, it seemed just right — not too big, not too small, not too run down. It was utterly silent and looked absolutely enchanting, wrapped in a pristine quilt of snow, the pale golden sun of winter dancing on its ancient stone.

So it was, that after a mere two phone conversations, we agreed that Stuart should go ahead and buy our little house. Six months later, I was able to see it for myself. Strangely, it seemed to me at first, despite now having our own *petite maison*, Stuart thought it made sense to rent a house nearby for the first fortnight. It was in fact a much-needed respite from now renovating on both sides of the world. We drove together from nearby Puymule for our first inspection together. The damp and gloomy day echoed my sense of misgiving. The picturesque photos in the snow had not quite captured the renovating reality. A few days later, we were back — to start the sheer hard work with a vengeance.

On our very first morning at Pied de la Croix, we both had a further foreboding sense of, 'What have we done?' Within a few hours, we were discussing whether we should put the house straight back on the market. It was not the idyllic rural farmhouse of our dreams: the traffic was constant and the flies were in abundance. What had happened to our key criteria of peace and quiet?

I was also totally overwhelmed by the amount of renovating required. A picturesque French *maison* it was not, and the land was so overgrown and neglected that we couldn't even walk around the grounds. The reality was so overwhelming that Stuart suggested I should steer clear of venturing upstairs to the attic and seeing it in all its years of neglect.

But we had no choice other than to accept our decision and push on. We had already spent a small fortune and were fully committed to at least turning it around and putting it back on the market in a renovated, desirable state.

Anyone who has ever renovated knows that the sheer hard work involved means that an indelible bond is created. So despite the despair and desperation we felt at times, and the punishing hours of intense hard work, we did fall in love with our now much-loved Pied de la Croix.

For me, it was the act of stripping the wallpaper and discovering the ancient wooden beams that became a feature of our beautiful new *cuisine*. I felt a palpable sense of bonding with our French farmhouse — it seemed to emanate a sense of happiness to have life breathed back into it.

And then there was the joyous discovery that the huge volume of traffic was simply due to a temporary diversion from the *autoroute* to Paris. It was this that cemented our decision to stay.

I often look back and laugh about our first renovating trip. What was I thinking? I seemed to have packed for Parisian *soirées*. Fortunately, a new friend, Marie-France, gave me some blue overalls more suited to the task than anything in my suitcase.

Without a mirror in the house, it wasn't until I saw the photos upon our return to Australia, that I realised the extent of the rips in rather delicate places. No wonder I drew the attention of the parade of *artisans* we had coming through the property.

And then there were the roofers. I sent a postcard to the senior girls at my school, to let them know they hadn't lived until they saw the young French roofers, perched high on the barn, shirtless in the searing summer heat and dancing to music blaring from their radios. As for our elderly neighbours, I observed them each day, their devotion to each other palpable.

People are fascinated by the fact we have a house in the Lot, and often ask about the difficulties or challenges involved. Apart from the fact we can't simply go for a weekend, the only drawback for me is the interminable flight each year. There is, of course, also the matter of my very limited French (where is the time to learn?), but my tendency for the dramatic — and my ability to mime — seems to carry me through.

Bureaucratic matters such as setting up a French bank account have their difficulties, as does finding a gardener that is not *très cher*. But our friends in the village are always willing to help us out, and we have learned to manage things from afar — all via email — such as buying a Renault, installing a pool and arranging for the planting of lavender and shrubs in our *jardin*.

Each time we leave Cuzance, our *petite maison* sleeps quietly behind its wooden shutters. Our French dream is, at times, about questioning the sheer magnitude of such an undertaking. Yet it is more than balanced by the joy of creating another life in France — one we slip into seamlessly each time we return. And so, the adventure, and our other French life, continues.

Oh là là, Technology and Renovating

Eight weeks before leaving, we book our train tickets from Gare d'Austerlitz to Brive-la-Gaillarde. It is always a source of amazement to me that we can print our tickets at home, all the way across the other side of the world. It is at this point each year that the countdown starts to become very real. I triumphantly email Jean-Claude to let him know our arrival time and hope that he will be able to pick us up. Meanwhile, Stuart has also been emailing him to sort out a better mobile phone deal. The year before, as we had not used our mobile throughout the previous twelve-month period, the number had lapsed. This caused huge dramas and dilemmas immediately upon our arrival, when we missed the train by a matter of a few minutes. With the disconnection of our number, we had no way of contacting Jean-Claude to let him know of our late arrival. As with many other French matters, we are determined to make our journey and arrival as smooth as they can possibly be this time.

It is only through the serendipity of our friendships and email communications that we are able to find out many things that would otherwise be virtually impossible. So it is that Jean-Claude had told us about a new *portable* phone deal that he had organised for Françoise rather than the outrageously *très cher* plan she had been on. He and Stuart exchange emails to sort a new SIM card and subsequent new number that will now be our permanent French contact. *Voilà*, another piece of the jigsaw puzzle that is our French life, will soon be in place. Once again, it is *merci beaucoup* to Jean-Claude. However, things do not quite go to plan. As seems to be inevitable, when it comes to us and mobiles, whichever country we are in our attempts to set up a new plan are not only complex but we seem to be thwarted at every turn.

It all started with Jean-Claude letting us know that he had found a fabulous deal with Free. Like Stuart, he too loves to shop around and get the best value for his *euro*. We could only agree that two *euro* a month was an extremely attractive option. All we had to do was let him know our bank account details and he would go ahead and sort it out for us. This way, he would send us a new SIM card, and *voilà*, we would be able to contact everyone immediately on arrival. If this time something went awry and we missed a connection — like the train literally disappearing along the tracks before our very eyes like last year — we would at least be able to call him. Many emails later, we did get a new Sim but it was a very convoluted and protracted procedure. It involved Brigitte and Erick, friends from our first trip to France, entering the picture yet at the same time, leaving Jean-Claude partially in the dark about the problems we had encountered. We did not want to hurt his feelings, for he is always there to help us in any way possible, and yet, the arrangement was not going quite as smoothly as hoped.

The SIM card Jean-Claude sent us, had not been activated. It now had to be posted back to France, this time to our technologically savvy friends, Brigitte and Erick to activate. By the time Brigitte and Erick received it, the period to activate it had elapsed. With much stealth, we had to convey this to Jean-Claude without him being aware that we had to seek further assistance. In return, he gave us the privileged access to his email account. The only way to get a new password was to do so in his name as he had bought the Sim. His curiosity was certainly aroused, so I just pleaded my usual technological ignorance, which all who know me well, perfectly understand. Getting the new password involved Stuart navigating his way through the *portable* site in French.

Meanwhile, all this had to be conveyed to Brigitte and Erick. This would be complex at the best of times, let alone trying to convey it simply for friends in a foreign country. After its third voyage across the oceans, our SIM card is definitely very well travelled.

I suppose however, it is a minor matter this year, compared to the significant role he assumed the previous year in buying our car by email and then the part he played when our long distance *piscine* was put in. Such is Jean-Claude's attention to detail, that when he replies after I let him know our arrival time, he tells me he will take us to Carrefour *supermarché* to buy some essential supplies on our way to Cuzance. He also lets me know that he has attempted to check the pipes in our cellar as, since the winter was so severe, many people have had serious problems with frozen pipes. Unfortunately he can't seem to find the right key, so it will be with a sense of trepidation, that we venture into the cellar ourselves to check on our first night. Will there be a flood or frozen wasteland? We already know that this year there will need to be a serious outlay of *euro* on the nasty *septique* problem as the smell is becoming ever-pervasive.

Two Lives Mirrored

In what also seems to be developing as a recurring theme and the mirroring of our two lives on either side of the world, our weeks before departure are consumed by renovating chaos. Not only are we in the process of now getting prices from Jean-Claude for the *salle de bain* window in Cuzance, oh what a surprise, our bathroom at home is now on a fine timeline. Now why does that not surprise me too? Despite the fact that Stuart has been working on our bathroom for literally months, it is suddenly imperative to get it *fin* before we leave. I am adamant that I absolutely do not want to return to a renovating site. Are we not, after all, about to embark on renovating in our other life? And so, we have found a tiler, a huge concession for Stuart to outsource any renovating task at all. However, the tiler seems to be having an inordinate number of days away from the site. Meanwhile — now here's yet another surprise — just like last year, with only weeks remaining, it's time to try to sell our car. Weeks pass without a single call. My stress level builds. Stuart, as always, remains implacably calm. As if this is not quite enough, with a matter of just a few weekends left, we organise to have a skip one weekend to get rid of all the bathroom debris. To add to all this, Stuart has two all-day bridge competitions and we are still sourcing and pricing carpet for two bedrooms. The aim is to have all restored for our return from France. Quite frankly, it all seems absurdly ambitious. This would however, seem to be the opinion of only one of us.

Some weeks before our return, Stuart also announces that he will have to contact Piscine Ambiance to clean the pool to have it ready for our arrival. I let him know that I will email Albert to mow the grass as near as possible to our return date. Its freshly mown appearance will hopefully be a stunning juxtaposition to our other experiences on previous arrivals, of an overgrown, rambling, utterly neglected *jardin*. A part of us never ceases to marvel at the fact that we are making arrangements for the *piscine* and *jardin*. Ordinary people, an extraordinary life, is never far from my mind.

A month before we leave, winter hits us with all the mighty force of the season we are soon to escape. Cyclonic winds, powerful surging seas and deluge after deluge of driving rain beats upon the house. When the electricity is finally restored, I log on to my email and am transported to our small corner of France. Albert has sent photos of all his latest work in our *jardin*, including mowing swathes through the waist-high grass. He tells me that rabbits have eaten two of the lavenders that he planted in spring. There is also sad news as one of our graceful silver birches has to be cut down or it will fall on our new barn roof. As the rain lashes the house and the wind roars ferociously, it's hard to conjure up summer days in France.

This year's plan is to get the paving well underway so we are no longer sitting in weeds, rocks and rubble. There is always a plan, whether it is our renovation at home or the long list of work in Cuzance. I discuss with Stuart whether I should get a quote from Albert to pave around the *piscine* or at least a quote to help him with the labour. Doing this will free up a considerable amount of Stuart's precious time. We already know from our vast renovating experiences, that a projected two-week plan to pave will in fact consume a month — no doubt in blistering heat.

Perhaps if Albert does the paving, we can instead work together on our *petite maison*. I don't need to even be there, to have the list ready in my mind, of what still needs to be done in the transformation of Pied de la Croix to completely become a welcoming home, full of charm and ambience. I must remind myself again though, not to be consumed by the thought of lists. However, I do know that the conduit needs fixing in the spare *chambre* as well as requiring new skirting boards. There is still painting to be done and this year — next? — the wall needs to be knocked out from the dark, box-like toilet to open it up into the bathroom and introduce a false element of light. While there is still no window in the bathroom, nevertheless the illusion should work. I have learnt many renovating skills over the years and have surprised myself endlessly by how much I in fact know and how much I can tackle alone. Conduits and putting in skirting boards are not in that category. As my mind ticks over long before our return, I realise that if Stuart's days are consumed by paving, I too will feel compelled to work. What though can I manage this year by myself? Not much it would seem. Ah, the *jardin*. How could I have possibly overlooked my return to that formidable task?

As with our previous discussions the year before related to the car, the *piscine* and the new roof on the barn, the element of utter surrealism adds a strong layer of incredulity that this has become our wonderful other life. I know that I will never, in all the future years to come when we make plans to return to Cuzance, stop being full of a sense of wonder that this now has become our French life. I reflect on the decades and the journey that have brought us to this remarkable point. The early days of marriage when we packed our sandwiches for a rare day out as we couldn't afford to buy lunch. Our first year together in Canberra, when Stuart's only income was our weekly market stall at Gorman House. We sold kilim cushion covers that we had shipped back from Turkey when we lived there, met and got married. I still remember the penetrating cold of those early winter mornings; your breath itself fog in the air as we scraped the ice from the windscreen to set off in the enveloping darkness to the markets. How we stamped our numb feet and rubbed our hands to try to warm up as we waited for a sale, that sometimes, never came all day.

Meanwhile, like the last few summers, we start emailing Stuart's brother John and our friend Liz in Wales, to take our 'bookings' for their arrival in Cuzance. I email Liz and say:

My thoughts when I am dreaming, often turn to you and hopefully, time together under the walnut tree when the days are warm and balmy. Books in hand, the piscine will tempt us to cast them aside for a while, then a rosé or two, followed by one of your beautiful meals when you do spoil us so. I do look forward very much to your pears in red wine and this year, I will not work or renovate your room when you are there!

We will have outings, we will buy perfume in the chemist in Martel, we will linger over our choices in the patisserie, we will explore Isabella's petite shop, and — we have an enchanting restaurant already lined up to take you to!

So, are you dreaming too during your wild, wet days in Wales?

In reply, Liz says:

My dear Susan,

How lovely. I now have all those images in my head and time won't go quickly enough! I don't know if we will manage the pears because I'm coming earlier in the season and they may not be ripe on your orchard trees. However, I'm sure I'll manage some other delights. I love cooking in your kitchen in France, it's such a social place to be. Shopping, cooking, relaxing, swimming, the possibility of the odd brocante...and I'll only have a few days to squash these heady pursuits into. I'm so looking forward to it.

After just a few years, life in Cuzance is taking on a steady and comforting rhythm.

La Piscine in Peril

How would we manage without the internet? It is not possible to imagine all that we have achieved without instant access to information, sometimes information that throws us into a spin. Not only did we buy a car by email, install a pool by email, and organise a new gardener by email, we also had to shoot emails back and forth rapidly in a frantic effort to save our *piscine* in the big freeze. While at home, most of the state was experiencing severe floods, the European winter was one of the worst in memory. Life at home was constantly awash in a never-ending torrent of rain that consumed our lives and conversation. Deep, deep snow and treacherous ice however, was not on our personal weather radar.

Meanwhile, throughout the year, every few days Stuart logged on to check the weather in France. This was mainly out of simple curiosity to see how the seasons were unfolding on the other side of the world, especially in our own special little place, Cuzance. It was primarily so he could announce to me the extremes of temperature and we would marvel from afar at the depths to which the temperature frequently plummeted. That is, until the winter of the big freeze; suddenly, sheer curiosity turned to extreme consternation. The temperature became an entirely different matter. It became personal — it was an inconceivable minus eighteen in Cuzance. The *piscine* was in peril.

Stuart sent an email to Piscine Ambiance. We needed to know urgently if our pool was at risk, not simply of freezing but if the pump was adequate, if it was likely to break down and if the new pool was likely to crack. As the previous summer had been mostly cool and damp, we had literally only used *la piscine* on a couple of occasions. It was not worth thinking about the possibility of our pool, sitting all alone in an empty orchard, possibly near the end of its days — frozen, broken, cracked and spilling a river of water across our *rustique jardin*. So now we had to call Piscine Ambiance as well, organising the time by email to ensure we were able to speak to someone in the office. This time it was not the president or Yannick or Nicholas, as in all our previous email communication the year before. It was a new young English girl, Hannah. She calmly confirmed that yes, it was indeed imperative to send a technician immediately.

Naturally, the night that the call is arranged for, Stuart is out playing bridge. He assures me it will be a straightforward matter. Naturally it's not. Hannah asks me a series of questions about the pump, the switch and the mechanism's operation. I vaguely recall that Stuart has told me the switch is set to go on for two hours a day. I frantically scribble notes and questions to leave for Stuart when he gets in late at night after bridge. At midnight, he too has to call Hannah to sort out the complexities of the long distance *piscine*. Now why doesn't that surprise me that he has to step in after all to sort it out? The next morning before work, I hastily check with him what's happening to save *la piscine*.

He fills me in and lets me know that a technician will go to Cuzance as soon as possible — snow and ice permitting — to check on the pool and the switch. I hesitate to ask how much this will cost. The *euro* conversion takes a while for me to calculate. Once I manage to do so it's not an attractive calculation, especially first thing in the morning. It is now that I raise the question — somewhat hesitantly — of why the technician who came on site to brief Stuart on the complexities of operating and maintaining a pool — especially long distance — hadn't raised this critical point. As it transpires, he most certainly did. However, and yes, I can understand this, it was on one of the few significantly hot days the previous summer that the technician came to discuss *la piscine's* maintenance and operation. Yes, the issue of extremes in temperature had been discussed, including the possibility of snow and ice. On a blazing hot summer's day, such a thought however, was inconceivable. Stuart chose not to have the switch installed that would prevent *la piscine* being in peril. And so, the technician ventured out on the icy perilous roads to save *la piscine*. As for the water pipes in the *petite maison*, on our return, we knew that would be another matter entirely.

The Moon, Whales and Stale Bread

When the whales return each June, swimming north to warmer waters, it signals our return to France. The first winter moon is always spectacular. It shines in a bright river of light across the ocean. As the darkness of winter creeps in ever earlier, the silver path of the moon is in a straight line to our kitchen bench. I gaze out at it as I stand preparing dinner. The next full moon I see peeps instead in a bright yellow orb, through our Cuzance bedroom window, late at night.

Winter seems far away once we arrive in Cuzance. Yet I know winters were a harsh time in days gone by in Pied de la Croix. I know this from the newspaper tightly packed into every single crevice of the old farmhouse. It lined each step of the stairs up to the attic and the gap between each outside door and the floorboards. One day, as I am tearing out this tangible sign of the bitter cold seeping in, Jean-Claude tells me about Madame de la Croix's attempts to stave off the icy fingers of winter. He kneels down and shows me how the old oak wood is exceptionally smooth and shiny in some places. Those gleaming spots are near cracks that are wider than others in the floorboards. Why do you think that is? Jean-Claude asks me. He likes to test my knowledge. I tell him I have absolutely no idea and couldn't possibly hazard a guess.

When he reveals the reason, to say I am astonished is a huge understatement. Apparently, Madame de la Croix, used to roll up small pieces of stale *pain* and then stuff the bread in the cracks to fill them up. The romanticism of days long gone dims with such tales that betray the ferocity of winter and a life lived on the land. I now have two summers, two rhythms and two lives. Yet the spirit of Madame de la Croix lives on in the dusty corners of our rooms.

Actually, while it seems far from Paris, in reality our *petite maison* is just a swift four-hour train trip on the TGV from Brive-la-Gaillarde to Gare d'Austerlitz. However, while in Cuzance, being in our *petite* village in the Lot, it is like being buried deep in the country. Rabbits bounce along the road right outside Pied de la Croix and squirrels scamper over the moss-covered stone wall opposite the French doors in our kitchen. While the alluring streets of Paris beckon brightly, it's just the way we like it. There is an encompassing sense of being far away from the world. Our friends find it even more so when they arrive to stay and to their dismay, they discover there is not even a *boulangerie*. They try to hide their disappointment, for after all, is not a *boulangerie* the quintessential essence of life in a *petite* village in France? On the eve of our annual departure to our *petite maison*, the enquiry from friends and colleagues is always, 'When are you going to Paris?' It seems that Paris is synonymous with going to France. We gloss over the fact that most times we simply land at Charles de Gaulle and the most we see of Paris is the metro.

While we no longer have a desire to be tourists in the other famous cities of the world, the romance and beauty of Paris will never lose its captivating charm. Yet given the choice of a Parisian apartment, or our old farmhouse, there is no question in my mind that I would choose Cuzance any day.

Apart from this year when we had a morning in Paris before catching the train, on the last leg of our journey from the other side of the world to Cuzance, we have not spent any time in Paris for five years. However, Paris will always be a city that has captured our hearts in a way that no other has.

Our other life in France, becomes even more astonishing when we start to discuss the details of how we can also spend a few days in Paris this summer. We can leave our Renault at the station and *voilà*, arrive in Paris for *déjeuner*. When we had stayed in the Melia Colbert Boutique Hotel five years previously, after I won a trip to Paris and five nights in luxury, we had discovered a small hotel round the corner that we liked the look of for future Parisian sojourns. Rather than search through my diary to unearth the name, Stuart goes on Google street view and indeed, just round the corner from the Melia Colbert, he finds the small, authentic Les Degres De Notre Dame Hotel. A virtual walk along the street shows a number of charming bistros and the comments posted for the hotel make it all the more enticing. Such is the immediacy of the internet that from the reviews posted we are able to decide that Room 51 will be ours, if it is available. It has a sweeping view of the Notre Dame Cathedral. As always, my mind works overtime, and my bag is packed for what I will wear in Paris. While in fact these plans do not eventuate, part of the joy is all in the dreaming, and, the plan will be in place for another year. Once again we are mindful of how privileged we are to know that we will indeed return. A night in Paris on our return leg home, will actually be imperative in the future, indeed, more than a mere luxury, to avoid the mayhem that ensues on this return trip and our almost doomed departure.

A Morning In Paris

The very phrase 'a morning in Paris' conjures up so many images and expectations. I was conscious long before our precious morning that we would have to carefully watch the time — or once again there would be a recurring theme and we may well see a train slipping away right in front of our eyes. On our first trip to Paris, one of the very first things I learnt, was that the last day of June is the start of *solde* season. Tempting as it is to be in Paris, the very morning the sales start, I promise Stuart not to be sidetracked and slip into any sales — just 'for a few minutes'. He tells me that I can always meet him at Gare d'Austerlitz if I want to shop while he wanders the streets of Paris, soaking up the atmosphere in a few short hours.

I decide against this tempting offer for several reasons, despite the fact that arriving on the very first *solde* day seems too good to be true. One, I have a terrible sense of direction. We both know that I would be highly unlikely to find the station. Two, even if I did; it's likely that I would board the wrong train and end up far away in Barcelona or Milan. Actually, perhaps not a bad idea after all for *solde* season. I also remember only too clearly catching the train home from Sydney one day — Stuart had boarded the train, the doors closed and I was left standing forlornly on the platform.

So, thoughts of *solde* delights are reluctantly cast aside. After all, Stuart has promised that this year (for we have once again been renovating at home) that our first week will be one of rest and relaxation. He has enticed me away from thoughts of shopping in Paris, with a possible *solde* trip to Limoges, a new destination. Last year we didn't even get to the sales in nearby Brive until they were well into their third week. By then, the racks were empty and desolate. Limoges brims with the hope of full *solde* shelves and racks, simply overflowing with French *chic*. Mind you, at home we would never dream of venturing on a four-hour round trip to shop. In France, however, it all seems to be quite different and our everyday selves are cast aside.

We have carefully planned our precious few hours for our morning in Paris, to absorb as much atmosphere as possible. The very name, Quartier Latin, conjures up images of bohemian Paris and the Sorbonne, which is not far away. The student atmosphere creates a lively collection of second-hand bookshops and *cafés*, while the myriad streets entice you to wander and simply immerse yourself in all that is glorious in Paris. However, we have to be careful not to fall too fully under the spell of the crooked lanes, for after all, there is a train to catch quite soon. The famous Luxembourg Gardens are also in this district, as well as Palais du Luxembourg, where there is a park with a large pool where children sail boats and Parisians read the paper or bask in the sun in striped deckchairs that you can rent. All of these enchantments will have to be for a future visit.

We take delight in the shops, restaurants and *boulangeries*, and as the lunch hour approaches, we join a patient, snaking queue for *baguettes*. A long queue is usually a reliable indication of excellence and we are not disappointed. We find a little park and sit on a bench in the shade, immersing ourselves as fully as possible in a fleeting taste of Paris. Time ebbs rapidly and we make our reluctant way back to Gare d'Austerlitz to collect our luggage. Our path takes us through the stunning Jardin des Plantes, three hectares of botanical gardens, and there is just enough time to linger and admire the outside photographic exhibition.

Our fleeting morning has been all that we hoped for; the sun shone, we had our first *espresso* and delicious *baguette* — and most importantly, the train did not disappear imperiously into the distance.

Portables and *Septiques*

We finally staggered into our *petite maison* at 8.30pm. This year, all went according to plan; a beaming Jean-Claude there to greet us and a hasty trip to Carrefour to stock up on the most basic essentials, wine of course being the top of the list. That in itself was overwhelming; the crowds and long queues of late Saturday *supermarché* shoppers — it was like the busiest supermarket in the world. It is absolutely the last thing you feel like after the interminable flight from the other side of the world. Then of course we chose the wrong queue. How was it though that it was so apparent that we were foreigners, that the cashier signalled to us that we needed a special Carrefour card and we were in the wrong line? I had even taken care to have a scarf in my bag to nonchalantly tie around my neck on arrival in Paris, in what I like to think is the essential French touch. When I point this out to Stuart, he declares that she must think we are from Paris and won't have the requisite Carrefour card. I decide that I like his explanation. So, to the express self-service checkout, a challenge for me at the best of times, let alone in a foreign country and consumed by exhaustion.

As with everything, Stuart takes it all admirably in his stride, though fortunately the express cashier is on hand to assist when we encounter problems. The *tomates* have to be abandoned as we have not weighed them. A small loss for at least we have our first bottle of French wine. Armed with *pain, fromage, jambon* and chocolate chip muesli, we set off on the very last leg to Cuzance. How can French women be so slim when they start their day with chocolate chip muesli, let alone the bread, cheese and ham we have hastily grabbed? That remains one of life's perplexing mysteries.

Shortly after, we arrive at La Vieux Prieuré, to be welcomed by Françoise's warm embrace. Françoise is short, round and always beaming. I am the opposite, yet when we hug, it is like two halves fitting together. Their *jardin* looks at its glorious summer best and over an *apéritif*, we truly feel like we are home again in Cuzance. However, it makes the difference even more pronounced when we finally unlock the door to Pied de la Croix. While it is altogether different to our first viewing of it together a mere couple of years ago, on a damp day with trucks thundering past, and while it is undeniably transformed, nevertheless, despite the dust covers, it is wreathed in cobwebs. There is a thick layer of dust on every surface and abundant evidence of the visiting mice in our absence. They have gnawed through the packets of coffee in the cupboard and even the toilet paper. I try to focus instead on the romance of the film set qualities when I first step inside again after a year, rather than raw reality, when I stand back and take stock more slowly. What could those *petite* mice have been thinking? No doubt the harshest winter on record for a very long time has driven them to such drastic measures.

Every year though sees a step further in our organisation for our return. Sheets are waiting in a plastic tub and it's the only task we can manage, to make up the bed after more hours of travelling than I can manage to count. A simple meal, a glass of *rosé* and it's absolutely lights out. The rest can all wait until a new day in Cuzance.

The first full day in France is a Sunday but even Françoise knew that it would not be a highly prized *vide-grenier* day. It will take at least two days to get the *petite maison* up and running. We wake before 5am in the pitch dark of our tightly shuttered *chambre*. First things first, we set up the coffee machine. Recovering from jet lag is hard at the best of times let alone without a strong *café*. Outside, it's eerily silent and darkness envelops Cuzance in a crisp chilliness. A squirrel scampers across the roof of *la grange*, the only other sign of life in the still-waking countryside.

While life at home already seems remote and another existence altogether, the uncanny resemblance of our two lives do not escape us. Mobiles and plumbing seem to be our parallel downfalls on either side of the world. Our new *portable* plan, that we had such high hopes for, means that in fact we can only connect with friends in France. Another perplexing puzzle to add to the list of things to deal with. Oh yes, just like in previous years, the lists have started already — and it is only day one. The most pressing problem though is the *septique*. At home we have to get a plumber as soon as we return for the dreadful plumbing problems. That though is nothing to compare to the devastating, all-consuming, all-pervading utter stench emanating from our *septique*. Oh là là. The smell fills our entire *petite maison*. It is just like being back in Turkey on our travels all those years ago when we first met. We knew it was going to be bad on our return for the *septique* problem had already well and truly flared up the previous year, but nothing could prepare us for the reality. For the moment though, we simply have to live with it. There are more pressing things to deal with, like, will our *petite voiture* start after sleeping for a year in the garage, in *la grange*?

Though your memory holds a thousand imprints, the reconnection with the minutiae holds infinite joy. The collection of old cutlery in a wooden trug, the exquisite heavy glass bowl that I bought for a song, the white enamel jug that holds *la cuisine* utensils. So many *vide-grenier* finds on so many occasions. After only a couple of years, we can't even recall the precise where and when of each piece of treasure. The accumulated pieces represent the layers that transform our *petite* farmhouse into a home.

I am sure that each year will be the same. A repetition of reuniting with beloved *objets,* balanced by the discovery of the forgotten and overlooked. Added to this are the other fragments of Cuzance life that have been cast aside in the year in between. Most striking is the soft constant cooing of the doves and the stratum of noises of other birds unknown to me, overlaid by the chiming of the village church bell.

The silence in the very early morning and late evening is the deep, deep silence of the countryside. The musical bird notes of the day fade gently away to be replaced by an occasional soft rustling in the dry, fallen leaves — field mice, hedgehogs and a slinking black cat slipping through the night shadows.

By early morning on our very first day, I abandon the cleaning. I'm rapidly worn out — consumed by jet lag and the lack of a proper meal, by now for several days. Airline food does not count in my book as a 'proper meal'. I slip under the soft comfort of the eiderdown and just like our first evening, within a few minutes, drift off into a deep sleep. Several hours later, Stuart tiptoes in to triumphantly announce that he has recharged the car. After a year, he's jubilant that it started the first time when he put the battery back in. The day of challenges he's set himself is well underway and it's not even midday. He flourishes a shopping list that he's already written and lets me know he's off to Martel to the *supermarché*. I murmur goodbye and sink once more into the Cuzance silence.

Much to my surprise, on our first afternoon while the house is still in a state of considerable disarray, Stuart suggests an outing to Martel. Although he has already been once to the *supermarché*, he feels like having a wander round. He seems to be fervently embracing the fact that we have declared that this year we simply will not slavishly work the whole time and that the first week will be a break. It is a quiet Sunday afternoon in Martel and while it is a small town, we discover quiet streets tucked away off the main square that we had not previously explored in the past two years. That in itself is a measure of how absurdly hard we had worked before. And so it is, on just our first full day, we are able to enjoy a leisurely stroll, admiring the abundant, bright window box displays. To our surprise, we also discover two more *boulangeries* that we had no idea existed. Over *espresso* and a *crêpe au chocolat* we discuss how it simply reinforces that we have certainly worked far too hard on our previous visits. We need to also remind ourselves why we are in France. It is not to merely renovate the entire time.

A Mouse in the House

On our second morning, as I sleepily stumble out into *la cuisine,* it suddenly comes home to me with a jolt, that just two years ago, all we had was a single table to not only prepare everything on but it was also our storage area. It would hold at any one time an eclectic array of items, like a surrealist painting; a loaf of *pain,* paintbrushes, *bricolage* catalogues, maps, screwdrivers, as well as our *petite* collection of plates, glasses and cutlery. Renovating and setting up a house in those basic conditions requires a lot of organisation, flexibility — and patience. The statement, 'two years' does not quite encapsulate all that has been achieved since then, for in reality, the total transformation until now, has all been achieved in a matter of nine weeks. While that time was spent in the longest days of sheer hard work imaginable, it was not even nine full weeks of solid work. There were the endless *bricolage* trips, the expeditions to the *Trocs* in search of second-hand furniture, the *brocante* and *vide-grenier* outings. I can only marvel as I gaze around at our new stylish IKEA *cuisine,* the cracked old leather Chesterfield sofa and chairs, the long wooden table and assorted array of old wooden chairs. How did we possibly manage all this I wonder?

After only one whole day back in Cuzance, our collection of *vide-grenier* finds are all unpacked and our *petite maison* is almost restored for another summer. The mantelpiece is decorated once again with everything that has been tucked away for a year. In pride of place, is my still-life painting, that I picked up for a mere two *euros.* I like to secretly believe that it is by a famous artist and worth two million *euros.*

I convince myself that it is and I will make our fortune by selling it at Sotheby's. The matching bright yellow jugs, the dark brown *espresso* cups and saucers, all lined up in a neat row, the beautifully carved wooden vase — all these things give me pleasure every day in our little French farmhouse. As I eat my chocolate chip muesli — surely not 'real' muesli but nevertheless utterly delicious — I discover that it is extremely addictive. I decide that it is far too decadent a way to start the day. Surely I should be more selective here about my choice of daily mouth-watering treats? I devour another mouthful of exquisite rich, small dark *chocolat* squares. For now, such momentous decisions can wait.

As I soak up the view of *le jardin* while I have my first *espresso* of the morning, I plan my day. Most pressing is to seek Jean-Claude's opinion on the source of the freshly dug, ominous mound of dirt in the cellar. I had only seen it in the fading light of the previous evening, yet what I saw was enough to sufficiently alarm me. I asked Stuart why he hadn't told me about it when he discovered it earlier in the day. In his usual inimitable manner, he told me he didn't want to worry me. It was probably only a rabbit he said. I don't know much about the habits of rabbits but I do know enough to think that it may be more disturbing than a mere *lapin*. However, I cannot begin to imagine what creature has been marauding in our cellar. In addition, there's some highly alarming noises emanating from the attic — dubbed last year, 'The Squirrel Room', due to the disturbing sounds of scampering and the sight of squirrels leaping across the barn roof. Stuart informs me he will venture up there later. He can go alone, I think. There is also still a mouse in the house.

In my sleep-induced, jet-lagged haze, as I had prepared my *petit déjeuner*, I had only just managed to remember where Stuart had decided was the only safe place for the *pain* and packets of food that may be tempting for a mouse on the lookout for a tasty takeaway treat. Where else but in the oven of course?

My day gets underway despite the possibility of creatures who have taken up permanent residence in our absence. While we get our bank statements and other French accounts delivered to us at home, it occurs to me that after a year, I should probably check the post box.

It wasn't until we got our regulation-sized, *Le Bureau de Poste* approved post box late the year before and attached it to the stone wall — under Jean-Claude's guidance about what position would be deemed acceptable by *Le Bureau de Poste* — that we were considered to officially exist in France. I discover a puzzling collection of very official-looking letters. They have been posted every two months from a government office in Cahors. We have absolutely no idea what they mean. They are put aside to ask Jean-Claude about when we visit for a late afternoon *apéritif*. What does bring me enormous joy is a welcoming letter from Kaitlyn and Ryan, my students at home. I am deeply touched by their thoughtfulness that a letter is here to greet me at the start of our long summer away. This too I tuck away to share with Jean-Claude and Françoise. It is yet another extraordinary fragment of my new life, the fact that two of the people I am the closest to are a 17-year-old Australian school girl and a 70-year-old French man.

Today I have to tackle the dust-covered linen and towels, yet even washing in France is not an ordinary experience. I venture down to the cellar and pull back the creaking, cobweb-covered wooden door. I always have to remember to stoop as I go in or I'll hit my head on the low stone doorway. I reach for my washing products that are placed in a handy little stone niche in the wall. The cellar has been here for one hundred and thirty years; like many other elements of our *petite* farmhouse, I wonder about all those before me whose footsteps I am following in the cavernous, cool space. Next I need to unpack. I have not even had to go near my suitcase yet for I've just pulled on clothes that I left in our *armoire*. What is already dawning on me, is that in my usual fashion, I have seriously over-packed. What on earth was I thinking when I filled my suitcase? In the depths of the country, I simply pull on a T-shirt and a pair of *pantalons* every day. I seem to have packed for the Riviera or a summer of Paris *soirées*. It has never been my forte. And let's not forget, I have been lured by the promise of *solde* in Limoges in our first week. Indeed, as I was packing at home, even I was struck by my sheer madness at bringing clothes back to France that I'd bought just the previous year. Like our well-travelled SIM card (which I hasten to add still doesn't work), it would seem that I also aspire to have clothes that travel the world more than most people I know. Seriously, I don't know what I'm thinking at times. Later, when Gérard and Dominique drop in to see us and I'm invariably in my less than attractive *rénovation* clothes, they actually ask if when we go home I can send a photo of what I look like when I go to school every day. That seems to sum up my lack of stylishness in France, despite my best attempts at times.

Over our *apéritif* with Jean-Claude and Françoise in the soft glow of the late summer afternoon, I make plans with Françoise for my first cooking lesson to make a *tarte aux pomme,* an apple pie that will also be a French lesson, as all my instructions will be in French. This is why I am in France after all. Sadly though, the summer will pass and our plans will be thwarted. 'Next year', that seems to be our catchcry for many things. As I obsessively work later in *le jardin* in the intense summer heat, I dream of how in the following year, under Françoise's expert culinary guidance, my *tarte aux pomme* will glisten in its honey glaze.

Before we leave their *maison*, Jean-Claude translates our official letters. They are related to the new *la grange* roof and enquire whether *la grange* will now be inhabited. Absolutely not, Jean-Claude empathically declares, and writes accordingly on the letter for us in French. He and Stuart conspiringly agree that we should not pay any more taxes than necessary. All that our barn houses is our *voiture*, and a car hardly counts. Views on taxes are clearly the same the world over. As we wish them *bonne nuit,* Françoise climbs the small wooden stepladder in the enchanting kingdom of her *petite la cuisine*. She reaches and stretches for jars of her gleaming homemade *confiture*. The most prized jar of jam is her fig one, labelled September 2009. We are then given a choice between *fraise* and rhubarb, all from her immaculate potage garden. While strawberry is a luscious choice on fresh *pain*, we choose the rhubarb as we have not tasted it before. It is touches like these, of the homemade gifts of *confiture* from the French kitchen of our dear friend, that make all the difference between simply having a *maison* in France and having a home. In such a short time, Cuzance is definitely home.

Restoring *la Petite Maison*

Stuart's promise of the past — which I had never quite believed — has proved to be true. He reminds me that he had absolutely assured me, that each year the renovating and hard work would get easier. To my enormous surprise, it is indeed the case. Well, at least so far. It's early days yet. At the start of our *vacances*, time seems to stretch to infinity. However, our frantic, feverish renovating seems to have decidedly been replaced by domesticity. On day three, Stuart tackles the enormous pile of paperwork — *voiture* insurance, the Piscine Ambiance contract we need to renew each year for opening and closing the pool, and of course, the official Cahors letters. I start to unpack our suitcases. It is telling in itself that after three whole nights, we've had no need of anything we packed.

Our tiny wardrobe is fitted into the wall of our *chambre*. It has handmade, dark wooden doors and is very small and narrow. I carefully apportion half the *petite* space to each of us. I then meticulously layer our clothes on the hangers. There is a trick to hanging everything properly; the coat hangers have to be ever so carefully placed at an angle. Who knew there was such an art form involved in hanging clothes so precisely?

Yet what do we wear each day in Cuzance? The very clothes that have stayed in Cuzance for a year. For two people who claim to rarely shop, it seems absurd to simply have so many. Just like the delight I take in unearthing our *vide-grenier* finds to display and decorate, once again, I pull on my much loved, well-worn, faded green *pantalons*, my soft-with-age blue and white striped top and my faded denim skirt. These clothes cost me only a few *euro* and must have been washed hundreds of times by their previous owners. They are my absolute favourites, for they are like meeting up with old friends. And the rest of the time? We pull on our old, stained, ripped work clothes to labour day after day in *le jardin*.

My life is suddenly so domestic this year, that my notes for daily life consist of asking Françoise why the water stays in the washing machine compartment each time I wash, and what is the word for stain remover. A far cry indeed from just a year ago. This however, although I don't yet know it, is all about to rapidly change. It would seem I have a false sense of idyll.

In the short space of a year, it is hard to believe that our early days on arrival, have changed so dramatically. It is also a source of irony to me, that now our *petite maison* is no longer an empty, bare shell, waiting to be renovated and furnished, and the more Pied de la Croix becomes a home, the more there is to do before we can even start this year's huge project outside. So it is not until day four, that the house is fully restored from its packed-away, boxed-up, dust-covered state. The books are out, the *objets* artfully displayed, and it is already such a home in every sense that every single item I go to reach for, whether it is in *la cuisine* or *la salle de bain*, that there is nothing I can't find that I need. I even have a hairdryer in the bathroom. How times have changed indeed!

I feel a certain sense of pride in what we have achieved — and in a foreign country. From just a sink and old wood stove as the entire kitchen in the first year, to a shiny new IKEA *cuisine;* a wall knocked down to create space, and the last vestige of the most recent *rénovation* in the 70s, the tartan wallpaper — all vanished. The toilet however, to my daily horror, remains a dark box, like a *petite* walk-in cupboard.

Such is our domestic devotion that we have even been to the car wash in Martel. Domesticity reigns supreme in Cuzance. What I am already realising is that our packing up at the end of our *vacances,* will take just as long. And, let's face it, there is a lot of work to get underway before that time arrives. What is also creeping into my thoughts is that perhaps we are simply avoiding what lies ahead. Nevertheless, there is no denying that this more low-key approach is certainly attractive — and indeed, seductive. No endless parade of *artisans* to '*Bonjour*' and offer *espresso* to every day. No garden crowded in a sea of *artisan* trucks, no — for the moment anyway — phone calls to *plombiers* that are never returned. The days start now with a calmer rhythm.

We start our own Cuzance rhythm to reconnect fully once again with our French life. So, it's off to the *boulangerie* in Martel for the first of what will be many weeks of indulgent treats. At only ten thirty the display of luscious pastries is almost depleted but we are more than delighted with our *abricot hibou,* savoured with an *espresso* at the *café* across the road. The pastry simply melts in our mouths, we breathe in deep sighs of utter contentment. The equivalent of our Danish pastry at home has this intriguing name as it means 'owl', named so for the fact that the two luscious pieces of apricot placed in its centre, represent the eyes of an owl. When we tell Gérard and Dominique about our latest *boulangerie* delight, they have not even heard of an *abricot hibou.* It is no small surprise to me that Dominique is not familiar with it. Someone as svelte as she is probably only ever steps inside a *patisserie* once a year for *Noël* celebrations.

We love the fact that it is perfectly permissible to take your own *petit déjeuner* pastry to a *café.* Within just a few minutes, we see two people we know — Monsieur Arnal, the owner of the Hotel Arnal in our village, and Nigel, an English friend of Jean-Claude and Françoise. While my French has sadly not progressed at all in the past year, I do know enough to grasp that Monsieur Arnal is eager to know if I can now communicate with him more fully. I shake my head, '*Non*.' It is a disappointment both to myself and him.

Then it's off to Intermarche, to discover that the *supermarché* has considerably expanded in the past year. The fish display is much larger and has soft jets of water spraying the fresh *poisson*. Like all our *supermarché* visits, especially the first time back, it is the wine aisle that we linger in the longest. Most exciting of all is how affordable champagne is. We buy a bottle for Liz's arrival the following week.

To round off our responsibilities, we go to Jean-Claude's on a mission, to use his internet. Such is his endless kindness that he lets us have his lengthy encryption code so we can use our own laptop. I've tried to use their computer on previous occasions but the different layout of the French keyboard means that my typing, never good at the best of times, is even more of a dismal failure than it normally is. It is a lengthy, tiresome afternoon of trying to connect with the world. It also proves to be true that if something seems too good to be true, then that is indeed the case. We finally log on and check why our new *portable* deal does not seem to be working. It would appear that our two *euro* a month plan does not have international access until the following year. And so, we are virtually cut off from the world for two months. Jean-Claude will be our conduit to the vast world beyond Cuzance. Truth be told, I love the sense of escaping from the world; buried in the country, reality seems to be another place altogether. We immerse ourselves in the slow pace of Cuzance village life.

Once technology is sorted in a fashion, we are able to relax over *apéritifs*. I am truly touched, when out of the blue, Françoise, tells me that she intends to whisk me away for a weekend to their apartment in Lyon. I had already gleaned from Jean-Claude in our previous chats, that it is quite grand. Now, when Françoise describes it to me, it seems even more so — parquetry floors, four *chambres*, study, *cuisine*, sitting room, *salle de bain* and a terrace. She tells me it is enormous and in the heart of Lyon. An invitation such as this is an honour. I simply can't wait. I don't have weekends away like this at home, let alone in France. While we spent several nights in Lyon, three years ago, the experience will be nothing compared to this insider's guide.

We leave in the early evening after another relaxing *apéritif* hour, this time, next to their *piscine*, soaking up the late summer sun and the beauty of their herbaceous border. I always marvel at the grandeur of their *maison* and *jardin*. I am conscious too that it represents over twenty years of love and hard work. I know that our *petite* farmhouse and *rustique jardin* will never be quite on this magnificent scale. Just as we emerge from behind their high stone wall we encounter Gérard, who we've not yet caught up with this year. He always reminds me of a big, friendly bear — with his shock of white hair and large frame. He's been out for a bike ride and invites us to go back and see Dominique. I plead *fatigue*, although their friendship is one we look forward enormously to rekindling each year. Seeing Gérard always warms my heart. Again, although I can't exchange as much conversation with him as I would like, he always makes me feel happy. He is perpetually beaming and the very essence of *bonhomie*. As Stuart says, 'As happy as a butcher,' for who has ever met a grumpy butcher? Jet lag still lingers though and we know to accept means that the *apéritif* hour will be extended by several more.

By the time Stuart serves *dîner*, I'm nearly falling asleep over my succulent pork chop and lettuce dressed with French mustard. I crawl into bed straight after *dîner* and indulge in one of my favourite Cuzance moments, gazing out at the verdant trees and pink-tinged sky. The moment is completed when the full moon bursts out from behind the soft puffy clouds. My reverie is broken when I see Jean-Claude striding past our *chambre* window. Though it's late evening, in his inimitable fashion, he has dropped in to check on the alarming activity in our cellar. Over our *apéritifs*, he had surmised that the digging and huge pile of dirt may be from a badger. He had even made a joke, 'Don't be afraid to badger me about the badger.' He and Stuart set off to the damp, cold cellar with a torch to investigate. Jean-Claude concludes that the digging seems to be from a rabbit. I am astonished that such a huge mound of dirt could be from an excavating *lapin*. Jean-Claude disappears into the night and Stuart comes in to let me know that his booming voice has carried back through the quiet night as he informs Monsieur Arnal that we have a *lapin* problem in *le cave*. It would seem that the whole village now knows. Such is the way of a *petite* village and it is part of what makes me love Cuzance.

A New Approach

It scarcely seems possible that only two years ago, on our very first morning, I fell off our air mattress in the room that would become our *la cuisine* the following year, and immediately started to pull down the ugly wooden lattice on our porch that served no purpose at all. We then launched into the debacle that was stripping the wallpaper off in our bedroom. Now, the start of our third working *vacances*, it seems to take me hours to start functioning properly, even with the kick-start of a couple of *espressos*. 'It can wait,' seems to be the new mantra of the day we have adopted. This time, there is still a glorious nine weeks stretching out in front of us. Little did we know, when time seemed to stretch endlessly, that we would not, in our usual fashion, reach our renovating target. After just a few days in Cuzance, already the real world has rapidly receded. We are absorbed seamlessly into our special little French world. A world where the day holds infinite promise of what it may bring. A world where the day ends in a golden glow of summer light. As the day comes to a close, I rediscover the delight of lying in bed, before darkness descends, gazing at the soft green of the trees in the Chanteurs' *jardin*, crowned by their magnificent walnut.

I have learnt from Jean-Claude that Madame Chanteur is in hospital in La Rochelle. They have been away for six weeks now. In such a short time, their meadow-like garden already has a sad air of neglect. I have bought with me a gift of a photo to give them. They are framed within their stone doorway and the love of at least fifty years of marriage shines from the soft, worn lines in their faces. I know without being told, that Madame Chanteur may never return home again. I know too that Monsieur Chanteur may well fade away shortly after. While I have only ever been able to exchange a few simple words with them, I took great joy in the past two years in observing them daily and seeing their great love and devotion from afar.

I ask Jean-Claude if he has an address for them in La Rochelle so I can post the photo to them. He tells me that Monsieur Chanteur is of the old school and would not reveal his address or phone number. I can only feel that our neighbouring *maison* has an air of doom enveloping it. The Chanteurs have only lived there for a year and before that, Anne Barnes, the English woman I would surely have become friends with. Yet she had died tragically in Haiti while working for the United Nations, just shortly before her planned retirement. I feel a sense of uneasy trepidation for whoever else may live one day in the house next to us.

On just our third day, we are even more fully immersed in domestic duties. Stuart finally emerges, declaring he's more than ready for his *petit déjeuner*. It seems that he too has developed a penchant for *chocolat* muesli. We then launch into further domesticity; it's hard to believe that only two years have seen such a major change in our daily routine. The *voiture* is a disgrace; full of dry grass from the previous year from our *rustique jardin,* so Stuart sets to work to clean it. Meanwhile, I reacquaint myself again with the dials and knobs of my French washing machine. The birds sing, the sun shines and we have a real French home that is no longer just a renovating site.

Le Supermarché

At home, supermarket shopping is not one of our favourite pastimes. When I do the weekly grocery shop, I tend to virtually run down each aisle, sharply swing the trolley into the next and throw the always predictable items into the trolley at great speed. I never linger and I never select new items. I play a little game with myself and time my once-a-week grocery shop from parking the car, to leaving the car park.

Nevertheless, while in Cuzance, even this usually mundane task takes on a new ritual and new dimension. Our local Intermarche is on the outskirts of Martel. It is one of the few drives that I can manage alone. However, we usually go together to share another part of our French life. We already have our favourite French items and brands that we buy each week. We don't just like French butter — we love it! The one we always choose is in red and white checked wrapping, while our favourite yoghurt is Bon Maman. There is a Bon Maman range of compote that we also buy in our village of Thirroul, where we shop at home. I find this quite amazing the way our two lives sometimes connect. Once we discovered the *mousse au chocolat* with this label, well, that became virtually an essential purchase each week. The list of treats seems to be ever-increasing.

Each week we aim to sample a new cheese as well as try to remember the names of all the *fromage* we have liked before. As I wait at the deli counter, I silently practise the names of the ones I am going to ask for. Each customer waits ever so patiently. We have certainly learnt though, just like the world over, never to shop on a Saturday morning, especially when tourist season is in full swing. Each customer is greeted in turn with a courteous, 'Bonjour Madame, bonjour Monsieur.' No one is ever rushed. If a sample is required before buying, it is politely proffered. While our *supermarché* is relatively small, there are still enormous wheels of soft camembert and huge wedges of harder, tasty *fromage*. The women behind the counter are immaculate in their crisp white uniforms, hair neatly tucked beneath their starched white caps.

In the larger *supermarché* in Brive, there are enormous displays of fresh fish, with cool jets of moist air gently spraying them. It is to Carrefour we head when we need extra items for our *petite maison*, such as the little white wrought iron table and chairs for our porch. However, there are some surprises too in store sometimes when we shop. Sometimes there are unexpected challenges in actually finding what we want. At times like these, logic does not come into play. On the rare occasions we need to buy *confiture* when our friends have not given us gifts of jam from their pantries, we have to remember that it is for *petit déjeuner* and so is on the shelves with the coffee, tea and sugar — because jam is what you eat for breakfast. Similarly, *apéritif* snacks initially proved to be baffling to find. Right — pretzels, chips and savoury biscuits are in the extensive alcohol aisle. There is in fact a sense of logic after all, for this is what you serve with a drink before *dîner*.

And then there is the wine. Like with many French customs, I try to learn by quietly observing. I watch as wine on the highest shelf is reached for and surmise it is for a special family occasion. I learn too, that just like anywhere, even in France, that the *rosé* on special is not necessarily the best available. Stuart also picks up a little trick for buying French wine. If the space on the shelf only has a couple of bottles left, he follows the lead of the French and scoops up the few remaining ones. He reasons that it must be a popular purchase to be virtually depleted and therefore, a wine worth buying. This technique certainly seems to work, for it has lead us to sample quite a few interesting bottles at a reasonable price. Well, perhaps more than a few.

Then there are the tubs and tubs of brightly coloured containers all lined up in the refrigerator section that present a staggering number of desserts. In this, the land of tantalising, sumptuous *patisserie* treats, it astonishes us that there is such a vast array of packaged desserts. When we have been invited to an informal dinner with friends, it is customary to serve a *crème caramel* or *île flottante* from the *supermarché*. We too, when friends stay, have sometimes adopted the custom and offer our beloved *mousse au chocolat*. It is truly so delicious that I'm tempted to carefully place it in a small glass dish and pass it off as my own.

A feature of our *supermarché* is that you have a discount card. However, like many other elements of life in France, its use is somewhat perplexing. We present it every time we shop, yet we never get a discount. This is very puzzling, particularly so when we buy our outside mosaic table and four chairs for a significantly reduced price. This leads Stuart to having a number of conversations at the information desk, in his attempts to find out how we activate our discount. Finally, he understands that the card must always be presented at the outset of the transaction to receive the discount when you are paying. Next time we will do this. If it was up to me to glean how this works, clearly there would never be a discount for us. Oh yes, my French is still lamentable.

Picking Up the Threads

Life in Cuzance is stolen time. Each time spent there is a precious gift; one to clasp in your hands, treasure and marvel at the many layers of our lives that have bought us to this point. With little effort or planning, the hours and days fill themselves and overflow in to the next.

One of the very first things we do each year on our market visit to Martel, is to drop into the *Office du Tourisme* to collect the season guide, *Saison 2012 — Brocantes* and *Vide-Greniers — Lot — Correze — Dordogne*. It is a list of the *vide-greniers* and *brocantes* in the Lot and surrounding *départements* of Correze and the Dordogne. We eagerly scan and highlight the markets we will visit. Each early Sunday morning is mapped out far in advance. I have the joy and anticipation of returning to our favourite *vide-greniers* such as Turin and Gignac. I can already feel the feverish obsession to discover treasure sweep over me. One of our first this season will be in Blanat, near the famous town of Rocamadour, one that in the past yielded tantalising treasure.

We are off to a flying start in planning our treasure hunts but discover there is a long-standing rivalry between Cuzance and the nearby village of Gignac. It is a rivalry based on their annual *vide-grenier*. Walking through the village one evening, we saw that posters had been put up to advertise the forthcoming Gignac *vide-grenier*. By the next night, on our evening *promenade*, we noticed they had disappeared. It is the custom throughout the *départements* in *vide-grenier* and *brocante* season for brightly coloured posters to appear everywhere, several weeks in advance, so that people from nearby villages and towns will flock to their clear-out the attic markets. We eagerly look out for these posters and plan our Sunday outings based on them. What was going on in Gignac? Even friends such as Jean-Claude, who do not make it a habit to visit markets, had Gignac on their weekend itinerary. Had it been cancelled? A little investigating revealed that there was friendly rivalry between our village and Gignac — hence the mysterious disappearance of the posters. Of course this made us even more determined to visit the Gignac *vide-grenier,* for we had heard from many people that it was a truly magnificent one. And when the day finally arrived, later in the *vide-grenier* season, indeed it was.

There is always a tremendous feeling of early Sunday morning excitement as you fly through the countryside to be among the first to explore the potential treasure. Often the markets are held in a farmer's field and for one Sunday morning a year it is utterly transformed. Row upon row of cars are all parked neatly in lines — often in an adjacent field. People tumble out of their *voitures*, consumed by the urge to be the first to fall upon coveted pieces of antiquity. And yet, tearing through the calm of an early Sunday morning, we are often mystified about how there can possibly be a *vide-grenier* at the end of our country drive, for the winding lanes are quite empty and it seems impossible that the remote roads will lead to fulfilment. Yet indeed they do. We turn a corner and there, at a time when most are still enjoying a leisurely Sunday morning, is a field full of possibility. The air is often cool and damp, yet there is also a palpable air of those like us, caught up in the exhilaration of a treasure hunt.

Wednesday and Saturday mornings are allocated to the fresh produce market in Martel, that originated in the 12th century. The arching roof is a huge, self-supporting wooden construction and the space underneath springs to life on market days. The abundant fruit and vegetables are fresh from the farmers' fields, literally picked only hours before, still glazed with early-morning dew drops. Once the market is *fin* in time for *déjeuner*, the only sense that there were hundreds of people lingering with their baskets over their arms, carefully choosing their produce, is perhaps a stray scrap of cabbage leaf, blowing in the light summer breeze.

Martel is a truly beautiful little town, that every single time we are there, I take pleasure in wandering around and gazing at its medieval past. There are lots of imposing doorways, beautiful arches, half-timber houses, wooden shutters and, of course, the towers. As you wind along the road from Cuzance, its seven towers give it a distinctive silhouette. It's known locally as the town of the seven towers. While most of the towns in our region began as a religious centre or a military site, Martel sprang up because of its position at a crossroads for the Paris-Toulouse trade and as a route for carrying salt and wine. It is also close to the famous town of Rocamadour and was an important stopping place for pilgrims. The sense of history every single time I am there, seems to seep up through the very cobblestones. On market day, the square comes to life like a film set with all the actors in place, as they have been for hundreds of years. Tradition and ritual are part of everyday life in France.

Meanwhile, we are creating our own history and enduring imprint on Pied de la Croix. Once again, before our return, Jean-Claude's attention to the details of our other life is touching and extraordinary.

This afternoon I had an appointment with a maçon for a quote for your bathroom window, but he could not make it; so it will be on Friday; to switch on the mains, the button is in the small shed at the back of your bedroom, isn't it?

Your plantations have almost done nothing, due to the bad weather ... and are outgrown by the weeds, except the catalpa which displays a single bud. Françoise is recovering from a bad cold caught in those freezing churches! She was wheezing until now like an old Ford T model! Concerning plantations, there is a surprise from me; but it is not doing better than the rest; so much for mysteries!

Love to you from JCC.

Jean-Claude's remarkable attention to details means that he is following up something that I had actually forgotten about asking him to look into for me! The *maçon* for my bathroom window. I cannot even begin to predict the possible cost.

French Protocol

After spending several summers in France, we remain conscious of French protocol and alert to the nuances between the two cultures. We are proud of the fact that in our small village, it was us who introduced Gérard and Dominique to Jean-Claude and Françoise. We noted however, with great interest that whenever we were with Gérard and Dominique, and Jean-Claude and Françoise came up in the conversation, they referred to them as Monsieur and Madame Chanel. With our casual Australian manners and easygoing ways, this formality is a revelation to us. However, we have learnt that this formality is deeply entrenched, particularly with older generations. They can in fact, know someone for thirty years and this form of address is still used. So, in Cuzance when we go for a walk round the village with Jean-Claude, we note too that he always greets the older inhabitants, such as Monsieur Dal, in a formal manner. In fact, I have also noticed that he always refers formally to our neighbours as Monsieur Chanteur and Madame Chanteur. When I think about it, I don't even know our neighbours' first names; perhaps I never will. Status too remains an important element in French life and it is still often the way, that the higher the person's status, the more reserved their behaviour is. Again though, it is mainly the older generations, and I'm sure one day, this element too will fade way.

What we have come to love, is the many elements of French protocol, such as when you are entering and leaving a shop. It is customary to always offer a greeting, *'Bonjour Madame, bonjour Monsieur,'* and on departure, '*Au revoir, bonne journée,*' — goodbye, have a nice day. I always find joy in the rhythm of these exchanges. If you don't offer a greeting, the French will simply think you are very rude — the service is usually in direct proportion to your politeness. Everyone appreciates any effort that you are able to make with the language and so, I always try to do my very best. Just like when I lived in Turkey, the very basic words go a long way — *merci, merci beaucoup, excusez-moi*. I have learnt too, that even if they understand English, the French may be wary of speaking it, unless they're fluent. In all respects, the French do not like to appear less than perfect. It is hard when we return home, not to continue the daily greeting, for after a few months, it is second nature. Likewise, I try not to kiss too many of my colleagues too often on both cheeks, though I must say by now, people seem to have become used to my adopted French ways. I frequently answer the phone at work with a bright, '*Bonjour!*' In France, it is in fact the custom to greet all your colleagues each day with a kiss on each cheek. Somehow, I don't think I will attempt to introduce that element into the workplace.

I look around, watch, and try to learn all the time. The French are always quite formal when they leave their homes. Even a trip to the weekly markets means that you would never dream of going out in what you wear at home; certainly there are no thongs or singlet tops in sight. When we stayed with Brigitte and Erick in their *chambre d'hôte*, I always noted that after they finished cleaning the *chambres* each morning and had done the daily washing of all the *chambre d'hôte* sheets, they would both change to venture out to the *boulangerie* and *supermarché*. They would always put on something smart. This too is a custom I am conscious of, apart that is, from the humiliating times I have dashed on an urgent mission through the village to Jean-Claude's in my renovating attire. Being conservative and smartly dressed is just another way of trying to fit into French life. It is something I have come to love, for all who know me, are familiar with my penchant for dressing up whenever possible.

Likewise, relaxing in a *café* can be altogether different. No matter how frantically busy or overflowing the tables are, there is always just a quiet hum of conversation. The tone is always muted, never loud. While drinking is a recognised French way of life, no one shouts or loudly laughs their heads off and the ring of a *portable* or a noisy child is seldom heard. It is not *chic* to behave in such a way. On the rare occasions we have lunch at our favourite restaurant in Martel, Le Jardin des Saveurs, although it is just *menu du jour*, the bread crumbs are swept off the crisp tablecloth after the first course. The waitress comes with a *petite* pan and brush to ever so discreetly whisk the crumbs away. This is the sort of attention to detail that I simply love.

When we are invited to *dîner* with friends, no side plates are used for the bread that invariably accompanies every meal. If we are lucky enough to be invited to Jean-Claude's and Françoise's, the *pain* is especially delicious as Françoise makes her own bread. The *pain* is simply placed on the tablecloth next to your dinner plate. Hence all French homes have a tablecloth that often stays on the table throughout the day. While I now have two tablecloths, both farmhouse checks, and both gifts, I don't think I will ever have a plastic one as many French households do. While very practical, I simply don't find them attractive at all.

The *apéritif* hour is something else I find especially civilised. Only one *apéritif* is usually served, at the very most two. Bread sticks or a small dish of olives or peanuts is always placed on the table, for it is rare to have a drink without some small accompaniment. We find this a great way to catch up with friends, as it is simply so easy and the protocol means that people rarely linger longer than an hour, for they then head home for *dîner*. This suits our style of entertaining just perfectly. When we are invited to dîner, usually just one *apéritif* is offered before eating, as there will be wine with the meal. Jean-Claude has a plastic carrier that was once used for milk bottles. When we have an *apéritif* on their terrace, he brings it out with *pastis*, gin and other choices in it. Despite the reputation of the French for drinking vast quantities of wine, in fact it is surprisingly far less than at home. *Vive la* difference.

Isabelle's *Petite* Shop

Visiting Isabelle's shop has become a part of my weekly ritual. As well as going to the twice-weekly markets to buy our fruit and vegetables, on Friday morning we now go to Martel once a week to do our grocery shopping. Such a prosaic task has become one of pleasure. We have now established the habit of first having our weekly treat of going to the *boulangerie* to choose a delectable pastry. There is always an immense pleasure in lingering at the counter and gazing at the sumptuous array of mouth-watering pastries. Then across the road to the locals' *café*, as opposed to the ones in the market square that tend to attract the tourists. While the *café* is right next to the road — we seem to be attracted to places situated on roads, just like our *petite maison* — like so many French towns, it overlooks tubs of brightly coloured flowers. We order our *espresso*, '*Deux café s'il vous plaît.*' Yes, I can actually manage the simple phrase for ordering two *espresso* ... and we linger over our melt-in-the-mouth *croissants*.

It is a chance to sit and observe the daily life of a small French town. The *café* is also a *Tabac*. There is a place to precariously park right at the front of the *café* and the locals dash in to buy their *Gauloise*. It is like a drive-through tobacconist. Once when I went in to pay for our *espresso*, I was puzzled by the fact the young woman behind the counter did not move from one end of it to the other, to collect my *euro*. After quite a while, I moved to the other end of the counter to pay. I told Stuart about the puzzlement of paying. Ah, the first end of the counter is the *Tabac* section and you can only pay for those purchases there.

Hence the dash-in-drivers who hastily grab their daily *Gauloise*.

Our bank, *Bank Populaire*, (literally, a popular French bank), is next door and on the other side of the *café* is *Les Marchands de Journaux*, where people grab their copy of *Le Figaro* to read over their *espresso*. Next there is the *pharmacie* and like all other chemists in France, it displays a poster of mushrooms to be able to identify those that are poisonous. Mushroom gathering in spring is a very popular pastime in France. Each year Brigitte and Erick tell us when they are setting off for a few days' break to pick mushrooms. By now, as we have our *espresso*, we actually know a few locals passing by and going to the shops, to exchange '*Bonjour, ça va?*' with. This simple greeting fills me with delight. In some small way, we do belong.

It was on one of our *café* sojourns the previous year that I glanced across the road and my eyes landed with happiness on a newly opened *petite* shop, complete with a hat stand and other second-hand wares out the front. I exclaimed with pleasure to Stuart that I simply had to go and investigate straight away. Knowing my predilection for any possibility of second-hand treasure, Stuart settled back with another *espresso* while I skipped across to investigate. A second *espresso* can only last so long, and by the time he thought my time for exploring had definitely been sufficient, I had my arms laden with potential purchases to eagerly share with him.

When friends and family come to stay, Isabelle's shop has now been woven into my personal itinerary. So now Mum has her pink jacket in *Australie* and Liz has a *petite* watercolour in Wales. As with all my treasure, I eagerly display my new *chapeau* to Françoise next time I see her. She duly shares my pleasure in my pretty pink hat. Not long after, when I go La Vieux Prieuré, Françoise and their youngest daughter, Bénédicte, show me what they have unearthed in Isabelle's shop, for they too call *la petite* shop by the name that I do. Just like last year, when

Dominique appeared in her first-ever purchase of second-hand clothes, it is when I introduce my French friends to sources of second-hand delights, that I truly feel a part of life in Cuzance.

Actually, I don't know the name of *la petite* shop at all. However, I always chat to Isabelle the immaculate and *chic* owner, so that is what I call her treasure trove. I'm thrilled to actually say it's part of my weekly routine in a new village, in a new country. To start to establish rituals, means that I feel a part of the rhythm of life in Cuzance.

Bon Courage

'*Bon courage*' are words that I would be profoundly grateful to never hear again. It seems that every passer-by, every casual drop-in, every *artisan* and all our French friends, utter this phrase when leaving our *petite maison*. No translation is needed. The meaning is absolutely clear. Underlying this seemingly casual, polite phrase is an undertone that distinctly conveys, firstly, that they think we are extraordinarily mad to tackle such a project and, secondly, how grateful they are that it's not them. Shades of one of my frequent thoughts, 'Is a working holiday a *vacances* at all?' rise to the surface whenever I hear this phrase. Somehow too it is always uttered in a tone of the utmost *bonhomie*.

As I continue to labour long and hard at whatever the current task is, I always gaze wistfully after their rapidly departing backs, knowing full well, that they are returning to relax in their *jardin* to linger over an afternoon *apéritif*. I can only begin to imagine the sage nodding of heads and absolute concurrence that yes, the madness of foreigners knows no end. My limited understanding of French would certainly not impede my understanding in this instance, of the speculation about a couple who come all the way from *Australie* each year to spend their *vacances* renovating.

As I get older, my penchant and inclination for renovating seems to rise in inverse proportion to the passing years. And so it is, that I find myself declaring with increasing vehemence — that next year when we embark on the bathroom — will be my last renovating push — ever. We will see. I seem to recall that those words have been uttered before.

Despite all that '*Bon courage*' implies, nevertheless when working life at home becomes challenging, I console myself with my escape clause — Cuzance. It reverberates in my mind, a place that somehow doesn't often seem real and yet real it is. Cuzance is indeed a place to return to year after year. A very real and very real different life, even if does hold the oft-repeated phrase '*Bon courage*'.

Our Belgian Friends

Time adds a rich layer of meaning to friendships from afar. A chance encounter on the streets in Trabzon, a small town on the Black Sea, twenty years ago has led to a friendship sustained through letters for many years and now emails. We had noticed Eric and Lydia on the small plane from Istanbul, as they were the only other tourists heading to a remote part of Turkey, at quite a dangerous time. It was the first Gulf war and there were bombs being dropped on Iraq. When we stayed in Trabzon, the four of us were the only tourists, so we all teamed up to share our adventures. There was a curfew each night; helicopters constantly hovered overhead and there was a real sense of imminent danger.

As with many of our friendships, chance seems to play a strong role. We had been booked to go on a ferry to eastern Turkey, but as I was heading back to our flat, after collecting my final pay from my teaching job — paid in cash and given to me in a large brown paper bag, just like real-life Monopoly — I encountered Stuart in our local market, also heading home to our flat in Besikatas. He had been to pick up our ferry tickets but on the eve of departure, we found out quite by chance, that the ferry had been burnt and destroyed. We made a last minute decision to fly instead and so, two new friends entered into our lives.

There was no way in those early days that I would have ever dreamt of having a house in France. Just a few days into our travels, Stuart spent all his money on a Turkish carpet, while just a few months later I paid for my own engagement ring. Who would have ever thought that

I would go from sleeping on a beach alone in Greece for three weeks to save money, to having a *petite maison*? We were both backpackers on a shoestring when we met Lydia and Eric. We stayed in rooms that cost only a few dollars a night; rooms that you would rather not glimpse in daylight. From soldiers with guns at checkpoints and in the streets and markets, to *châteaux* glimpsed as you round a corner on the way to the *supermarché* from Pied de la Croix. What a long way we've come. Life is truly an adventure when you take risks and push the boat out from the safety of shore to sometimes turbulent seas and uncharted territory.

As with many of our travels over the years, we have met up with people along the way, spent a few days exploring together, traded life stories, and shared meals. Most of these people are just transitory travel companions, bound by the place and time. So it was that after meeting Lydia and Eric, we spent the next week with them exploring eastern Turkey. This has been a special friendship that has spanned almost two decades. The years have seen us both renovate our many homes and share our unfolding life stories, including that of their two children, Jorn and Eleni. Then finally, after many years, we all met up on our first trip to France.

It was the time we rented a house for a fortnight and we seized the opportunity to gather our family and friends. There was a little studio at the bottom of the garden, so Liz, our friend from Wales, was booked into that. Stuart's brother John, was in a nearby *gîte*, a short bicycle ride away, while Lydia, Eric and the children were able to camp just nearby. And so, for a week, eight of us gathered each evening for meals in the *jardin* under the damson tree. This is not the sort of thing that comes readily to us at home, yet, across the other side of the world, somehow this is now woven into the French part of our life. Time dropped away, we laughed and filled in the gaps of the intervening years, and now, once again we are to be reunited in our own *petite maison*.

Just a matter of a few weeks before leaving, Lydia emailed to let me know that their summer holiday in the Basque country meant that they would also be able to visit us for a few days. What did I think of that plan? My fingers flew across the keyboard in excitement to let her know that is exactly what we hoped Pied de la Croix would be, a place for spending time with those we love. Somehow, again completely unlike the person I am at home, it doesn't matter that we don't still know John's plans; whether there will be eight or ten of us in our *petite maison*, that there aren't enough beds, enough linen and one *petite* bathroom. We simply know that it will all be perfectly fine, it will all work and our everyday selves at home will be transformed by the seductiveness of summer days in France.

The Figeac *Caravane*

Things really started to fall into place before we left this year. Weeks before heading for Cuzance, we decide to check the route for the *Tour de France*. Much to our excitement, the route goes though Brive-la-Gaillarde, a mere twenty minutes from us. We speculate about the back roads that the *Tour* may take and wonder if in fact it may go straight past our *petite maison* — after all, our house is right on the road! Last year I had strenuously resisted Stuart's entreaties that I go with him to watch it in Figeac. I simply couldn't imagine anything more tedious than a bunch of bike riders whizzing past at great speed, a blur of coloured jerseys, gone in a flash. I kept saying that he should make arrangements to meet Erick as I was sure it would be a perfect outing for them; much like my vigorous attempts to not be involved in any canoeing trips. The thought of a day in the *jardin*, even if it did mean literally sitting in a pile of weeds and rocks to tug and pull at them, was infinitely more alluring. However, like many of Stuart's ideas, once I finally capitulated, it turned out to be a brilliant day.

Figeac is a beautiful historic town on the banks of the River Cele, surrounded by charming villages. It's an unspoilt town centre, with a delightful range of medieval houses that are both stone and half-timbered. The site of the old *halles*, or markets, is where *cafés* now spread their tables. After a visit to the *Office du Tourisme*, to check the route, we joined the throng of the soon-to-be *Tour de France* crowds, and with just enough time before the race came over the bridge, had the *menu du jour*. Just as we were finishing our *café*, the heavens opened and it looked like our experience of the atmosphere we had only ever viewed from afar at home, was to be a rather damp one. However, the downpour was short-lived, so we crossed the river, caught up in *le Tour* excitement, and positioned ourselves in a perfect viewing spot, ready to see the riders swoop around the end of the bridge and then race up the hill. As it turned out, there was an hour of unexpected build-up of atmosphere and anticipation with the arrival of the *caravane*. This was something we had never seen at home when the *Tour de France* was shown and we had not heard anything about it, even from our French friends. It turned out to be tremendous fun. Truck after truck roared past with loud music blaring from speakers, young French people dancing on the floats and banners flowing in the breeze to advertise different companies. To add to the festive atmosphere, the dancers on the trucks all had samples to throw to the crowds: biscuits, magazines and if you were really lucky to grab one, a *Tour de France* cap from the large *supermarché* chain, Carrefour. So, this year, we knew what to expect.

Last year after the *caravane* had passed, we decided to move our vantage point to higher up on the hill. It turned out to be perfect. Just like in our *petite maison*, we were right on the road, close enough to feel the whoosh of air from the bikes that pass in a blur of movement and colour. The whole race was in fact so fast that we were not even sure it was finished. Finally, some French tourists asked the policeman on his powerful motorbike in front of us whether it was *fin*. We understood that *oui*, indeed it was. So it was in fact that at that very moment, Dave texted us to let us know he was watching the *Tour de France* on a cold, wet day at home and thought that the countryside looked very familiar to Cuzance. Were we thinking of going to see it at all? We texted back triumphantly to say, 'We are here and Cadell Evans has just gone past us.' And so it was, the *Tour de France* that I was so reluctant to go and see was the year an Australian won — and it was a day out that was far more enjoyable than I could have anticipated. Perhaps I should review my thoughts on a canoe trip after all.

Le Grand Jardin

Every single time I spend time relaxing in Jean-Claude's and Françoise's glorious *jardin*, it takes my breath away. Every single time, I feel a sense of privilege to have entree to such an enchanting kingdom. The high limestone walls and solid wooden gates, right on the street in the heart of Cuzance, do not give a hint of what lies beyond. The upper *jardin* is adorned with garlands of mauve wisteria and sweet-smelling honeysuckle, and on the right, a large, flagstone terrace leads to their stunning seven-storey *maison*. I find out later from new friends we make in the village, that it is known by everyone as 'the castle'. It is not until you are in the lower sweep of the garden, beyond *la piscine*, that you can gaze up and see it spread out before you. The tower climbs high into the sky and is balanced by the towering dark green fir trees planted on the boundary. When friends come to stay, I make sure that a visit to La Vieux Prieuré — the Old Priory, so named because it is literally opposite the church — is on the itinerary.

Apart from the neighbour's tractor, occasionally gathering hay, it is only the constant musical notes of birds that stir the peace and quiet. While I love Pied de la Croix, returning to our French home is always something of a jarring note. Although just a short walk, it is worlds removed. However, what I do need to remind myself, is that just three years ago when we first arrived, we couldn't even walk around our property. Although I'm still dismayed by the profuse proliferation of weeds, it is already a far cry from my first glimpse of our new French home, on a cold damp day, one that definitely matched my mood. I remember only too vividly my utter sense of wondering what on earth we had done. Now at least in our absence, Albert has planted a border of lavender and photinia next to *la piscine*. Thanks too to my vigorous pruning efforts last year, the orchard is flourishing. As the days grow warmer, the walnut tree is a perfect place to escape from the afternoon heat. It is even more perfect when Stuart makes the trek back to our *petite maison* in front of *la grange*, and returns with afternoon tea on a tray. *Espresso* and *citron tarte,* under the spreading limbs of the 80-year-old walnut tree; a slight breeze stirring the air. Life simply does not get much better than this moment on a languid French summer afternoon.

After over ten years of *rénovation*, I'm at last learning to adopt Stuart's philosophy, that it can all wait until another day. I've learnt too from his approach, that half the work is in the reflecting and planning. So, we take the opportunity on this stolen afternoon, to discuss the paving plans for *la piscine*. On his white plastic *chaise longue* — no French home is without them — he has a pile of house magazines gathered from *vide-greniers*. He pores over the pictures and explores the options. We pause to gaze at the golden stone of *la grange* and the immaculate new slate roof. While it took at least a week on our last working *vacances* to find the time to venture into the barn, this time we manage it on our third day. Though only a few steps from our *petite maison*, domesticity has consumed the daylight hours until now. While an absolute extravagance to even contemplate its conversion, it still remains at the pinnacle of our *rénovation* dreams.

Literally as we finish weighing up the merits of paving or decking round *la piscine*, Jean-Claude appears. I had only just said that once again we would need to get his help sourcing a concrete supplier and *voilà*, he appears round the side of *la grange*. As with all our pursuits, he enthusiastically embraces our crazy paving plan and with just a brief interlude for a hasty Kronenbourg, he whisks Stuart off to the nearby village of Cressensac to start investigating prices and all the possibilities. Though on the verge of seventy, there is never any time to be lost where Jean-Claude is concerned. Perhaps indeed it is the very fact that seventy is looming means that he embraces each day with enormous delight and enthusiasm.

Two Worlds

At home, through choice, my week day has life more or less an unvarying rhythm. I go to school, I return home, we walk Henri, tend to household tasks and the demands of daily life; renovate; friends on the weekends, family from afar in the holidays. In the early hours, as the day breaks and pink light floods the sky and sea, I write before going to work. A very simple life, a comforting sameness. In Cuzance, our world is utterly different. In many ways it mirrors our early renovating days in Sydney, more than a decade ago. We worked virtually every waking hour. As soon as we arrived home from work, we pulled on our renovating clothes. I learnt how to mix concrete, I ferried wheelbarrows of bricks from the front of our terrace house to the back, I loaded skip after skip with renovating debris. And we lived without a kitchen for nine whole months. Yet somehow, we had huge reservoirs of energy. It meant that we went out frequently for dinner and despite the punishing labour and arduous hours, we found ourselves in a large circle of new friends. Moving to Sydney from Canberra was a new life in every possible way. Just like in Cuzance, friends dropped in frequently and often lent a hand.

So it is now, many years later and on the other side of the world, that suddenly we also have a circle of new French friends who also drop in to check on our progress and invite us to *apéritifs* and *dîner*. The endless hours of summer sun, means that each and every day, holds any number of possibilities. That is one of my strongest memories when I return home to a more sedate, prosaic life. That on a morning when I wake in Cuzance, the day holds the promise that anything at all is possible.

Despite my utter lack of attempt to learn any French at all in the intervening year between my two lives, I utterly astonish myself when the few words and phrases I do know surge back into my memory. On the morning I wake with the intent of writing my postcards I bought on our morning in Paris, my waking thought is that I have already assembled the sentence in my mind to go to *Le Bureau de Poste*. 'Hello, three stamps for Australia please.' Later, as I stand in the queue — as is my habit on such occasions in a French shop — I rehearse the sentence in my head. *'Bonjour, trois timbres pour l'Australie s'il vous plaît.'*

And always as you leave, *'Merci beaucoup, au revoir,'* which conveys, 'Thank you very much, have a nice day.' While my inflection is incorrect, nevertheless the woman on the counter in *Le Bureau de Poste*, graciously acknowledges my effort with a warm smile, and by the end of our summer, also greets me with a smile when I enter to buy *timbre*. Each customer in every shop I go to, is greeted with customary courtesy and is politely farewelled as they leave. These rituals never cease to please me.

A Country Life

After only a few nights, my body clock seems to have adjusted to being in a different time zone. Just like at home, I creep out of our *chambre* just before dawn. The tall, curved street lamps are still lit and the birds are only just starting to melodically greet the new day. The sky gradually softens and lightens and as I venture out, rabbits are bouncing through the grass, their white bob-tails bright in the damp greyness. The neighbouring black cat emerges from one of our outbuildings and peers at me in surprise. It's welcome to sleep there I tell it, but you could at least be doing a better job with the mice.

It is drizzling and cool on the very morning I was planning to start tidying the *jardin* in front of our *petite maison*, including wrenching out the year-old weeds that have sprung up in the cracks in the rounded front steps. Just like in previous years, we have to glean the weather report from people we encounter. Last year it was the roofers or Ann-Marie, our bank manager in Martel. This time it was Nigel, who told us the day before that the weather would turn cool and cloudy for the rest of the week. Right on cue, it changes. This does not suit my plans at all.

Thank goodness we had our precious afternoon under the walnut tree. We remember only too well the days we spent working in the searing heat last summer. The day Stuart and Erick spent twelve hours straight installing *la cuisine* when it was forty degrees. I also recall only too vividly that not only did I toil relentlessly in the blistering heat in *le jardin*, but also in the rain. There will be no such madness of foreigners this year, I resolutely remind myself. Another thing we have reminded ourselves this year is to make the most of the days that peel away from the early morning chill and unfold into days of glorious sunshine. It would seem that once again the seasons are confused and we need to adjust our *rénovation* plans to meteorological vagaries.

Though *petite*, Cuzance is an interesting amalgam of people and *maisons*. It's a true rural village. This is reinforced when we go for an evening walk — though usually very late — it's still uncannily light. The fact that we are surrounded by French farmers is evident in the hushed silence hanging over the freshly mown fields and groves of walnut trees. A young famer wishes us '*Bon soirée*' as he comes out of his *maison* to draw his heavy shutters tightly closed so he can block out the last of the summer light and sleep before his early dawn rise.

We are lucky to be surrounded by an abundance of walking trails, with names such as '*Tour de Cuzance*'. We walk past the *Marie* and Hotel Arnal. Though only nine, not a soul stirs in our sleepy little village. We choose a trail on the outskirts that loops around the village and at the end of the walk, emerge at one of the many true working farms. There are pieces of farm equipment scattered everywhere and several tractors to plough the fields and gather the summer hay. Like most French homes, it has an extensive vegetable garden where lettuce, *tomate* and cabbages flourish. A *petit chien* bounds towards us, wagging its tail vigorously. It has a friendly, endearing face, the sort of loving dog that you could simply scoop up and take home. As the day draws to a satisfying close, it's the time when rabbits race homewards through the fields. They certainly better not be heading to a burrow in our *la cave*.

On each of the six approaches to Cuzance, there are newly built *maisons* constructed from wood and with sloping roofs. They have been designed and built to blend with the centuries-old stone *maisons*. There is however, no mistaking the fact that we are in a rural landscape when the very distinctive farmyard odour periodically pervades our *jardin*.

There is also the raucous squealing of pigs, on cue, at feeding times, early in the morning and then in the evening. The full moon shines on us as we end another happy day in Cuzance; the only people in the empty night as we head home along the quiet lanes.

Martel and the Markets

Today is market day. I'm not quite filled with the same sense of eager excitement that I am on *vide-grenier* mornings but nevertheless, there is a feeling of anticipation about once again filling my basket with fresh produce. I don't think that I will ever lose my sense of joy each year at rediscovering all the things that we have come so quickly to love.

On Sunday afternoon, sauntering around Martel, the market square was empty after the *déjeuner* gatherings. Now, on market day, it is bustling and lively. My secret hope is fulfilled when the middle-aged couple, both short, round and cheerful, whose stall we most frequented last year, recognise us and welcome us back. They must serve thousands of customers every year. To be remembered, truly makes me feel as if we belong.

When we return home, our basket is brimming. It is laden with more treats that we look forward to enjoying each year during our French summer. At the stall specialising in the walnuts of our region, we've bought *trois* products: *Noix Caramélisées* — their crunchy sweetness a perfect accompaniment with the *Apéritif Noix* we sip in small, delicate glasses after *dîner*, while the *Huile de Noix Vierge* will be used for salad dressing. We also buy soap for gifts — *Savon Au Lait D'Anesse* — soap from donkeys. It's the first time I've ever seen it and I find it fascinating that soap is made from donkeys' milk. I am especially fond of donkeys and the soft braying of one that I occasionally hear from a neighbouring field. As we unpack our straw basket, we bury our noses in the tantalising aroma of the ruby red *fraise*. Inhaling the freshness of succulent strawberries, brings summer to life in our *cuisine*.

I'm starting to make small steps forward with my language skills, for when I write the *supermarché* lists, I write what we need in French: *beurre, sucrer* and *jus*: butter, sugar and juice. Stuart's first words when he got up were, 'What will we have for *dîner*?' I remind him that is precisely what French people think on waking, for I remember Martine telling me that when we stayed at her home in the Loire Valley. I suggest a roast chicken and write *poulet rosti* on my list. Food is definitely a religion in France. It is one we fervently embrace.

Pied de la Croix's Stories

At home, everything we have bought and accumulated has a story attached to it, like when we lived in Newtown and there was an evolving element of recycling. Some of our street finds were fabulous, like the immaculate sixties Formica table I found one day in the alley behind our house. In France, the sense of an accompanying story is even stronger. The prosaic task of hanging out the washing on my makeshift line in the carport is made meaningful when I reach for the pegs. I've chosen to put them in a faded old battered tin that is punctured with tiny holes. Who once used it and for what purpose? I imagine it was a French child from long ago — grubby knees, torn shorts, searching in the long grass on *vacances* at his grandparents' farm, collecting insects and giving them holes to breathe, lost in the endless days of a childhood summer.

I spend a lot of time each day, letting my gaze drift and linger on the beloved *objets* we have gathered. I frequently muse about their past and who else once loved them. The price I've paid has nothing to do with my fondness for each and every item, for in fact, nothing cost much at all. It is what they represent and their unknown history that makes them valuable to me.

Last year, every waking moment of every single day, was consumed by the endless lists. We were utterly engulfed by them. What to buy, what to do and in what order. Everything was imperative, everything was a priority. It bordered on the tragic when we had to use masking tape to attach the most urgent tasks for each day, to the inside of the front door. Literally right in our face, there was no way possible each time we opened and shut the door that we could overlook the urgency of contacting the *plombier* yet again or face a potential flood in *la cave*. We are profoundly glad those days are behind us.

It is true that a year can make all the difference in the world. Our mutual waking thought is that we have to buy toothpicks. Can such mundane thoughts possibly be a greater contrast? We have invited Gérard and Dominique for *apéritifs*. We have bought the melon and prosciutto for the *amuse-bouche* — how I love that term for a snack served with drinks — but have overlooked the critical toothpicks to assemble everything. We take care to check the word for toothpicks in the dictionary before we head out to shop. While very good at gesturing, indicating and miming while in the *supermarché* and I can't find an item, I don't quite fancy the actions that would be involved in pointing at my teeth.

I wake from my afternoon sleep to be greeted by Stuart's announcement that he has moved four wheelbarrows of dirt, courtesy of Monsieur *Lapin*. Seriously, doesn't the rabbit know that we have more than enough work to do? After my *espresso*, I pull on my work clothes. What a wonderful reprieve to wait until day four this year before doing so. It was only last year that I would fall out of bed at daybreak and pull them on straight away from our very first day. A rapid *espresso* and it was off each day to *le jardin* to set to work with the dawn chorus greeting the new day. I know that Dominique's immaculate *jardin* will have a colourful profusion of summer *fleurs*. I'm determined that before their arrival, I will finish tidying up in front of our *petite maison*. I always have to remind myself though, that no matter how many weeds I wrench out and how much ivy I hack down, that it will always be a *rustique jardin* befitting an old farmhouse. A *château* it is not. However, since we have two months luxuriously stretching out in front of us, we plan to buy two baskets of pink petunias to decorate the front of *la grange*. They will hang from the iron trellis that was used to support the grapevines. In its former life, *la grange* was the hub of the farm where the cows lived and were milked.

Brive-la-Gaillarde and *Le Jardinière Chantalat*

We sleep in, we sleep in very late. I'm confused as I creep out for the light is dim and sombre. Still swimming up from sleep, I turn the *portable* on to check the time. The soft grey light tells me it's about seven. I repeat several times to Stuart that it is in fact after nine. Sleeping in is fine but it also means that it is a frantic rush to get to Brive before the shops shut at twelve. This is something you learn very quickly, shops shut on the dot of twelve and remain resolutely closed for the full two-hour *déjeuner* break. Dominique and Gérard had invited us to a pre-*déjeuner apéritif*. We'd declined, saying we were off to Brive to shop. Thank goodness, we agree or we would have segued straight from *petit déjeuner* to an *apéritif* in an exceptionally short space of time. Not that we are ever opposed to an *apéritif* but the time has come to accept that we are on a working *vacances* after all.

Over the *apéritif* hour the evening before with Gérard and Dominique, we had learnt some more about French customs. While they are very comfortable with us and seem to enjoy our Australian sense of humour, they are more formal in their approach to the ritual of the *apéritif,* than Jean-Claude and Françoise who casually offer us a beer while we are all relaxing round their *piscine*. As we chat happily with Gérard and Dominique for over an hour and an half, only one *apéritif* is ever accepted. In many ways, this sense of protocol suits us perfectly — we like the way it defines the time as a certain ritual before parting ways for *dîner*. As we get to know them more though over the summer, the French 'rules' seem to relax more and Gérard is certainly happy both to accept, while at our *petite maison,* and also offer another drink, when we visit at the *apéritif* hour.

We have made plans with them to go a *ferme auberge* for lunch. It's an outing they are very fond of and last year we had listened wistfully as they described the *degustation* delights of a seven-course *déjeuner*, all produced from the farm fresh fare. We are astonished that so many courses are only sixteen *euro*. I almost jump up and down with excited anticipation.

For now, though it is on with the business of a renovating life. Despite taking the wrong *autoroute* exit into Brive on our first trip for the year, and despite by now the very limited time before lunch, we have a very successful trip to *Jardinière Chantalat*. At home, we rarely go to nurseries except to buy seedlings for our vegetable garden. Now, we have two yawning acres that have been neglected for many years. Somehow, in the damp drizzle, we manage to squeeze four tall Laurier, two photinia, two hanging baskets and a tray of orange marigolds in to our Renault. The daily stop for *pain,* home for our usual simple *déjeuner* of *pain, fromage, jambon* and *tomate*, then off to *le jardin* in the rain. Despite the fact that it gets heavier and heavier, and we're soon quite drenched, we press on. I remember from last year that once I started working, the more I did, the more I wanted to do. This could well be, that despite having found Albert to mow and help while we are away, the fact remains that our land is huge and there is still more than enough to do. Although there are still swathes of weeds and brambles, the transformation in just two years is amazing. On our very first visit, it had been so overgrown that we couldn't even attempt to walk around our property and we left for home without even seeing it all. From once a small terrace garden in Sydney, to Cuzance, when days can pass and I don't venture to all four corners of our garden. Life's journey has been both entirely unexpected and extraordinary.

I start with a tenacious vine at the front of *la grange* that has grown rapidly in the past year. It is in danger of taking over and crawling into the gutters and rafters. Its tentacles reach into the gaps in the stone and over time, its invasiveness will cause the stone to crumble. Pretty as its bright orange flowers are, it has to go. I have to get the stepladder out and pry my secateurs into the crevices. When I step back, I'm very pleased with my effort — even if I am soaking wet by this stage. Time for afternoon tea and a new *mousse au chocolat* to sample. Mmm, *La Mousse Gourmande Au Chocolat*. It more than lives up to its gourmet label.

We gaze out through the rain-soaked windows and admire the bright orange marigolds that Stuart has planted. They are in an old stone trough built into the low stone wall near our *très jolie* front steps. We think the old trough was originally for the farmer's pigs to feed from. The baskets of pale pink geraniums hanging up high either side of *la grange's* huge wooden doors are a perfect complement to the pale gold stone. There were already five iron extensions protruding from *la grange's* walls, complete with hooks, just waiting for our *fleurs*. In less than a week, our *petite maison* looks more like a well-loved home every day.

When Gérard and Dominique arrived the previous evening, they stood for a few moments inside the doorway, while they took in all that we have achieved. Despite not visiting for a year, the fact that they notice our new lamp impresses us. We bask in the warmth of their compliments. The gift of new friendship is like a beribboned, special occasion, glistening white box from the *patisserie,* tied in a shining bow.

They told us how our nearest neighbour, Monsieur Chanteur, had intently questioned them when they had stopped in spring to take photos of our *jardin* for us. Who were they and what were they doing? Despite not being able to communicate very fluently with him, we're touched that he apparently keeps such a vigilant eye on Pied de la Croix in our absence. However, we are not at all pleased that he has chosen to plant five fir trees on our shared boundary. Eventually they will be enormous and block both the restful rural view and precious light from our *chambre*. Jean-Claude fills us in on why he has chosen to plant them so close to our *maison*. He says that he is an 'old school architect' and is apparently offended by the sight of our outbuildings and particularly the addition of our new water tank. We find this quite perplexing. After all, have we not all chosen to live in a rural setting?

More amusing are Jean-Claude's accounts of our Parisian neighbours across the road. He deems them to be very 'special'. This is his disparaging word for anyone who is at all different and does not quite fit in. We feel very fortunate to have escaped having this label applied to us. It would seem that the people from Paris scorn the bourgeois who own a second home. Stuart points out that this is a particularly strange attitude, for after all, their *petite maison* is where they escape to avoid the Parisian summer heat.

Even more entertaining is Jean-Claude's account of Monsieur Paris who took on a controlling role for the Cuzance *vide-grenier*. This extended to telling an old woman from the village that her stall was somehow not to his liking. This story sheds more light on why there seems to be at times a great divide between people from Paris and the rural French. We discover later, that perversely, Monsieur Paris is not held in high regard in the village as his home is always surrounded by piles of discarded junk. As his house, like ours, is right on the road, it is an ugly sight indeed.

We have planned to go with Gérard and Dominique to an evening *vide-grenier* in nearby Baladou. Just before we are about to leave, Dominique appears on our doorstep to tell us that they had discovered it is a barter-only *vide-grenier*. We have not encountered one here before but it makes a lot of sense in a rural community. Dominique explains that you can swap any number of things — shoes, clothes, *confiture*, even your labour such as work in *le jardin*. We have nothing at all to swap and it is the *apéritif* hour after all, so that's what we decide to do instead. I certainly don't intend to labour in anyone else's *jardin*.

As Dominique is inviting us for a drink, Jean-Clause drops in on one of his daily visits. She says they have not seen much of him at all since they returned to Cuzance for the summer. He explains that he must devote all his spare time to us while we are here. Everyone is gathered inside the doorway — Stuart and I stand each side of them to watch their animated gestures and *rapide* conversation. They joke and laugh together; it's like watching a lively stage play. As Dominique leaves, I tell her she could have called us on *la portable* rather than trek through the rain to let us know about the change in plans. She tells us it is always a pleasure to visit us in our home. They admire our *fleurs* as they leave together and I feel elated that our *petite maison* is being transformed so fully into a welcoming *maison* and reflect on what a far cry it is from the past two years when all we did was relentlessly renovate. There has not even been a single *bricolage* trip yet and it is only today that a hardware list has been started. By this time last year, the *bricolage* was already Stuart's well established second home. As we later meander home through the gentle rain after our *apéritif*, I am once again filled with a sense of joy to have two lots of *amis* in our village to share our other French life with.

Le Chien Quest

Jean-Claude has enthusiastically embarked on a quest for a dog. On Monday afternoon, perched on the old wooden chair in the corner of Françoise's *petite la cuisine*, I asked her what the chart on the wall meant. She explained that it was a diet plan from her doctor but confided that she was finding it difficult to follow the strict regime. It's no wonder she found it hard; cooking is both her forte and passion. I told her that when I get home from school each day I always feel tired but having Henri means I have to take him out for his daily walk. When I get back, I feel rejuvenated. While Françoise struggles to exercise, she agreed with my suggestion that by getting a *chien*, she too would be able to go for a gentle stroll each day through the village. This would go some way to combating the exquisite *cuisine* that Françoise conjures up for her friends and family.

We searched for Jean-Claude in *le jardin* to tell him of our plan. He has had dogs in the past and loves their company. He is the essence of all that a dog owner should be. Always working in his *jardin*, always on walks through the village, stopping to chat to all he knows; characteristic pipe in mouth and checked cap perched on his head. Walks with Françoise and a *chien* by his side would complete the picture perfectly. His only reluctance to agree with the plan is that in the bitter winter months they spend in Lyon, after their summer sojourns in Cuzance, we all know that while ostensibly Françoise's *chien*, it will be Jean-Claude who takes it out in the early morning and evening sleet, snow and ice.

By Thursday, *la chien* project is fully underway. Jean-Claude has found the perfect King Charles spaniel, four months old, in Cancon, a two-hour drive away. It was born in April, just like me. Maybe I will have a say in the name. I am filled with great satisfaction that my plan is so quickly coming to fruition. What we are also excited about is that in some small way, we will share their *chien* on our summer *vacances* and so have a French dog to return to each year. We decide, that as we will meet it straight away, when it becomes a much-loved part of Jean-Claude and Françoise's life, it will associate us with its new life too. We already look forward to it rapturously greeting us on our return to Cuzance in the years ahead.

Much to my amazement, I discover that all dogs born in a certain year in France, must have a name starting with the same letter for that year. Stuart explains that this way, you can tell how old a *chien* is. So, when they get their puppy, this year it must have a name that starts with 'H'.

Later in the week, I am surprised by the extent of my disappointment when Jean-Claude tells me that all the puppies have gone already. They have searched further on the internet and there will be none available for two more months — just when we leave. It would seem that I truly did see it partly as our *chien* too.

Solde in Brive-la-Gaillarde

Last year, it took us three whole weeks to find time to go the sales in Brive. Being in France in *solde* season and not being able to shop does not seem quite right to me. This time, I'm delighted that we are actually able to go before our first week even ends. Yet again, the changes in our Cuzance life in such a short time, never cease to astonish me. Even our friends have remarked that they are pleased we are not completely consumed by *renovateur* fever this year as soon as we arrive.

While Jean-Claude is on his *chien* quest, my quest is for the perfect pair of knee-high black boots. There is some confusion in translation when I tell Dominique what I'm looking for as she thinks they are to wear while working in *le jardin*. Since they usually only ever see me in my battered gardening attire, I can understand the confusion though it is a rather odd concept. I assure her that this is not the case but rather for when I go to work at my *lycée* at home. I always like the sound of my job in French as a teacher in a school library; I think it has a rather grand ring to it: *enseignant dans une bibliothèque de l'école*.

Fortunately for Stuart, the two-hour lunch break that still exists in our region, means there will not be endless browsing. While in Paris and the south of France, the luxury of a long leisurely lunch has been phased out, it is one of the things we most love. While it often means certain adjustments to our daily routine, when we too have time to indulge in a two-hour lunch, there is nothing in the world quite like it. Stuart also has to be back in time to meet Françoise to play bridge in Souillac. Last year, on one of his endless *bricolage* trips, he completely forgot the bridge plans he had made with her. Not this year; this year everything is different. I manage to dash in and out of a few shops and hastily grab a few bargains, then the sacred lunch hour descends. Shutters are closed, doors are locked and a quiet reverence for *cuisine* settles over the once bustling shops of Brive.

While the shops did not hold my coveted boots, it was enjoyable to finally have more time this year to stroll around Brive and explore its architectural beauty. As with every city, town, village and hamlet in France, there is also a strong sense of history. During World War II, Brive-la-Gaillarde was a regional capital of the *Résistance*, and was the base for a number of clandestine information networks and several of the main *Résistance* movements, including the *Armée secrète* (or 'Secret Army') and the *Mouvements Unis de la Résistance* — the 'United Movement of the Resistance'. Now, the medieval centre is full of shops, restaurants and *cafés*. It is a far cry from the days of spies, secrecy and subterfuge.

I remembered the story of Madame Jouve who lived in Cuzance and was accused of being a collaborator. With other women, she was taken to Brive to be paraded in the streets as a traitor. The cobblestones we walk upon would have been witness to events that we simply cannot conceive.

After just a few hours and a taste of city life, we were glad to once again return to the peace and quiet of life in Cuzance. Well, maybe not all is entirely different this year. Let's not forget there is still work to do — a lot of it. The renovation is still far from complete. It's not all shopping trips, indulgent *déjeuners and apéritifs*. Jean-Claude has told us there is a *maçon* working on the house opposite them. He has already kindly organised a quote from another *maçon* for a bathroom window. He had left the previous quote inside Pied de la Croix for our return. He has now discussed with their neighbour's *maçon* to give us another quote. It is just as hard to get *artisans* in France as anywhere in the world, so we are grateful when the four of us squash into our *salle de bain* to measure and discuss where my longed-for window will go.

However, while hopes were high for this *maçon* and a window for this summer, once again, the oft-repeated phrase of '*Non, non,*' rings out in our *petite* bathroom. It would seem that he too is fully committed before his summer *vacances*. I can't begin to imagine the difference that one day, having light and air will mean. For the moment, it remains an airless, dark box. It looks like it is going to stay that way for quite some time. Mind you, the fact that it is perpetually dim means that despite my exhausted appearance when I do renovate, the mirror is deceptively flattering. Perhaps I don't want a window after all.

Our *chambre* shutters are so dark and heavy that they make it impossible to discern the time. So it is, that in less than a week, my body clock has fully adjusted and is once again in a steady rhythm. It often means that I'm up for hours — usually while it's still dark and I've done several hours of work before Stuart emerges. I prune, I hack, attack, dig, wrench, tear down, and move piles of stone. He can often only hear a rustling when he comes out to find me and is fond of asking if we now have a goat, for all he can hear is a steady movement in the undergrowth. My progress can be traced from the mounds and piles I leave in my wake. While backbreaking at times, it is also strangely soothing to work away in the quiet country stillness, far removed from the world and its cares. Just like pulling on my much-loved second-hand clothes, when I return to Cuzance, I also greet my *jardin* tools like old friends. I'm especially fond of my indispensable pruning saw that Jean-Claude gave me. Its old piece of blue twine, cunningly attached, helps hook down branches, to meet my vigorous pruning efforts halfway.

The *prunier* tree is weighed down almost to the ground with its harvest of dark-blue plums. In the damp cool of the morning, just after the soft grey light has crept across the fields, my cold fingers grasp the damp plums to gather for Dominique to make *confiture*. Within minutes, my colander is full. All my French friends make their own jam. I've never picked a plum before, let alone made my own jam.

So far we have only had one hot day and that has been enough for our two rose bushes to unfurl into pale pink beauty, tipped with sparkling drops of early morning moisture. I pick *petite*, exquisitely formed buds to place in the tiny antique *digestif* glasses Dominique gave us for a present when we arrived. Their soft pinkness is a perfect counterpoint when I place them on our dark wooden table. Even the rain is soft when it falls. Our Cuzance world is wrapped in a haze of gentle beauty.

Resuming Relentless Work in *Le Jardin*

For some reason, we seem to be avoiding the renovating that remains to be done. The list is not short by any means. It includes finishing the spare *chambre* in readiness for the first of our summer friends to arrive when Liz comes to stay. However, there is a lure to be outside, despite the fact that it remains very cool and overcast.

We tackle the planting of our new shrubs that are to provide a much-needed screen for *la piscine*. From the village centre — which consists of the Hotel Arnal and the *Mairie* — our block of land and the pool is on full view to all the villagers, and there is a direct view from the upstairs windows of the *Mairie*. While I want to have a close relationship with the inhabitants of Cuzance, this is not quite what I had in mind.

Stuart uses an old pick with an ancient worn wooden handle that Erick gave us, to attack the stony limestone ground. It remains hard and unyielding. The pick must be at least fifty years old and has seen many years of hard labour. Once again, I wonder who once used it. I imagine an old farmer, stooped with age and worn by the weather like his pick, meticulously tending his vegetable *jardin*.

As I wrench the invasive weeds from the new bed of lavender, I reflect on Jean-Claude's immaculate garden. There is a huge emptiness in the middle of the vast expanse of grass where he had to recently fell a dead walnut tree. He told me that it will be the last Herculean task that he performs. The thought fills me with sadness.

There is a strange peculiarity to the light in Cuzance. No matter how gloomy or overcast the day, invariably the sun bursts through brilliantly at nine each evening. The *petite maison* is filled with pure bright light. On one such evening, before bed, we walk through *la grange* and stand in the doorway at the back, looking out at the orchard. The soft rain falls gently and is pierced by the last rays of glistening sun. There is an otherworldly quality to it. It is an utterly magical moment, a moment to tuck away into the box of precious French memories.

I am invariably in bed just before the light fully fades. I rarely reach for my book straight away. Instead, I lie against my soft pillow, and watch the puffy clouds scud across the still-blue sky. At home, our white walls are filled with paintings and artwork. Here, in our tiny *chambre,* just like our *cuisine,* the walls have been left unadorned in their white-washed simplicity. The oblong-shaped windows, surrounded by dark wood, frame the view of the trees, sky, clouds and ever-changing weather. No art is needed. Cuzance itself is a still-life.

The Morning of *Le Maçon*

The morning of the next highly-anticipated *le maçon's* visit with Jean-Claude, dawns clear and sunny. Of course we have no idea when they will appear. Such is the desirability of *artisans* that it is impossible to pinpoint a time. This makes it difficult to leave Pied de la Croix and go to Martel for our daily *pain*. Stuart points out that I could always go by myself. After a week, I've still not driven our *voiture* and am reluctant to do so on a busy market morning. I learnt the word for car very quickly last year when the roofers were always asking me to move it from in front of *la grange*. Just like all my stumbling attempts to grasp French, a word only penetrates my vocabulary out of necessity. I did however, quite quickly learn all the essential words for all the delectable cuisine. *Canard* rates highly though duck is not a word in my grocery shopping lexicon at home. Of course, like *artisans* the world over, the *maçon* does not appear. There are shades of last year and the oft-repeated cry of, 'When will the *plombier* come?'

There is a strange symmetry between our renovating days in Sydney and buried deep in the French countryside. Without going anywhere at all, I still manage to have several 'chats' during the course of the morning. A walk to the communal bins brings a lovely encounter with Marinette, the matriarch of the village. She is sitting on a wooden bench under the shade of a chestnut, cane by her side and wearing her well-remembered blue and white straw *chapeau*. *Le Bureau de Poste* van stops and delivers her letters to her while we sit companionably together on the bench. Marinette points to her last name 'Barre' on a *lettre* and tries to get me to pronounce it. I attempt several times. Marinette purses her lips to show me how to produce the correct '*ooh*' sound. She laughs kindly at my clumsy attempts. I simply cannot twist my mouth in quite the right way. I know she secretly thinks that a three-year-old child would do better. After her sixth attempt, she accepts that I have failed miserably. She shrugs her shoulders in a very Gallic gesture and abandons my elocution lesson. It is precisely what happens when Jean-Claude tries to get me to pronounce Cuzance correctly. I can never, ever pronounce the '*ooh*' sound the right way.

I try to convey that I will be attempting to improve my French by having cooking lessons with Françoise. This way — or so my ambitious plan is at this stage — is that I will use all the accompanying French words to produce my sure-to-be magnificent *tarte aux pomme*. I already know the words for butter and flour — *beurre* and *farine* — so clearly I think I am about to be a Michelin chef in no time at all. At this point in our *vacances*, I still think I have all the time in the world, for the summer seems to stretch endlessly. Clearly, I have romantic visions of wafting through the village in my summer frock and *chapeau*, French market basket over my arm with apples from our own orchard in it. It is well known that I tend to live in a fantasy world of romance-induced visions. As I leave Marinette on the bench, she utters the oh-so familiar words, '*Bon courage.*'

Yesterday when Jean-Claude dropped in, I checked whether the apples from our orchard were suitable to eat and cook with. '*Oui*, your *pomme* are fine,' he assured me. Another glorious thought; my own apples for my own private cooking lessons. Measuring quantities in French will be an altogether different matter. I still struggle with simple counting and days of the week. I rather suspect Marinette knows about these deficiencies as well. Still, when I got married in Turkey, my dress was made by a seamstress who did not speak English and just like now,

Our House is Certainly Not in Paris

I had only a few faltering words of Turkish. My dress was still however, the fairytale one I imagined. While languages and I do not seem to be a perfect match, somehow I always manage.

As I clear the weeds and leaves from the past year from outside the doors of *la cuisine*, I go to say '*Bonjour, ça va?*' to Monsieur Chanteur. I was so happy to see that they had returned the previous evening, for we all feared that Madame Chanteur would never return after her long hospital stay. I am careful to be formal in my greeting, as well as taking care to refer to Jean-Claude as Monsieur Chanel, for I have taken note on several occasions that Jean-Claude has pointed out that our neighbour is very 'old school'. I do my stumbling best to convey how pleased I am to see him and to enquire after the well-being of Madame Chanteur. I also make sure that I include '*très merci beaucoup*' for keeping a watchful eye on our *maison* in our absence.

I am also mindful that Jean-Claude has told me how apparently offended they are by the plastic tank that squats like an ugly toad at the end of our carport. I'm conscious that it is in their line of sight as the Chanteurs resume their daily ritual of *déjeuner* and *dîner* under their walnut tree. It is the only space I have for my line of twine to peg our washing. Perhaps the open display of washing also offends them? It is possible, for now I think about it, I have rarely seen washing flapping freely in the wind and sun as is our custom at home. This is another aspect of French protocol that I simply have no idea about.

The sun finally shines and as the washing flaps away — no doubt offending French niceties — I start to pile my rickety old wheelbarrow high, Jean-Claude's gift from last year, and set off for the first of many precarious trips across *le jardin*. The front tyre is as wobbly as a child's front tooth but there will be no tooth fairy to rescue me if it falls off. It is a day of true French domesticity; washing, gardening and the final finishing touch, Stuart cleans the windows of Pied de la Croix. They sparkle and gleam. The *petite maison* becomes even more a home with each passing day, especially when people from the village pause to commend our efforts and admire our *fleurs*. It means the world to me that they have accepted us so fully into their small *commune* for I know this is not always the case with foreigners who suddenly appear in their rural midst.

Next door, on his first morning back in Cuzance, Monsieur Chanteur loses no time either in starting to catch up on the months of neglect while they have been in La Rochelle. Though white-haired and perpetually stooped, at eighty-eight he has the vigour of a man half his age for he is always active and energetic. I often pause in what I am doing, to glance across at him in his *le jardin*. I am full of admiration for him, both for the way he works so hard and the loving, devoted care he shows his wife. When *déjeuner* and *dîner* time arrive, it is Monsieur Chanteur who nimbly scurries back and forth to their *maison* to collect their fare and carry it on a wooden tray.

Last night, when going to bed, I had seen Madame Chanteur for the first time this year, through our *chambre* window. She was poised in their doorway, a red cardigan draped round her shoulders, a hand against the stone to support her frailty. She was peering across her rain-soaked *jardin* and it was a sight that warmed my heart, for I knew innately that her heart had longed for the sight of her Cuzance *maison* — at least one more time. I am absolutely sure it was what kept her heart steadfastly beating and keeping its tenuous hold on life.

Summer Daze

Marinette pauses on her morning *promenade* to praise Stuart for the grapevines growing each side of *la grange* doors that he is training on wire to create a graceful arch. She says she likes them as they are in keeping with the rural look of the village. It pleases us enormously to be accepted and to fit in — despite my *petite* French. I take pleasure in always wishing both her and Brigitte Dal, '*Bon promenade*' as they go on their daily strolls. That is a word I especially love for it seems to capture all that is idyllic about life in a French village. Time to meander slowly, time to chat, time to not think about the outside world or let it intrude. Time stands still in Cuzance.

Once summer truly starts, the heat is startling in its intensity. Sunlight creeps in ever earlier to all the corners of Pied de la Croix. The rooms are washed anew each day by the bright shafts of summer sun. The hay-gathering season is in full swing and huge tractors lumber past, their trailers packed with enormous, tightly bound rolls of golden hay. By now, the tourist season is at its height and cars full of holiday makers wend their way past our house, sometimes stopping for directions. Most of the time I even manage to help them on their way to Martel or Rocamadour. I practise my à *gauche* and my à *droit*, making sure to use hand gestures to indicate turn left, turn right. Before the village clock even strikes twelve, we know the *déjeuner* hour is imminent. At ten minutes to noon, the *voitures* start to scurry frantically past, to be seated at the table in time for the precious lunch hour.

The days take on a heat haze. We take on a daze from the heat. The grass browns rapidly. The puffy white clouds have all disappeared. Now, it is only possible to work in *le jardin* in the early morning coolness and the late evening. Even the constant backdrop of birdsong is more languorous.

There is nothing more splendid than a drowsy summer afternoon spent under the walnut tree. And surely, there is no better way to start a day than our first *vide-grenier* outing for the season. We have even agreed that, like in previous years, it is worth setting the alarm so we simply don't arrive too late to scoop up bargains. Our efforts are rewarded. We round the corner, to find row after row of *voitures* are parked in the farmer's vast field. We gasp aloud with excitement as we race along the narrow lane and there before us, are row after row of 'clear-out-the-attic' stalls. After just a few years, Blanat is one of our favourite places to rummage in the pursuit of true French treasure. Last year, the perpetual rain meant that there weren't many stallholders prepared to face a deluge. In a strange echo of last year, the day has turned cool and gloomy once again. It is only thirteen degrees when we set off, our spirits buoyant despite the menacing black clouds. While the weather is sombre, we are elated. This is one of our favourite pastimes in the whole world.

This year, the sun breaks through just in time for the village to have its annual household clearance. As always we have an eclectic list: a letter opener for post at Pied de la Croix, old linen as gifts for friends, a watering can for our new plants. Then of course any riches we stumble upon. We resume the *vide-grenier* approach we have adopted from previous years. Stuart sets off on a brisk reconnoitre for any must-not-be-missed bargains. We then go on a more leisurely stroll together to pause, pick up, examine, choose or discard *objets*. The scoop of the day is a silver soup ladle, a song at one *euro*. It's from the stall of Gérard and Dominique's friends. They tell us later that they did indeed sell it to me at an *amis* price — a special price for friends. As soon as we get home we scrutinise the tiny hallmark. Surely no piece of treasure will ever surpass this? We lay out our finds and examine the pristine linen and *école* notebooks — old school exercise books from long ago classrooms that were never used. Who was meant to write in them and what stories of childish imagination, dreams and hopes may have been contained there? As I cradle the ladle, my heart feels warm, just as the soup will be that I one day stir in our *petite maison*.

Over *dîner*, the disturbing noise from the previous evening ominously returns. We had been to Souillac for our first meal out — of course we chose our favourite steak, *frites* and *crème brûlée*. By the time we are home, tucked up snugly reading, the thunder starts to roll in waves overhead. And then, the alarming sound of loud scratching penetrates even the thunder. Last year, noises emanated from the attic, a place we have not set foot yet this year, even though it is just up a short flight of stairs from our *salle* where we occasionally have time to sit in the late evening on our battered Chesterfield. Though neither of us have actually said it, I think we are both nervous about investigating an attic that has been shut up for a year. This sound though is much closer — and far more alarming.

We grab the feeble, flickering torch and tiptoe out to investigate. On cue, like a drum roll in a film, the thunder intensifies. The shutters close the night out — and thankfully too it would seem, the marauding creature at large. There is no way to investigate the noise more closely — and certainly no great desire to do so — for we have now identified the source of the noise. It is much closer to home than we originally thought. It is not outside at all. No, the scurrying, scratching sound is behind the blocked-in metal guard in front of *la cuisine* fireplace. We remember the trepidation of the thought of a badger in *la cave*. Are there bears in France? We know about the *sanglier,* when in certain seasons it is not safe to go for a walk in the country, in case you encounter a wild boar. Surely it is not the season for *sanglier*? Our knowledge of French wildlife is a bit hazy.

It is late Sunday evening; everyone has been gathered for their family *dîner*, we dare not disturb our friends at this hour. There is nothing at all we can do. It is times like these that I fully realise how deeply buried in the country we are. We creep back into bed and pull the covers tight. Maybe it will just simply go away. The head under the covers technique seems to work for indeed, to our profound relief, the ominous scratching sound does in the end simply stop.

The Days Unfurl

On Jean-Claude's daily visits he frequently regales us with stories — accounts of the village, our neighbours and *soirées* they attend and give. His stories would be sufficient to fill a book of their own. One day, he told me about a recent *dîner* they attended. There was a young woman there, the same age as their son, Patrick, on holiday from Paris at the time. She too once lived in Paris and apparently she and Patrick got on very well. In fact, Jean-Claude reports that he later overheard them making plans to meet for *café*. This later causes some degree of excitement for both Françoise and I, as we are collaborating to find Patrick a lovely girlfriend.

He goes on to tell us that she worked as an eye re-educator. None of us are at all sure what such a job possibly means. Whatever the job may entail, clearly there is no call for it in the country, as Jean-Claude tells us she does not get much work at all. He concludes his anecdote by telling us she now finds herself living with her parents and with little diversion or income, in a *petite* hamlet. It has the highly amusing name of La Sotte, which literally means 'stupid girl'. While I keep my thoughts to myself, I can only conclude that it is a perfectly apt name for the girl who came from Paris, to a remote village, and now has little work.

As he has told us on previous occasions, Jean-Claude once again reminds us that in a *petite* village, absolutely everyone knows absolutely everything you do. And if they don't, they are eager to find out. As he *promenades* through the village each day, he is inundated by curious queries about us. Everyone it would seem is very anxious to know when we are going to 'open' our *piscine* for the season. Underlying this, is the implication that Australians have very strange ways, for after all, we are here, and in their minds the pool should be open. Damp days and drizzle do not seem to enter into it. They are perplexed as to why we have been back a week and not yet removed the cover. I am sure they are bemused by much that we do. All I can say is that the laurier hedge better have a rapid growth spurt — and soon.

On another day that he drops in, Jean-Claude shares more stories with us about our neighbours, the Chanteurs, but he tells us that it is in strict confidence and that I am not to breathe a word of it. When they walk past as we are sharing an evening *apéritif* on our porch, I am shocked to see how frail Madame Chanteur has become in the intervening year. I am touched anew by Monsieur Chanteur's loving protectiveness as he holds tightly onto her arm to support her. They too stop to admire our *fleurs*. However, once again I feel frustrated and on the outside as I simply can't communicate with them the way I would like to. At the *vide-greniers* I certainly know how to ask the price — '*Combien il est?*' — but I fail each time to understand the answer and always need Stuart on hand to tell me the price. At least I know enough to wish them '*Bon soirée, bon promenade*' as they continue on their gentle night-time stroll.

The next day we continue our combined onslaught in *le jardin* against the invading sea of weeds and brambles. A week of intermittent sun, interspersed with short, sharp showers, has meant that the weeds and grass have sprung up in front of our eyes. It is virtually impossible to hold the tide back. In only a week, the focus of my life, has narrowed down to our little Cuzance world.

All that matters now is the garden and my obsessive tendencies are in full force. I waste too much time wandering round the vast expanse in search of my digging implement that I have flung down carelessly. I almost cry with frustration. My indispensable *jardin* tool now means more to me than my coveted pair of French boots. I have lost precious time working and before long, the rain plummets down again and I am quickly saturated and driven inside. Our gardening clothes are soaked through and we have to wait for them to dry out before we can do any more work in the garden. Once again, I wonder what we were thinking. One set of work clothes each yet enough clothes for a month of Paris *soirées*. When we retreat to the house, there is now an ominous smell emanating from behind the fire grate. There is no way at all to see what is causing it, for it is impossible to even attempt to wrench the grate out. Thoughts of the suspected badger from *la cave* return. Or, possibly worse.

A New Week Beckons

Last year, Monday mornings invariably meant a visit to the *Maire*. There were mountains of paperwork to be approved and signed off. There were heart-in-the-mouth moments and a huge sense of trepidation. The work on the roof was well underway but did not have the official sanction. Would the work on the roof have to stop? Would it take weeks and weeks to have the official stamp of approval? And, worst of all, would it be *fin* before our departure? Now it looks like there will be more bureaucratic moments in store.

After deciphering our solemn-looking *lettrès* from Cahors that required us to state whether *la grange* was now being inhabited after the addition of its *nouveau* slate roof, we receive yet another official *lettre* from the government *département* in Cahors. We need to provide verification that *la grange* is not a *nouveau maison*. How will we prove this and how will we provide the proof? We choose to shelve the intricacies of French bureaucracy for the moment. There is simply too much to do.

Meanwhile, Mondays start with continued efforts in *le jardin* to stem the tsunami of weeds engulfing our new plants. It is heartbreaking to see this happen in front of our very eyes and, indeed, in the blink of an eye. It has only been a matter of days after all that we planted them. To protect them, Stuart climbs the ladder to the storage space above the carport and the very handy bales of hay that have been left by the previous owner. Mulch in an instant. He tosses down bale after bale of crisp, dry hay. Little were we to know that this would prove to be a perfect source of propagation for another influx of choking weeds. So much to do and so little time.

We then gather rocks from the land to edge the beds. There are lumps of limestone everywhere; no garden supply centre is necessary when you live in Cuzance. The land provides all that we need. We utilise all that we can that we find. Even the old blue twine from the hay bales has a second life when it is used to tie up and train the grapevines. This is recycling in its natural element. In fact, Stuart even remarks that he has not yet made one *bricolage* run. By the start of the second week last year he would have made at least five trips in this time. Freed from his endless work on *la cuisine* that consumed his life our previous summer, this time we are able to work side by side. While not as relentless — yet — in our efforts this year, for it would be impossible to sustain year after year, Brigitte from the village on her daily walk, does kindly enquire if we ever have time to simply *promenade*. I try to convey that we are certainly going to try to more often this year. While we are not completely consumed and driven by the desire to *rénovée* like previous years, nevertheless the days still ebb away. The difference is that this year we have found time for stolen hours under the spreading shade of the walnut tree.

La Dinette

While the inability to communicate with the outside world due to the failure of *la portable* is at times frustrating, nevertheless our lack of technology means that we are able to fully immerse ourselves in life in the country. At times however, the world beyond does bring a layer of responsibility and commitment to friends and family. On such occasions, I wander down to Jean-Claude's to check my email. I am an incongruous sight, walking through the village clutching my laptop, for in many ways, time has stood still in Cuzance and the outside world does not seem to intrude or impinge. It is something I particularly love, the immersion in my own special little world; a world where for a while you can divorce yourself from reality. While inevitably it laps at the edges of our rural backwater, I indulge myself in pretending it does not exist at all. We can dance to our own tune while we are here.

Stuart has gone to Souillac to play bridge with Françoise. A quick check of my email extends into a six-hour visit, ending with *la dinette*, for on their return, Françoise invites us to stay. *La dinette*, she tells me, is an informal, impromptu meal and casual invitation. This is more flattering than an invitation to a *grand dîner*. There are five of us, as Patrick is still on *vacances*. We gather round their outside table, overlooking the upper terrace festooned with wisteria. As a Parisian landscape gardener of growing repute, Patrick has not been able to resist some vigorous pruning and training. He and Jean-Claude have differing views on landscaping and the generations sometimes collide.

For a simple meal, to us it is extremely impressive that there is still a procession of courses. *Saucisson* from the markets — a type of cold sausage, thinly sliced, this one infused with the regional walnuts — homemade *pain*, ragout, *fromage* and then homemade *crème glacée*, *chocolat* tart and orange sauce — remains from their splendid Sunday *déjeuner*. These are not quite the leftovers we are used to in our home. The meal is made especially memorable when Françoise declares that we are part of the family. Our sense of acceptance and privilege to be so lovingly absorbed into our French life, is added to when Patrick offers us the use of his apartment in Paris when we return next year. It is like being offered the keys to the kingdom. There is no other phrase that exists with quite the same ring as, 'An apartment in Paris.'

We are puzzled though when Patrick reminds us that he made this offer when we met him the previous year. It is mystifying to both of us how we could have possibly forgotten such an exciting prospect, for after Cuzance, Paris is the only other place we would choose to be in our other French life.

As the heat builds up to a crescendo, so too do the flies who have taken up permanent residence in Pied de la Croix. Stuart sets to work in a frenzy of fly swatting. Like most other words I learn, it is in the context of necessity. So it is that *les mouches* is quickly added to my vocabulary. Like the weather, *les mouches* is a frequent word on our friends' lips. No discussion of international politics or worldwide events; no, in the country your world is narrowed down to the vagaries of the climate — 'Will there be a storm tonight?', 'Will it rain tomorrow?' and the marauding *mouches*.

Ferme Auberge

Scattered throughout the countryside in our region, is an abundance of signs for *gîtes* and *ferme auberge*. There are rural *gîtes* and *gîtes* in *châteaux*, and then there are the signs that point down enticing rural lanes to *ferme auberge*. Like many other experiences, it is not until this year that we have time to experience one. We had often been told by Gérard and Dominique of their fondness each Cuzance summer to eat at a *ferme auberge* at least once a week. Today they are taking us to their favourite one, near Souillac. They represent the essence of all that is celebrated in French rural *cuisine*, farm-fresh food, grown, picked, cooked and served by the family in their *maison*. Each *département* in France is justifiably proud of its own regional produce. What all *départements* have in common is that food is an art form, a religion, the essence of existence. What French people choose to eat each day underpins the rhythm of their daily life.

As always in France, the drive is as much a part of the experience as the destination. This one takes us past the well-remembered towering limestone cliffs, down winding narrow lanes and then, up a gravel drive to a large and picturesque house, covered with ivy and steps decorated with welcoming pots of crimson geraniums. It is set high on a hillside and has a sweeping view of the summer crops below, neat green fields of abundance.

In a *ferme auberge*, everyone gathers round one long table and everyone is served the same meal. There is no need for a menu although there is a choice in the main course. This is not a meal for the height of summer for the food is rich and heavy. It is redolent of the fare prepared for true farm workers, when *déjeuner* is the main meal of the day to build you up for a solid afternoon's work in the fields. Now, as the tourist season starts in earnest, the lunchtime gathering of up to thirty people, can be a smorgasbord of nationalities. In the evenings it is even busier, when *dîner* is also served on the outside terrace and sixty people can be served in the course of an evening. All I can say, is that after a seven-course meal at night, they must roll home like a big bale of hay.

We are seated in the prime position, next to the window, overlooking the beds of yellow roses. The first course to arrive is a hearty vegetable soup, followed by *rillettes*, a thick, coarse type of *pâté*, served on crunchy, oven-fresh *pain*. Next, there is a choice between goose and roast lamb. Gérard is an aficionado of goose and heartily recommends it. Dominique and Stuart opt for fat, corn-fed goose and I choose soft pink, tender lamb. It seems to have jumped straight from the fields to my plate. We toast each other and promise to make an annual pilgrimage to *la ferme auberge*. There is a green salad and *fromage* followed by Gérard's absolute favourite dessert, *île flottante*, which literally means floating island. Despite our love affair with all that is a dessert in France, *île flottante* does not rank highly on our list. It is a strange concoction of meringue floating in an ever-so-sweet syrup. It is cloying and does not rate a look-in in our echelon of favourite French desserts. Gérard assures us that the *ferme auberge* one is utterly different. We remain to be convinced. I am even less sure when he says it is also known as 'eggs in snow'. I am instead given a plate of *abricots* and walnuts. I discover I have made a mistake. They persuade me to try a mouthful, and I am swept away by its smooth lusciousness. Trust a Frenchman to be *au fait* with his desserts.

We head home thoroughly replete, through the pretty villages of Cresse and Gluges. The *voiture* is swamped by the formidable rock walls and we hug the narrow road as it curves in right under the soaring cliffs. I breathe in tight in case we encounter another car. Somehow,

I think this may make a difference. The Dordogne flows calmly next to us, kayaks flash past and kites wheel lazily overhead. We drive next to walnut groves, the trees as straight as silent sentinels, and as we go through the small village of Saint-Sozy, Gérard and Dominique point out La Terrace, a three Michelin star restaurant. Who would have thought that there was a Michelin star restaurant right on our doorstep? I later discover there are in fact six in our *département*.

The meal has been so big and hearty that all I want to do, when we finally arrive home at four, is to curl up and sleep. However, I had started to paint the hallway opposite the bathroom in the morning. To pack it all up now and resume another day, represents as much work as simply getting on with it and finishing it. So I press on, until weariness overtakes me and Stuart steps in to finish, painting until late evening. Last year this was our normal daily template; we hope this is a one-off.

We wake to a freshly painted hallway; an effort well worth it. It frees us up to go the markets, have a hasty *café* and delectable *abricot hibou* before racing in to Brive before the twelve o'clock cut-off. By now, we know our way round so our buying trips are swifter and more successful. The find of the day at Carrefour *supermarché* is a *solde* whipper-snipper, essential for slashing through the long grass that is creeping ever-higher. As we leave, like a synchronised moment for a Carrefour ad, a man in an open-top Peugeot has a matching whipper-snipper propped on his back seat. He toots his horn, waves and we all smile. It's like a perfect script for happy French homeowners. As soon as we arrive home, Stuart puts it to work straight away and there is a wonderful transformation from a shabby farmyard appearance to freshly cropped grass in front of our *la grange*. It is ready just in time for Liz's arrival the next day.

We mop and sweep and dust and clean in readiness. It will be the first time she will have seen *la cuisine* installed and all the furniture in place, for last year it was still very much a renovating site when she stayed. While we work hard, it is not at all the same as housework at home. Somehow, it feels more like cleaning and setting up a doll's house. There is definitely still an air of novelty to carrying out everyday tasks in Pied de la Croix. I can only hope this always continues to be the case. I even pick sprigs of lavender from our new plants to adorn the table. It is like designing a stage set.

That's when it strikes me that it's like playing in a doll's house, for it's when I tidy and straighten and place and decorate, that I realise the layout of our *maison* is a perfect square shape. Perhaps that is why it is so perfectly pleasing. As you enter from the rounded steps that everyone admires and says are *très jolie*, you walk straight into *la salle* and *la cuisine* lies to the right, all open-plan now that we have knocked a wall down. It is quite unlike traditional French homes where the sitting room and kitchen are rarely all open and flooded with light. There are two *chambres* at the back with the *salle de bain* in the middle. The symmetry and squareness is echoed in details such as our new shining white porcelain sink. It all reminds me of longed-for childhood dollhouses or those I have peeped at in museums. Perhaps it is why I feel like I am simply playing house.

I am so happy that Pied de la Croix is flooded with light for none of our friends' *maisons* quite have this quality. It is an element from home that we cherish — bringing in the sky and light. I often pause in what I am doing to watch the sky in all its ever-changing moods and the trees bend and sway. When storms lash the house, our unusually large windows let you watch the tempest flare up and then wear itself out. The only sounds at night in the country are those of the farm animals settling down to sleep and nature in all its unpredictability and beauty. When the wind abates after a furious storm, our *petite maison* seems to sigh with contentment and relief.

The Great Surprise

Jean-Claude, Françoise and Patrick arrive for an early evening *apéritif* in *le jardin* with the softest, cutest, most adorable bundle I have ever seen, clasped in Françoise's arms. I am so overcome by sheer excitement that I fail to even greet them properly with two kisses each, one on each cheek as is the custom each and every time we see them, so enraptured am I by the puppy and its entirely unexpected appearance.

She is called Ophelia — with the emphasis on the 'H', as this is the letter all puppies born this year must have a name starting with. However, in the *voiture* on the journey home after going to choose her, they have changed her name to Henriette. They have called her this in tribute to our little Henri, far away on the other side of the world. To say I am touched is an understatement. Gérard and Dominique pull up in their tiny green Twingo and join us at the table we have set up in the front garden outside *la grange*. The sun peeps through at the end of the day and a golden glow is cast upon our happy gathering. Henriette is passed from lap to lap and we all fall instantly in love with her.

It is Patrick's first visit to our *maison* this year and, ever the professional landscape gardener, he goes off to inspect our new plants. He returns alarmed. The hedge will be far too high, it will block the sun, we should have consulted him. '*Non, non*, Patrick, you are on *vacances*,' I assure him.

Then as always, for we are far from Paris after all, and *jardins* that are grand designs, the conversation turns to the two inevitable topics:

les mouches and the weather. Jean-Claude shares his trick of dealing with the flies. He sucks them up with the vacuum nozzle from all the surfaces. This is particularly successful he tells us, if they are crawling and swarming on the flat surfaces of windows, where they have been attracted to the light. I later adopt this method myself and find it has a high hit-rate. It always strikes me as exceptionally odd that *les mouches* problem is ever so much worse here than at home. I also always find it amusing that we have such endless conversations on this topic, but then again, we are in rural France. There are no highbrow discussions about art and literature; yes, our house is certainly far from Paris. I wonder though how we will be able to contribute to conversations when we are indeed in Paris next year with Patrick and his friends. Time will tell. I expect though, not to hear the dreaded *mouches* word once.

Meanwhile, Stuart has rapidly taken on the characteristics of a mad man, consumed by his daily pursuit of flies. He swats them frantically, to no avail — we resort to hanging ugly strips of old-fashioned fly paper; we spray noxious fumes in a fury. Finally, one night, he spots sneaky little *mouches* buzzing through the open vent for the old stove. He stuffs it thoroughly with plastic bags. *Voilà*, the next morning instead of getting up to a swarm of *mouches*; a veritable invasion, there are only one or two. The change to our sanity is both instant and remarkable. Such is daily life in Cuzance.

Friday the Thirteenth of July

The swallows are now swooping in wide circles through the pale blue sky — surely a sign that at last summer is imminent. We have a slow, relaxed morning after our impromptu *dîner* party the evening before with Patrick and Liz. When Patrick had wandered back to Jean-Claude and Françoise's to tell them he would be staying for *dîner* after our *apéritifs,* he arrived bearing a plate of freshly baked *rhum baba* that Françoise had just whipped out of the oven. We fall upon the plate with glee. The spontaneous *dîner* party is complete. It is nights like these I treasure, gathered round our long wooden table, French wine flowing, laughter and conversation spilling out into the quiet country night. The hoot of owls is the only other sound to punctuate the stillness.

When I later thank Françoise for her delicious dessert, as on many other occasions, I cause much merriment with my pronunciation. I say *merci beaucoup* for the *rhum baba,* for this is the name I know the dessert by and think it is universally known as such. But no, in France it is called *baba au rhum.* Jean-Claude is so highly amused by this that he then often asks me afterwards to pronounce the dessert by the name I know. Each time I say *rhum baba,* he falls into fits of laughter. A small thing in itself but who would know there was a world of difference in the trifling difference of a dessert. I wonder what they call trifle?

As Stuart and I are having our morning *espresso* on our *petite* porch, Jean-Claude arrives bearing his beloved new bundle. Marinette, on her daily *promenade,* supported by her cane, stops to admire the adorable *la chien.* While I perch on our moss-covered, stone wall as we all chat,

I hold Henriette as she snuggles up to me and falls asleep in my arms.

I carry her carefully inside to show Liz. The *salle de bain* is like a Turkish bathhouse. I'm dismayed by the clouds of hot steam for Jean-Claude has just told me it is highly unlikely that the first *maçon*, whose quote is now looking hugely attractive rather than in fact *très cher*, will also not be able to put our window in the bathroom this summer as I had hoped. He has left yet another message on the *maçon's portable* but tells me he is probably already on his summer *vacances*. *Oh là là, maçons*, I fume silently. I well remember how the month of August is when virtually the whole of France is on *vacances* for the entire month. If you need anything done, it has to be organised far in advance of this sacrosanct summer *vacances*. We are about to have our friends from Belgium to stay, and then there will be six of us. I am anxious about how our decrepit, dark bathroom will cope — especially our *septique* and toilet in its tiny box. To call it a room would be generous.

Jean-Claude continues his morning of gloom. He is perturbed when he discovers that I have not signed and posted the *maçon's* quote to let him know I have accepted it. This is a detail about French protocol that I have completely forgotten from the previous year when we had the roofers. I'm disconcerted as this will mean even further delays.

Thoughts of *maçons* are soon forgotten when Liz, Stuart and I set off to the picturesque village of Montvalent for *déjeuner*. It is again true that the journey is in equal pleasure to the destination. Sharp, curving bends that Stuart always has fun skilfully swerving round; glorious *châteaux* glimpsed from afar, sheltering under the edges of the chalky limestone cliffs; tiny churches with steeples piercing the sky; row upon marching row of perfectly aligned waving stalks of corn and vineyards, straight as railway tracks, stretching to the horizon. The smooth surface of the Dordogne glides beside us; the rural charm is picture-perfect; truly it is one of the most beautiful *départements* in all of France.

Once again, the restaurant has been recommended to us and, just like last year, it was Anne-Marie, our bank manager, who told us about it. At home, we don't even know who our bank manager is. If it is anything like Bon Famille that she had also highly commended last year, we will be more than happy. She has told us that it is run by a young couple who started it the previous year. I always have high hopes that these rural restaurants are where chefs destined for the bright lights and enviable *cuisine* of Paris, are starting out. We are not disappointed. As always, we choose *menu du jour*. We are served succulent skewers of duck and peach, a superb combination of flavours, followed by pistachio *crème glacée*. The sun shines, life is good. As we are relaxing over our glasses of *rosé*, Gérard and Dominique call to invite us for *café* and *gâteau* for afternoon tea. We manage to leave our leisurely lunch in time to dash into the *supermarché* on the way home. *Voilà*, there is a *solde* mosaic table and chairs that will be just perfect for behind *la grange* when the paving is *fin*. It is always fortunate that we have such clear powers of imagination, for the paving is yet to even begin.

We walk through the village carrying a bowl of plums, freshly picked from our *prunier* tree, its branches so laden they are snapping off. A brief chat on the way with Monsieur Arnal, who remains oddly perplexed as to why after being back for so long we have still to remove the cover for *la piscine*. Surely he has other thoughts to occupy him? We gesture at the ever threatening grey clouds and tell him it is still far too cool.

We gather for *gâteau* round Gérard and Dominique's table in their cosy *la cuisine*. When we visit them, there is always a sense of formality, for the table is always beautifully set in readiness and the *café* and cake is served ceremoniously. Dominique has been out to buy special *gâteaux*, a choice of *chocolat* or *fraise;* my hand always hovers when luscious chocolate or strawberry are both on offer. All our friends well know my weakness for French pastries. As guests, the choice is ours first. If only all of life's decisions were this simple; *chocolat* wins every time. The sense of protocol in the serving of afternoon tea is balanced by the laughter and jokes we share. I always try to remember to take my dictionary when we spend time with them but on the occasions I forget, we still chat like old friends, although we have only known each other just a couple of years. They too love the *vide-greniers* and the following day we are all headed to Padirac. By now, they are very familiar with my bargain hunting ability, and Gérard never fails to ask if what I am wearing cost one *euro*. I have asked them to keep a look out for a *girouette,* for I am still sad that our weather vane mysteriously went missing when our barn roof was replaced. Despite all our enquiries, nobody claims to have any knowledge of it. Patrick later suggests we should go the *gendarme* about it. This is not one of his better ideas. I shudder to think how this would affect our standing in the village. Perhaps not.

Brigitte's Birthday

We feel hugely honoured to be invited to Brigitte's sixtieth birthday celebration and to stay the night in their *chambre de hôte* in Villefranche de Rouergue. The day starts with an early morning expedition to Padirac, the first *vide-grenier* we have been to that is also a *Marche fermier*. It means that instead of a quick dash to Martel on the way to buy our fresh produce, we can buy it there. As always, I have already put my eclectic list for my treasure quest in my large straw basket. Today we are searching for nut crackers, a candlestick, ice tongs, a chopping board, an English dictionary and, of course, highly coveted old linen.

There is at last a glimmer of sun as the three of us set off early. It is Bastille Day and the day looks full of promise, as if the weather may at last break; perfect for Brigitte's party in the evening. For the past fortnight, the average daily temperature has been the same as at home in winter. Liz, fresh from Wales, tells us that England has had never-ending rain for months on end and there are widespread, record-breaking floods. We hope the rain doesn't wash over the Channel to our little corner of France.

However, as soon as we arrive in Padirac, the hint of sun fades and the chill once again descends, wrapping the *vide-grenier* in a cloak of grey dampness. France and summer? The two words seem incongruous. Memories flood over Liz and I as we wander round, stamping our feet and rubbing our hands in our efforts to warm up. This was our very first *vide-grenier* that we visited together when we met up in France four years ago. We can even recall the *la robe* she bought. She tells me the dress is still one of her favourites.

It is a superb *vide-grenier*, full of fascinating stalls. We find five fabulous gardening books, including a *nouveau* one by a gardener of repute. This will be a perfect gift for Patrick when we stay in his apartment in Paris. I spend a long time poring over exquisite old linen pillow cases, all hand stitched and many with initials embroidered on them for days-long-gone, *trousseau*. These are the moments I love, for they conjure up so many images of young girls, hair tumbling over their shoulders, as they sit by the light of an old oil lamp, each stitch a measure of love for their imagined future life.

As I linger over my linen choices — trumped by an imperious French woman — when I am finally given the price for my selections, the stallholder directs a questioning glance at Stuart. I have been madly calculating what choices I will sacrifice. He later tells me she was concerned the pieces would be far too expensive. I live for the clear-out-the attic days.

I am always hesitant to ask, '*Combien il est?*' for I think the price will be *très cher*. It is not. I am in fact astonished that they are not expensive at all. I scoop up sets of pristine white pillowcases to take home for friends. I move on to find a pair of ice tongs, another tick on the list. They will be used with the Suze ice bucket we found last year, when we serve *pastis* for summer *apéritifs*. It is an essential part of any French household, for *pastis* is the drink of choice for many of our friends.

Returning home, with baskets brimming, we're startled by the sight of a bride in the front passenger seat of a white van, her flowing veil fully covering her face. Even behind it, we can see her face is pale and taut. On the narrow country road, it is an especially startling sight. The trees arc and meet overhead; the roads are slippery after the overnight rain. The way the trees meet so closely, creating a tunnel of gloomy darkness, is a sure sign of how treacherous these roads would be covered with winter ice and snow. I hope they are not a symbol for what may await the bride in the van.

The dark black clouds roll overhead and we stop in Martel just in time to see the fire brigade — *la sapeurs-pompiers* band — and veterans marching to the Cenotaph to commemorate Bastille Day. There is a stirring sense of pride and patriotism in the reverent crowds lining the streets.

The afternoon passes quickly before we set off to our party, leaving Liz to spend the night in Pied de la Croix and immerse herself in the solitude and peace of a Cuzance country evening. And so we have another French evening of utterly marvellous memories. There are so many fragments of the night that lies ahead yet all so smoothly orchestrated to achieve the perfect sum total.

There is the drive itself to Villefranche; the winding roads that by necessity impose slowness and thus the savouring of the rural landscape, as it changes and unfolds around us. There are flatter, drier fields near Gramat, bordered by limestone walls. When we pass the sign for Roumégouse, it never fails to bring a smile to my face. It was certainly one of our more memorable adventures when we set off on a forest walk one day with John a few years ago.

Ah yes, a relaxing walk in a French forest that would bring us out at the end of the trail near Rocamadour, one of the most-visited towns in France. From the outset of our country amble, it was apparent that it was not going to be a simple stroll in the park, so to speak. We drove in off the main road to where we had been directed for a leisurely stroll. The track rapidly became increasingly narrower and the limestone rock walls bordering each field, were in danger of imminently scraping the sides of the car. It was also becoming quickly apparent, the further we ventured, that before much longer at all, the track would simply become so narrow that there would be no way to turn around or even reverse. Before the adventure had even fully begun, it seemed doomed. We stopped. We parked. We set off. The track descended steeply; it was not at all what we had been led to believe from Catherine, who we had rented our house from and whose suggestion it had been. From the outset, the track seemed endless, and confusing in its apparent destination. I spied a length of abandoned blue twine and tied it round my waist. It was destined to be our marker to tie around trees and mark our return. As we plunged ever further down the steep sides of the towering deciduous forest, I took even more care with my Hansel and Gretel trail of blue twine. Before too much longer, as the summer heat wrapped itself around us in the ever-thickening stands of trees, I declared that there was no way I was going to complete the arduous intended round trip. No, John and Stuart, after fortifying themselves in Rocamadour, could trek back, get the car and then collect me. As we continued, we stumbled across several ancient crumbling water mills. The midst of nowhere, yet still the surprise of past relics. Several hours later, after what was proving to be an extremely strenuous hike rather than the intended pleasant forest stroll, it was clear no one would be completing the return trip. Perhaps there would be a bus from Rocamadour that would take us back to our starting point?

As we trudged endlessly through the thick forest, the tranquil sound of a stream lured us on. It was a perfect place to pause for *déjeuner*. Thankfully we had come prepared with tasty *baguettes* for our forest adventure. Far from anywhere, we perched gratefully on enormous boulders and let the tranquillity of the forest seep into us. It would seem the tranquillity and isolation were not quite what we thought though. Apparently alone in our cathedral of trees, the serenity was harshly broken by the entirely unexpected appearance of three dirt bikes that roared along the narrow trail in a blaze of speed and dust.

One of the many attractions of the medieval town of Rocamadour is its stunning views over dramatic vertical cliffs. These cliffs are not quite as attractive when viewed from below and the only option is to scale them. We had all definitely had quite enough of the natural beauty of the Lot. There was no option but to catch the *très cher petite* tourist train to the top. This option did not mean however, that we were prepared to descend again and march back through the forest to retrieve the *voiture*. And of course, there was no bus service. And so we started walking in the blazing heat, along the main road, tourists streaming merrily past, oblivious to our interminable trek back. So, with the universally recognised symbol of an extended thumb, we tried to get a lift. At last, dressed in the readily recognised outfit of waiters the world over, a young student picked us up. Relief flooded through the three of us. However, our driver was perturbed and puzzled by our destination, in other words, not a destination at all. We tumbled out when we spotted the Roumégouse sign on the main road, for all we had to do now was trudge along the track and *voilà*, the *voiture* would be waiting, to whisk us home. After a few minutes, we heard the roar of a car behind us. Although obviously already late and racing to get to work, our waiter who rescued us, was so concerned that he had literally dropped us in the middle of nowhere, that he had raced back to ensure that the three odd foreigners were actually where they wanted to be — that is, in the middle of nowhere. We assured him we were. With a final puzzled shake of his head, he raced back along the track, no doubt for an evening ahead full of shared bemusement at the antics of tourists.

I smile at the memories as we continue our drive to Villefranche. *Petite* hamlets are then strung out throughout the green folds of hills: Capendac, Faycelle and Cajarc and one of the names we love the most, Compolibat. The Lot river, sheer limestone cliffs and if it is early morning, the mist, all merge into one. Next are the small villages clustered on the approach to Figeac, each with a church spire that reaches up to the now blue sky and each unchanging for centuries in their quiet rural pace. The expansive views are ever-changing; depending on the season, the

Our House is Certainly Not in Paris   123

small medieval villages surrounded by plunging cliffs and steep wooded valleys. The fascinating medieval villages pass in a mere glimpse; time has not touched them for hundreds of years.

Then, there is the well-remembered sense of arrival in Villefranche at La Closerie; through the heavy wooden gates, along the gravel path bordered by profusely blooming roses, the long table with a heavy white linen tablecloth, set for sixteen and another table with an array of *apéritif* glasses. The scene is set in their pretty *jardin* for a magnificent party. We greet Erick, Stuart's French *rénovation* counterpart, for they can both turn their hand to anything at all when it comes to renovating. Erick's most recent renovation is the conversion of the old bath house that was used by travellers long ago, and is now a charming apartment.

We are introduced to some of the other guests, a number of who have come from Cannes in the south of France, where Brigitte and Erick are originally from. Everyone else at the party is French, so we feel even more special to have been invited to celebrate Brigitte's birthday. We make our way up the stone stairs to wish Brigitte *bon anniversaire*. She is surrounded by a cluster of her female friends in *la cuisine*. As one, the women all turn startled glances our way. Brigitte calls out frantically to us, 'Non, non,' and we are shooed away like chickens in the wrong farmyard. It is clearly evident that they are in the middle of frantic, last-minute *amuse-bouche* preparations.

We make our way back to the garden where champagne and hors d'oeuvres are being served. Some women disappear to change into pretty party frocks. Liz and I have spent a long time deliberating about what may be appropriate to wear for such an occasion in France. I simply have no idea. The steps of Pied de la Croix were the scene of an impromptu fashion parade as I tried on a range of possible outfits to model for Liz, reclining in the front garden; somewhat different indeed to my usual dishevelled state at our *petite maison*. Even the house seemed to raise a wry eyebrow in astonishment to see me attired in clothes fit for a *soirée*. We may not be in Paris, but it would seem there was a reason after all for my unreasonable packing.

By ten however, there is a damp chill creeping across the garden from the Averyon which flows next to their *chambre de hôte*. The women collectively disappear again to grab wraps and change into warmer clothes. Sartorial elegance is abandoned for comfort.

Stuart and I have been placed at opposite ends of the table. He is surrounded by people engaged in a very fast-flowing, impassioned debate about politics and the recently elected new President, François Hollande. Despite Stuey's infinitely better grasp of French and ability to usually follow and take part in conversations, he later tells me that he was completely lost in the rapid fire volley of political comments. While I still struggle, nevertheless later, I am able to exchange conspiratorial knowing looks with Kitty, across the table from me, about our no doubt rapidly expanding waistlines at the end of the rich gourmet *dîner*.

Dîner is served. The three-course meal is a tribute to Brigitte's extraordinary culinary skills. I am absolutely sure that her restaurant in the south of France, would have had a loyal and devoted following of regular clientele. I know this from the very first exquisite mouthful. Around me is a collective sigh of appreciative murmurs. I eat as slowly as possible to make the *entrée* last as long as possible. It is a sublime medley of light-as-air puff pastry with a layer of *foie gras* adorned with sweet, melting *abricots* that have been poached in butter and sugar. Silence reigns over the table.

The men have gone upstairs to collect the *entrées* from Brigitte's *la cuisine*. When we finish, the plates are all whisked away in a wide wicker basket, hauled upstairs on a pulley system that Erick has ingeniously devised. The women then trip upstairs in a clatter of high heels to gather the main course. If it is possible, the main course surpasses the *entrée*. Slowly cooked aubergine with roasted *tomate*, frittata and rare roast beef, cooked to utter perfection, in a smooth, succulent sauce. The sauce is made from highly prized *cèpe,* imbued with the dark, secret places of the woods surrounding Villefranche. Only those who are passionate about mushroom gathering, know the secret caches of the forest and where to unearth them. French people guard their *cèpe* secrets closely, for they are the jewel in the crown when cooking.

Dessert is truly the *piece de résistance,* a *gâteau au chocolat* simply oozing with decadent richness. Again, a reverent hush falls over the long table. When every last luscious morsel has been devoured, there is a clamour of requests for the recipe. I glance around at the gathered *amis* whose friendships span decades. I notice how French women gracefully wear the lines upon their face like a badge of ageing beauty.

A mere ten minutes after everyone is utterly replete, and has been plying Brigitte with questions about her culinary secrets, there is a distinctive sound of fireworks exploding. We leave the table en masse to gather in groups next to the river. There is room for a few of us to crowd together on the terrace of the upstairs *gîte.* The bridge arching the Averyon is crowded with hundreds of people, who I am sure, have been waiting patiently for hours. For us, it simply unfolds in a seamless sequence from an exceptional *dîner.*

The fireworks last half an hour, huge explosions of colour that rush towards us in all their spectacular infusion of bright light and colour. A single white swan glides serenely back and forth across the river. It is the culmination of both Brigitte's birthday and Bastille Day.

The frenzied motion of the fireworks sets the scene for champagne and dancing on the low wooden deck in *le jardin.* It is normally a place for quiet contemplation in the *chaise longues* lined up in a row. These are now hastily cast aside while Erick's son, Maxim, plays music of our generation — The Rolling Stones and The Bee Gees. The unseasonal coolness of the late evening does not dampen everyone's high spirits.

There are protracted fond farewells in the morning and an

invitation to stay in Cannes. Despite being the only foreigners, we have bridged the gap in a long-established circle of French *amis* and made to feel again that we are truly a part of our new French life.

When we head home, a line of Sunday traffic is stopped on the main road through the town. It is the strangest position for a restaurant I have ever seen. It is located on one side of the busy road and the tables and customers are on the other side. Surely it is the most dangerous job as a waiter in the world? We watch as one hurries across, tray perched precariously aloft. Each time he serves a new customer, he has to traverse the pedestrian crossing. Now there's a waiter who certainly deserves his gratuity.

We arrive home in the late afternoon. Dominique and Gérard pause as they are driving past in their *petite voiture* to let us know they are on their way to an evening *vide-grenier*. We are simply too weary to join them after the *soirée* that extended until the very chilly early hours of the morning. More ominously, Liz had told us that a ghastly smell has now developed behind the fire grate. We enter our *petite maison* in trepidation, to discover that the smell has pervaded our entire house. Once again, we decide there is simply nothing to be done and fervently hope that it will just disappear. Besides, we have our own private *vide-grenier* to unpack, for as we were leaving, Erick plied us with gifts, including a 100-year-old Singer sewing machine table, complete with the original Singer machine. He has also given us an ancient door knocker for Pied de la Croix and a heavy stone urn that I plan to plant bright red geraniums in. It is only much later when Gérard and Dominique drop in with a jar of *confiture* from our own plums, that they tell me what the urn is really for. It is intended to hold ashes. This is a detail that Stuart chose not to disclose. They add that they have found us a *petite* present that they will give us another time. We are surrounded by the riches of renewed summer French friendships.

Summer at Last

The weather in all its varying moods continues to dominate daily conversation. It is the most common thread that ties us all. We have been told in Villefranche and now again back in Cuzance, that yes, finally, tomorrow will be hot. The daily weather in Cuzance can change literally within the space of mere minutes. The clouds scud rapidly across the sky, then the sun bursts through in a blaze of late afternoon brilliance. Liz and I race outside to bask in it on our matching *chaise longues*. We know it will not last. Sure enough, we retreat rapidly as the wind whips up and the sky once again darkens. Brigitte had told me that on their wedding day in September — surely the height of summer — it had been twelve degrees. They had to abandon their *jardin* party and continue the celebrations in their *maison*. Yet, just two days later, the temperature rose to thirty. *Encroyable*, as we would all say. However, I have also been told the heartening news that the day after Bastille Day, the temperature starts to soar and stays that way for a month, until the middle of August. Right on cue, to our enormous relief, this does indeed prove to be the case. Incredible indeed!

As summer starts in earnest, so too do our *rénovation* plans. It is time to face the music. It is Monday but fortunately not as in past years, a day to visit the *Marie*. Instead Liz and I head to Martel to shop while Stuart goes to Souillac to order paving, sand and concrete for *la piscine*. He returns very pleased with himself on two counts. Everything will be delivered early the following week and like he does the world over, he has bargained for a better price. Once again too, this was all in French at a local business where no one speaks English. Seriously, is there no end to his talents? The extent of my French is feeling confident enough to buy a *baguette* in *la boulangerie*.

Stuey celebrates, though not 'officially' opened, by having his first dip in *la piscine*. All however, is not serene in Pied de la Croix. By now there are again more *mouches* in *la maison* than outside. We simply have no idea where the flies are now swarming in from. At Gérard and Dominique's, their proximity to the local pig farm means they are perpetually engulfed by *mouches*. They are so invasive that they can't even enjoy their evening *apéritif* in *le jardin* and take pleasure in their sweeping view of countryside and fields.

As the days start to offer a hint of summer promise, the boughs of the orchard trees are all fully bowing to the ground. We now have to pick endless buckets of fruit to save even more branches from simply snapping under the weight of the copious pears, plums and *pomme*. No wonder you never see *prunier* for sale in the markets. Everyone must have their own plum trees, or at least their neighbours' or *amis*' trees, to make their summer *confiture*. It is a strange position to be in, such abundance, and the words that never cease to fill me with surprise, 'our own orchard'. The mystery of how life unfolds is something I am always conscious of in my own little piece of France.

Our *vacances* is over, let the work begin. The sun shines without a single cloud in the sky to start the new week. It seems to be true what we have been told, that the day after Bastille Day, summer will start in earnest.

The last morning Liz and I have in Martel together is all that we hoped for and planned in our emails across the oceans. Sometimes as I log on in the evening at home, Liz and I find ourselves emailing each other at precisely the same time. Liz remarks that she often reflects on the fact that she is just about to have the day that I have just had on the other side of the world. I had never thought of it quite like that.

Off to *Le Bureau de Poste* at long last. How is it possible to have had postcards written for ten days and not had a chance to post them? We are not working after all, it seems inconceivable. Even I can't account for it. What I do know, is that the hours in the day rush past at a frightening pace. The church bell strikes, must dash out and get fresh *pain*, I think, and then proceed to load another wheelbarrow of weeds. Lunchtime arrives; stale *pain* yet again, redeemed only somewhat by trying to transform it in the toaster. How does this keep happening in the land of magnificent *boulangeries*, is our constant refrain. We are on *vacances* after all. How would we ever explain this at home? There is no possible answer.

Liz and I return after *pain au chocolat* and *café* at Mespoulet, to be briefed on Stuart's expedition. Before heading back to Souillac, he tells us he dropped in to see Jean-Claude, who yet again swung into action. A call is made to a man who used to live in the village. His job is to deliver gravel. He is nearby. *Voilà*, Monsieur Moreau arrives within half an hour as promised, to give a quote. It is unheard of. An *artisan* never arrives when he says he will. In fact, sometimes they simply never arrive at all. It would seem that we will have gravel delivered by the end of the week. Before long at all, it is another word that I become only too familiar with: *castine*. Once again, I muse to myself, is '*castine*' a word that one would usually encounter on *vacances*? Perhaps not.

As we later walk round our garden in the unexpected and welcome sun, the intermittent sun and rain has meant that the weeds and grass are yet again growing ferociously. I have completely transferred my interior renovating obsession to my sprawling *jardin* this year. The orchard trees too have come alive with burgeoning fruit, while the *prunier* trees are now breaking, they are so rich with fruit. Yet at least this year I can see the grass for the trees, so to speak.

We often find out critical information by sheer chance in random conversations. We were sure that the people from Paris in the neighbouring *maison* would simply have a local farmer in to cut the waist-high grass before their annual return. We thought that it would be an equally simple arrangement to have our grass also cut by a farmer and his tractor. After all, we are not aiming for a cultivated garden and have accepted that it will be *rustique* for ever after. It will be easy, efficient and cheap. Our costs are certainly something that need to be reined in. It is something we were very, very close to organising. It definitely made sense to us.

Like many of life's big decisions, it is only happenstance that I mention to Jean-Claude that I am about to search for a local farmer. '*Non, non, non,*' he emphatically tells us. Unless you make it absolutely clear that it is a one-off arrangement, (which we knew that we would not have the skills to convey by any means), the farmer will assume he has entered into an irrevocable contract with you. This means a number of things. Firstly, that he can come onto our land whenever he chooses to gather grass for his cows.

This arrangement would be fine — except for the second part of the contract — which means that when we come to sell one day, the farmer will be the first to be entitled to buy the land. This sounds not only hugely complicated, but could well have some very tricky ramifications. We are strongly advised not to take this course of action. Instead, Jean-Claude very practically suggests buying a ride-on lawn mower.

Our house is certainly not in Paris.

French roses in full bloom.

Grape vines on the barn.

Looking into *la cuisine*.

Our new kitchen

Weed prevention measures

Rebuilding an old dry stone wall.

'Light duties' in *le jardin*

Looking back at the barn

Off to market, past our *petite maison*.

Road test

Huge truck delivers sand and cement

Group meeting to discuss kayaking.

Another barrow full.

Friends relaxing by *la piscine*.

Finishing touches to the drainage channel.

Bales of hay in Cuzance.

Lunch at our *vide grenier*.

The Work Starts in Earnest

The sun seems to be a good omen. While Stuart spends the afternoon at *le bricolage*, Liz and I spend an afternoon under the walnut tree. Last year, she had grave fears that such an afternoon would never again come in her life. She has survived all that life has thrown at her and here we are again; just as I believed we would be.

By now, I am actually ready to work again in earnest. My first significant task is to gather more limestone rocks from the land. The soil has considerably subsided round *la piscine*, and now all the edges have to be shored up with stones. Five days on end without renovating or relentless working in *le jardin*, is the longest stretch in our history in our little house.

I have not glimpsed Madame Chanteur for days and have been anxious that she may again be in hospital. Monsieur Chanteur's *voiture* is gone for hours at a time, which is unusual in itself. Perhaps too, like it has been for all of us, it was simply the damp days that have kept them inside. Now, as the sun shines, the village comes to life and I see my neighbours in their favourite *dîner* place under the shade of the spreading walnut tree. I seize the opportunity to present them with their gift — a photo that I took last summer of them framed in the doorway of their *maison*.

The contrast between the woman in the photo and the woman at the lunch table, in the space of just a year, is a harsh and stark one. Her hands tremble as she attempts to unwrap the soft tissue paper. Her husband gently takes it from her. That they are clearly touched by my gift is palpable. Monsieur Chanteur repeats several times, '*Enchante, enchante,*' and gestures at the photo of himself and his beloved wife. As I leave, he says, '*Merci encore.*' So few words shared yet gestures transcend barriers of language. The church bell strikes, the birds sing, the sun continues to shine. Life's rhythms are an ongoing circle. Yet, melancholy also fills me for what I know will soon inevitably follow. It wraps me in a cloud of sadness as I move from the shade of the walnut tree in to the glittering sunlight.

Days in a French summer seem elongated. They seem to take on an elastic quality — one that only snaps off at the end of a long, long day of bright summer light. It's hard to comprehend how much one day can possibly hold. At least this year we are not working until midnight and have managed to have more *promenades* after *dîner*.

Cuzance is criss-crossed by literally dozens of walking trails and enticing paths that lead next to fields and walnut groves. As the sun sets, a yellow glow is cast upon the wheat fields — now beds of short, sharp stubble and decorated with enormous cartwheels of harvested hay. It is the ethereal light of late summer evenings in France that is the picture I hold in my mind when I am far from Cuzance. The other lingering memory is the utter silence that envelops the countryside. At home, the sound of the ocean is ceaseless so it is never completely still or quiet. In the rural landscape that has virtually remained unchanged for aeons, the stillness is only broken by the sound of *lapin* scampering home through the fields. The world is far away. A sense of peace infuses my soul.

The Summer Heat Surges

With Liz's departure, the summer heat surges, just as predicted by all. Ironically, this coincides with the return to sheer hard labour — in fact, convict style, for our most pressing task is to continue to glean the land for even more limestone rocks and gather them. We work for three hours straight in the burgeoning heat. I carry bucket load after bucket load of heavy stones. My job today is to carry on filling in the edges round *la piscine* where the soil has significantly subsided in the past year. Stuart lays out planks of old wood, salvaged from *la grange* and sets out bright yellow string to delineate where the huge truck will deliver the gravel.

As the church bell reverberates at twelve, it especially seems to be tolling for mad foreigners working in the midday sun. Unlike true French *artisans*, we don't immediately heed its note of caution and down tools. If I am honest, we are labourers, not *artisans* at all. We instead continue working until it's essential to prepare a hasty *déjeuner* before the much-anticipated arrival of the next in a long line of *le maçons*.

As soon as he arrives, I am struck by his beaming, friendly face. Jean-Claude has hastily finished his *déjeuner* to be on hand to translate. I leave it to the three of them to discuss the important position of the bathroom window. However, I am soon summonsed to the critical consultation and the four of us crowd into the *petite salle de bain*. There is much discussion of the height of the window and need for privacy from the road and passing traffic. Much hand-gesturing on my part once again indicates what I think will be appropriate and what will most certainly not be acceptable. As the road is often heavy with tourist traffic, I have no desire to be a feature on the tourist trail.

Impatient as always, I of course want the window in now. I would preferably like it before the arrival of our Belgian *amis* when there will be so many of us sharing an airless box. '*Non, non,*' it is not possible. Naturally, *le maçon* is also soon to go on *vacances* like the rest of France for the sacred month of August. Now, why is that a surprise? The phrase, '*Non, non,*' and *artisans* seem to go hand in hand. While disappointed, a skill I have taught myself over the years is to turn situations around. So, I now think that it will instead be wonderful to return next year to find a *nouveau* window in our *salle de bain*. Jean-Claude, the custodian of the keys to Pied de la Croix, will take care of all the arrangements with Monsieur Moreau. The oft-repeated phrase is again reiterated on their departure, 'What would we do without Jean-Claude?'

Before that point, I gesture again to *le maçon* to follow me as I have another query. The four of us troop out into the burning heat. I convey my concern about our crumbling outbuilding, the last in a row of four, starting with our very own *pain* oven. Now, maybe that's a skill I should learn and we would never again be without fresh bread. Then again perhaps not. After all, there is enough to do. Besides, I know full well that bakers rise at the unearthly hour of 2.30am, to ensure that their *pain* too rises in time for their first customers of the day, the loyal *petit déjeuner* clients who line up early for the array of breakfast pastries: *pain au chocolat, croissants* and *chausson aux pommes*, the delectable light pastry filled with apple. The dedicated *boulangerie* bakers then bake bread twice more throughout the day for the *déjeuner* customers and then again in the evening for *dîner*. There are so many selections, that just the act of buying bread becomes a decision making mission. What to choose today? Will it be *brioche*, the sweet bread, *pain de seigle*, rye, *pain de campagne*, bread in the shape of a ring, a *flûte*, which is twice the size of a *baguette*, or, one of our favourites, *ficelle*, which is a long and very thin loaf? To say that the French love their fresh bread is an understatement. It is a daily ritual that is as much a part of them as breathing. Indeed, the tantalising smell of newly baked *pain* is like no other in the world, as it drifts in perfumed clouds along the streets. To step into a *boulangerie* is like being wrapped in a layer of aromatic sweetness and fragrant freshness, for the pungency seeps into your very pores.

I quickly abandon my *pain* flights of fantasy as we examine the dilapidated building. I keep in mind too my well known lack of prowess in *la cuisine*. Indeed, I have been known to burn toast. Stuart dismisses my desire to preserve our old outbuilding, for all he sees is *euro* signs flashing before his eyes. I, however, am adamant and insist on a quote. It is interesting that my insistence transcends the language barrier. The two French men say that it is just the same in France. It would seem that it is universally accepted that women have the last word. The three men shrug and smile.

My decision is verified when we learn the ancient red tiles on the tumbledown building are in fact rare and valuable. How we can dismantle it tile by tile, to replace in precisely the same pattern as we have been carefully instructed, is something I am not at all sure how to tackle. I am also not sure how we can possibly find the time for this exacting task for now the paving is our consuming focus. It is, however, imperative to save this rural relic.

After they leave, we rest for a while under that shade of the gnarled walnut tree. It's a day to remember. Now into our third week, Stuart has finally and officially 'opened' *la piscine* and was up to clean it in the coolness of the early morning. Later in the afternoon, we wander down to visit Jean-Claude and Françoise before their family arrives from Berlin, Paris and Lyon for their summer *vacances*. Once again, Jean-

Claude entertains us with a story from his inexhaustible hoard. This time, it is about his elderly neighbours — Georgette and Paulo D'Britte. I wonder about the use of the word 'elderly' from a man on the verge of seventy — and then he mentions they are ninety.

So it was that last summer, the D'Brittes were about to depart on their annual *vacances* to their apartment in Collioure, near the Spanish border. There were cries across the neighbouring hedge, 'Where are the keys; where are the keys to the apartment?' They were literally about to leave in their battered *voiture* but it would seem the keys were lost. Finally, hours and hours later, at the *dîner* hour, the keys were found — in the bottom of Madame D'Britte's bag, the very bag in which they had been placed the previous evening. And, the bag had already been placed in readiness in the *voiture*. In the last minute relief, panic and confusion, the map that Monsieur D'Britte had been clutching in his hand, was mislaid. Despite the lateness of the hour, they were still determined to set off.

Apparently, as he was once a *gendarme,* Monsieur D'Britte refuses to travel on the *autoroutes* as he knows all the speed traps. And so, they choose to travel on the slower, more circuitous minor roads. It is not traffic that overtakes them but bewilderment. The muddled, delayed start has caused considerable confusion and consternation. They become very lost.

As I raptly listen to the tale unfold, I know precisely what the experience must have been like for them, for this too, has happened to us on the buried back roads of rural France. And I am sure, elderly or not, the longevity of their marriage notwithstanding, I can certainly hear the '*Merde, merde,*' echo through this story. Oh yes, this has indeed happened to us on more than one occasion. The ramifications are indeed, *merde*.

By now it is late, very late. Monsieur and Madame D'Britte then called their son for help. He couldn't assist them at all, for they had no idea where they were. 'Are you facing south or north?' he gently probed them. They could not reply. They simply didn't know.

As too has been the case with us on similar misadventures, the kindness of a stranger saved them. He came across the old and cold couple on a lonely byway and stopped to rescue them from their plight. He drew them a map. The map is for directions to their home. So it is they return to Cuzance, in the early hours of the morning. Jean-Claude only knows all this from Michel in the village. What the D'Brittes tell him is that they decided not to go on *vacances* after all but come home instead. At ninety, it was quite an adventure. The thought now of a *vacances* is simply exhausting.

Fling Open the Shutters

There is a trick to getting up early. We leave the *chambre* door wide open so the light filters in like slowly creeping fingers throughout the *petite maison* from the *salle* windows. The sitting room is the first room to be filled with the soft dawn. It lights it up with a rosy hue and flows across the ancient wooden floors with a pale pink tinge. Unless we do this, our bedroom is like a dark silent box — much like the bathroom. This strategy is now necessary as we need to wake up when the sun does.

A hasty *petit déjeuner*, then it's off to the heavily dew-soaked *jardin*. One trip across the rough land to empty my wheelbarrow and my shoes, socks and the bottom of my work pants are saturated. It's hard to believe that within a few short hours, the sun will be burning too fiercely to continue working outside. We now have to reassess our work schedule. There are hours and hours of work to put in before the *castine* delivery. And really, we have no idea when that will possibly be. What we do know, is that we have to be ready. The form work has to be in place, copious weeds sprayed — yet again — the string line adjusted, and the huge expanse of weed mat measured, cut and put in place. It's a daunting task for two people in a very short timeframe.

Everything picks up speed. The leisurely days are already a distant memory. We now rush everywhere. Even going to the markets in Martel often becomes a race against time before they finish at twelve. The days of sauntering to select the freshest, ripest, most succulent produce are long gone. Now too the tourists are abundant; gazing in delight, cameras slung round their necks, ready to capture the quintessential French market moments. There is none of this for us. We have more pressing demands; for us, *rénovation* season is in full swing.

What balances the imperative ticking of the clock that now dictates our every action, is the sense of being a part of our *commune*. Even when we now go to Intermarche, several shop assistants greet us warmly, with the ever-courteous '*Bonjour Madame* and *Monsieur*'. The same greeting is exchanged with locals when we walk through the narrow, picturesque streets of Martel on our way to the market. Our sense of village life is even more special when we encounter Jean-Claude and Françoise in the *supermarché*, working through their long list in readiness for the arrival of their large family.

At the end of a long summer day, the shadows subtly soften and now the threads of light creep imperceptibly across the silent fields.

To Market, to Market

This year we buy our luscious *pêche, cerise* and *melon* from a new young stallholder. Although he always has an eager queue, it is never an impatient one. There is a sense of solemn, subdued occasion in calmly waiting, breathing in the aromatic, heady scent of fresh, succulent peaches, cherries and melons. No customer is ever rushed. There is a feeling of reverence in a French market for the land and its bountiful produce. The richness of the land seems to resonate through the centuries, for this has been the way of life for hundreds and hundreds of years.

We love the question, 'Is the *melon* for today or tomorrow?' The selection by the stallholder depends on your answer. He picks them up carefully, feels them in the palm of his hand, looks at the colour, assesses its ripeness. Only after this, is the *melon* handed over. Prosciutto wrapped around golden slivers of *melon* has become our favourite *apéritif* accompaniment to serve our *amis*.

Through these simple, everyday transactions, my confidence in communicating is starting to improve. While I can now manage straightforward requests in the markets, I still stumble with simple numbers and amounts. A *demi-kilo* of *cerise* is however, a must to know. Half a kilo of ruby red cherries is after all, one of the highlights of a French summer. The waft of pungent lavender, bound in raffia, floats above the smell of fruit picked at dawn. It is the distillation and essence of all that I remember when far away.

As the sun sets in a brilliant golden orb, the black cat with the enormous green eyes, watches us stealthily, crouched in the long grass near *la grange*. She is watching our every movement. Stuart tells me that he noticed she is slim again. I know what this means. She must have had her kittens. The question is, where? Stuart had seen her earlier, trying to get in to the barn. As we were sitting in the last light on our *très jolie* steps, she hesitated, not used to the presence of people in our usually empty *maison*. We finally leave the steps leading to the front *jardin* and *le chat noir* pauses to stare at us. She now imperiously enters *la grange*. I grab our feeble torch. It seems to only ever be used for investigating disturbing noises and animals. I peer inside the barn. There is the distinctive mew of newborn kittens. Of all the places she has chosen to have them, it is the ancient cow manger, still strewn with straw. The last thing I need is the responsibility for French kittens in a foreign land.

French Kittens

My day starts in a way I could never have possibly predicted. In the morning light, I'm able to investigate the litter of kittens in the barn manger. There are four *petite* tabby ones, as small as my hand. Clearly, they are only a day old. I have absolutely no idea what to do about the unexpected appearance of four French kittens. For the moment, I shelve the dilemma. There is work to be done.

Fortunately, on this allocated work day, the temperature has plummeted by about ten degrees. Ironically, it is a day we fervently hope the sun doesn't break through the grey, gloomy clouds. My job is still to collect stones to fill in the edges along the sides of *la piscine*. The gap is so gaping that I'm concerned I have nearly depleted my supply of stones gleaned from the land. Then — and I don't know how I could have possibly overlooked it before — I find a mother vein. These are the sorts of things that make you jubilant on a day in Cuzance.

The cistern wall has been concreted over at some point and there is a huge pile of concrete debris. I fill pail after pail, the clouds of concrete dust, swirling and choking. However, despite scrabbling in the dirt and weeds and concrete, the source of my in-fill makes me ecstatic. I consciously realise how quickly the focus of my world has changed. We have indeed gone fully 'off the grid' as Stuart has declared to people he is doing when he heads to France. However, we discover that our rural backwater is now colliding with the twenty-first century when we find out that the Hotel Arnal now has wifi connection. It is an incongruous sight when I walk past one day and see foreigners connected to the world on their laptops. It remains a world that we avoid as much as possible. Every now and then, I pause in my labouring, to peep in at the soft bundle of French kittens.

It's been a whole year since I worked so vigorously and relentlessly. It soon comes back to me however. I have resorted to lying fully stretched out in the dirt next to *la piscine,* to carefully place the larger rocks along the wall of the pool. I then scoop in buckets full of small stones. The hard work balances the daily delights of *abricot hibou* and *pain au chocolat.* I work as if I am human digger. I scrape and dig and lay and shovel. The wood pigeons, perched high on *la grange* roof, peer at me in puzzlement. Their soft cooing seems to be a murmuring background of incredulity at my strange actions.

Stuart has set off after *déjeuner* to the *bricolage* to buy a cement mixer. This is exactly the sort of purchase that is on everyone's list when they go on *vacances.* Across the now silent *jardin,* I hear the unusual sound of Monsieur Chanteur's raised voice. I can make out the words, *'Je t'aime, je t'aime.'* These are words the whole world knows. His tone is both anguished and passionate as he declares his love for his wife. From glancing across at them daily as they move ever so slowly from their *maison* to *le jardin* for their meals, I know it is his sheer strength of will and enduring love that is keeping his wife alive. As they make their way at the pace of an *escargot* to their table under the walnut tree, Monsieur Chanteur firmly grips his wife's elbow to support her faltering steps. Even from afar, I can see his loving grasp is far firmer than last year. Madame Chanteur may be fading before our very eyes but their enduring love is clearly not.

In my musings about his fervent declaration, I decide that over *déjeuner,* perhaps Madame Chanteur has declared that it is simply too much for her equally elderly husband to continue to care for her in his steadfast way. His declaration that carries across the *jardin* is a cry of protest. I have always known that he will walk by her side with utter devotion until the very end. An end I fear is near.

As I wait for Stuart's return with our shiny red cement mixer, I consult the dictionary to compose several sentences that I certainly never expected to have to use. I carefully check my construction with Dominique when they drop in. Very fortunately, their visit coincides with Stuart's triumphant return, our *petite* Renault Scenic staggering under the weight of our mixer. I too would have been staggering if Gérard was not on hand to help haul it out. We are all astonished at what our *voiture* can manage to squeeze in. We all duly admire the cement mixer before I ask Dominique if I have the correct words for our new French family of a cat and four kittens in our *grange*.

I then leave on my French kitten quest through the village, clutching my piece of paper with the vital words. Marinette is sitting with a group of *amis* in her front *jardin*. She calls out, '*Bon promenade?*'

Always conscious of protocol, and knowing my questions are highly unusual, I politely respond, '*Bonjour, non, non. Ça va?*', 'Hello. No, I am not promenading. How are you?' before I launch into my 'Do you own a black cat? Do you know anyone in the village who does? If so, it has had four kittens in our barn.' Just to be quite sure that everyone grasps exactly what it is I'm saying, I also hand over my note that Dominique has written for me. *Bonjour, avez-vous une chat noir*? And so the note continues, explaining my French kitten dilemma. It does not change the outcome in the slightest.

Accompanied by many gestures as usual, I make sure that the piece of paper with my carefully constructed sentences, is handed round to everyone present in my attempt to explain the reason behind my walk. I am fervent and anxious. I simply cannot leave a black cat and four French kittens to fend for themselves when we leave. Their response is to collectively laugh heartily. Quite clearly, I am the highlight of their afternoon.

My quest includes visiting the *maison* in the lane behind our *grange*. I have at times seen *le chat* disappear through our orchard, headed in this direction, so I have high hopes that the cat and kittens belong very nearby. I cautiously unlatch the gate, very conscious that there is a sign attached: '*Attention chien*'. This is something I clearly understand; to be on alert, that there is a dog present. Engulfed by fear that I am going to be savaged by a dog — while trying to save my French kittens — I tentatively creep up the gravel path and knock hesitantly on the door. Indeed, there is frantic barking, but to my enormous relief, it is a jumping bundle of white fur that greets me rather than the savage barking *bonjour* I am dreading. My relief is not matched by the fact that my neighbour has no knowledge of *le chat*; it is certainly not his and he has no desire to adopt my four French kittens.

What happens next when I continue through the village, stumbling through my several straightforward sentences? Everyone else I encounter simply laughs too, just like Marinette and her *amis*. Yes, they all know the *noir chat*; yes, they are very familiar with its *promenades* through Cuzance, but no, nobody owns it. Everyone seems to have the same suggestion. While my French is very limited to say the least, there is no mistaking the general consensus. Asphyxiate *les chats*. I convey the full extent of my horror at the thought.

My last stop is at the Hotel Arnal where there is quite a gathering for the *apéritif* hour. I repeat my routine and entreaty. While the people in the village collectively already think we are quite mad for our endeavours — to come from the other side of the world and *rénover* on *vacances* — my request simply cements in their minds their opinions of our foolishness. Yet I continue, imploring everyone to ask their friends and neighbours if they will adopt our kittens. Despite the laughter at my expense, I end with what I am sure will be a seductive selling point. I conclude persuasively by reminding everyone that cats are excellent for mice in the country.

I return and sink disconsolately on to our *très jolie* front steps. I gather my thoughts about our French kitten quandary. Gérard and Dominique return for an *apéritif* and even they cannot quite understand my sense of responsibility for the cats. They are leaving soon for *la plage* and we are invited to a farewell *dîner*. Thoughts of them relaxing at the beach do not lift my spirits. Not only will I be working relentlessly in the summer heat, I now have an unresolved dilemma. What I do know is that it is out of the question to smuggle four French kittens home.

Talk turns to lighter matters. French people love talking about food; *cuisine* underpins their very existence; buying it, preparing it, eating it. We have bought a can of *Confit de Canard* in the *supermarché* yet we are not clear at all about how to cook duck that comes preserved in a can. I go inside to get both the can and a frying pan for an impromptu 'cooking' demonstration on our little porch. We want to be quite sure about the instructions for creating an authentic French meal in our own *cuisine*. Gérard explains that you drain all the *confit* to roast your potatoes in the duck fat. I'd forgotten that detail from when we had *dîner* with them last year and now the memory of their crisp, delicious flavour, floats back into my tastebuds. I am looking forward immensely to this meal of our region.

The *chat* saga does not disappear however. In the following weeks, every time Jean-Claude encounters Monsieur Arnal outside his hotel, he gleefully enquires whether I have yet succumbed to smothering my French kittens. On my behalf, Jean-Claude indignantly reiterates each time, '*Non, non!*' Long live *le chat*, I think each time he repeats his tale to me.

Le Tour De France

On the morning of our much-anticipated outing to watch the *Tour de France* in the nearby town of Souillac, I vigorously resist venturing out to *la grange* to check the kittens; they are not mine after all. It has not made matters any better though when over *dîner* the previous night, Stuart glanced out the window and remarked that 'our cat' was walking down the road to the village. '*Non, non,*' I protest. 'It is not our *le chat.*'

The *Tour de France* is going to pass just three kilometres away from Cuzance in the nearby village of Cressensac. There has been much discussion and speculation for weeks with our friends about the best vantage point. Stuart has long had his strategy worked out. He's determined to go to Souillac to see the cyclists tackle the steep hill just over the Dordogne. While Cressensac is very close, it is flat and they will simply pass by without the challenge end exertion of a vertical climb. He has even worked out precisely where to park, at Point P, Materiaux de Construction — a place he is very familiar with from ordering our sand and gravel. It is on the outskirts, will not be crowded and we should easily find a place to park. When Dominique and Gérard give us a copy of the local paper, *La Dépêche,* it is exactly the place that is suggested for locals to park. Our strategy and time to leave is further revised when Jean-Claude tells us that the main roads into Souillac will be closed from 9.30am. He advises us to go on the back roads that only locals know, a circuitous route that goes through the hamlet with the delightful name, Le Pigeon.

Day after day, the sun plays hide-and-seek with the clouds. On the

Tour de France day, we are very lucky — it is not wet nor too cold or hot. The weather gods are on our side. We park on the outskirts of Souillac an hour before the *Tour* whizzes through. As we walk from near the ancient, soaring stone viaduct, to find a viewing position, an efficient, alert *gendarme* enquires where we parked. I am able to reply '*Derriere, du pont*,' — 'Behind the viaduct.' So simple, yet I am so pleased with myself to be able to tell him.

With a throng of other followers of *le Tour*, we walk to the edge of the town centre. Our plan is to walk up the steep hill near a roundabout at the end of the main street, so we can see the cyclists pick up speed and swish up the incline. As we near the roundabout, there are thick crowds already lining each side of the hill. Clearly, many have been there for hours, judging by the way they are set up with their folding chairs and picnic hampers. It is then we spot the perfect vantage point, a curved, arching wall that runs parallel to the hill. Behind it is a narrow road, lined with houses. Astonishingly, given the ideal view it offers, there are still spaces left. It is a superb spot, for you can see right along the main boulevard of Souillac where the cyclists will first appear, before ascending the hill right in front of us.

We don't have long to wait at all before the hour-long *caravane* starts. This is a feature of the *Tour* that is not shown at home but we had been told about it by our friends and seen the *caravane* the previous year when we watched *le Tour* in Figeac. It is a lively procession of advertising floats that builds up an atmosphere of anticipation. The floats blare loud, catchy music and energetic young dancers perform enthusiastically on the back of them. The atmosphere builds quickly. There are cars and vans and open-back trucks, advertising Carrefour, Vital and other big French brands. Sweets, key rings, caps and journals are tossed to the exuberant crowd.

It is then the helicopters hover into sight. You know that soon

Our House is Certainly Not in Paris   149

the cyclists will appear along the Boulevard Louis Jean Malvy, the main street of Souillac, adorned in their bright jerseys. The floating helicopters move closer and lower. The anticipation builds in equal proportions to the incessant whir of the whizzing helicopter blades. The nearby bystanders tell us that the first cyclists will appear in two minutes. By now, there are six hovering helicopters. I jump up and down and vigorously wave my arms. I have worn the brightest dress in my wardrobe in my attempt to stand out in the sea of people. I want to be spotted and seen by everyone at home who are avidly following the *Tour de France*.

Before the cyclists shoot through Souillac, a cavalcade of *gendarme*, motorbikes and dark-coloured cars with deeply tinted windows appear. At the roundabout, on the pavement opposite us, there is also a significant cluster of *gendarme*, their swaggering sense of importance, plainly discernible. Cleary there is someone *très* important in the cavalcade. Then, only one hundred metres away, a swelling murmur of excitement in the crowd indicates that it is the *nouveau* President of France, François Hollande. We are told that he was born in Tuille, where the *Tour* will stop overnight before its final triumphant ride into Paris. There has been no mention of the President's appearance in any *journal*. It has been a closely guarded secret and is a surprise to all present. As we are so close when he steps out onto the sun-warmed pavement, vigilantly surrounded by a posse of black-suited, burly bodyguards, and the first cyclists appear in a blur of motion, I wonder if we will be pinpointed by a helicopter and beamed across the world.

Dominique and Gérard visit us after our exciting afternoon with an *apéritif* invitation and just before we head out again, Jean-Claude also visits to tell us that Henriette has just seen her first *Tour de France*. It certainly is a dog's life.

Life in Cuzance is a non-stop social whirl. In three weeks, we can count on less than one hand, the nights not shared with friends over endless *apéritifs* and *dîners*. Such constant *soirées* could not possibly be sustained at home while we work — and yes, also renovate. Is there no end to our renovating across the continents and oceans? In France, it's quite a challenge to find the time to do all that we want to do; visits to new places, *vide-greniers* and *brocantes*, precious time with *amis*, and all the work that simply must still be done. It is just as well the daylight hours seem to stretch to infinity.

Two Trees and a Cupboard

When we return to our other life, Jean-Claude and Françoise remain a constant presence. There is simply no end to their continuous kindness. Our *petite maison* remains in the care of their loving hands. Emails wing their way across the miles bringing joyous news. The day before our twentieth anniversary, my Inbox announces 'Furniture'. In my Monday morning bleary-eyed state before work, I think that like last year, some friends of theirs have some furniture for sale and he is kindly letting me know what is available. No, it is far better than I could have anticipated. They have been involved from afar on a quest for us. The measurements have been provided and the cost determined — a different price from both of us; of course, mine has been higher than Stuart's and of course they both know that mine will prevail. They have found our longed-for cupboard!

YES! SENSATIONAL! We found in Sarlat the piece of furniture you wanted! It is awaiting you in the sitting-room of la petite maison and will fit quite properly the place you meant it for! It is made of cherry-wood, with a glass front and a drawer; it is certainly not one metre deep but will accommodate plenty of articles and books — and it cost 180 Euros (we had a rebate from 200); sorry, there's no bill since I paid cash in banknotes; sorry we can't send you a photo since both our cameras are out of order. In the same stand, Françoise found her Noël present — a Moustiers fountain.

It was the most challenging of quests. The *armoire* is to fit in the corner next to the fireplace in the *salon*. Its measurements are very precise for there is a cupboard attached to the wall above. The cupboard on the wall is hand-painted with bucolic scenes. The paint has been so thickly applied that it is impossible to open. I always contemplate it as a source of potential treasure. Within just a few months of our return, they have been successful where we failed. I am quite sure too that they have visited far more *brocantes* and *vide-greniers* than they usually would, especially in such a short space of time.

Then there is more exciting news.

Yesterday afternoon I bought your two mûrier-platanes and planted them, and watered them thanks to Mr Chanteur's watering-cans and pond (he had left them for my use since he had sown grass by his pond; when I bought them they advised me to buy buttressing equipment (sorry I don't know how to say 'tuteur' in English) so that the wind should not fell them. Also, as I had told you earlier, I bought two bags of earth for the one tree that is in the rock by the pool; so that the bill is steeper than you expected (of course I will leave the detailed shop's bill in la petite maison).

While we were delivering your furniture, Françoise saw that your bedroom shutters were not tightly closed so we went in again to close them. The wind is still blowing so that, in spite of the buttresses, the mûrier-platanes tend to lean into the wind — I am trying another way of buttressing them.

And so, through our email exchanges, Cuzance is always close.

Trois Vide-grenier

We eat *dîner* at a seasonably yet unreasonably late hour. It is often so late that I simply fall into bed straight after eating. Despite how much we always seem to fit into every single day, the days still slip away like sand running through your fingers. The church bell tolls, the day moves on.

There are two days in a row when we wake with a palpable frisson of excitement. A weekend that holds *trois vide-greniers*. It is unheard of to have three treasure quests within the space of a single weekend. All is carefully plotted and planned. Thanks to Gérard and Dominique, who always read the local Lot *journal, La Dépêche*, we have been told that there are several not listed in our *Office du Tourisme* guide: Theminettes, Saint-Felix and Betaille.

At the markets, I continue to pore over piles of old linen. Once again, there are exquisite hand embroidered pillowcases, each stitch in each seam a story of love and hope, for often such delicate pieces that have now found their way to the markets, were once part of a long-ago *trousseau*. I wander with my market basket, lingering to pick up and examine fascinating relics from the past: old paintings, battered tins, delicate china and pieces of ancient glass. There is simply too much to buy that holds the tantalising appeal of long ago days in France. Our *petite maison* is already full to the brim with treasure, even after such a short time. Now that would look lovely in the converted barn of the future, I find myself frequently thinking.

We end our outing by driving to Montcuq and have an *espresso* at an outside *café* with a sweeping view over the green hills and grey slate rooftops, before heading to the fresh produce markets. The nodding, dinner-plate size sunflowers add a burst of bright yellow to the lively scene. There are rows of lettuces, wilting in the warm sun. An old woman scrutinises them; prodding, lifting, examining. The young stallholder grimaces at us and mumbles under her breath. Her impatient gestures transcend any language barriers, especially when she beckons her *maman* to serve the demanding elderly woman, with what will clearly be considerably more patience than she has on this sunny Saturday morning.

The afternoon is filled with delicious sunshine so we finally fling open all six doors of *la grange*. The light floods in and transforms the cavernous space. The threads of sunlight even penetrate the ancient, thick wooden rafters that arch high overhead like the inverted hull of an enormous old wooden fishing boat. The history and beauty of the barn seep through every stone. After not seeing it fully opened for a year, I fall in love with it all over again. I am enraptured and enchanted anew and consumed by the desire to transform it.

In a piece of accidental planning yet with serendipitous symmetry, we discover that the rear, far left door of what will be *la cuisine* one day, lines up exactly with the new lavender bed stretching neatly beyond in a pleasing straight row. As this is the first time we have ever opened this door, we feel tremendously pleased with the effect of our *jardin* design and the planting by Albert in our absence. Beyond, the graceful curves of the orchard trees, draw the eye.

The barn roof soars up by at least ten metres to the apex and *la grange* is about twenty metres long. There are enormous cream-coloured flagstones along one wall that one day can be carefully removed with a crowbar, to place in the *grand* entrance. I am always both pleased and quite amazed at how clear my vision is for the transformation from a cow barn to a magnificent *maison*. The *euros* to achieve this and the hard work and energy required are something I tend to conveniently gloss over.

The walls have all been painted white at some point in the 107-year history of the barn. Though encrusted with dirt all these years later, and festooned with trailing swathes of cobwebs, just sweeping an old straw farm broom across the walls, removes the outer layer of grime. An initial quick clean leaves a prefect patina of white wash, every designer's dream. We have tried before to replicate this effect by experimenting with sanding and white paint on wood. It is impossible to ever achieve; only time and history and the life of a farm seem to create this in a natural state. Perhaps paint marketing teams should set up their creative design teams in old French barns. Or maybe not. Stilettos and old cow manure are not a perfect match.

We discuss and plan and dream. We know it will be *très cher*. What we also know is that it will be the *piece de résistance* of all our *rénovée* years. From Canberra, to Sydney, to our village on the south coast of New South Wales, an old French barn was never on our life itinerary, and yet, it always seems to be so perfectly right that life has led us to this unexpected place. Cuzance seems to have always found us rather than the other way round. And now that it has, it fills our imagination, hearts and hopes. Just like our *petite maison* was not that long ago, for now, *la grange* remains an empty shell, full of old farm debris, walnut husks and French kittens. Yet it exudes a tangible sense of warmth and extends an invitation to be transformed into a *magnifique maison*.

A Wedding in the Village

In the most absurd juxtaposition possible, I abandon my Saturday afternoon outfit of weed spraying ensemble, complete with a blue and white check tea-towel tied over my mouth, to hastily throw on a frock and straw *chapeau*. I run through the village to our church. There is a wedding and Françoise is singing in the choir. As a mark of respect to our friendship, I have promised to go.

The church bell clangs ceremoniously, for me, signalling alarm. Have I misunderstood the time to attend? I clutch my *chapeau* as I hastily make my way to the *Mairie* where all are gathered. In the upstairs window, *le Maire* can be glimpsed. I had forgotten that this is part of the French marriage ceremony, that first the bride and groom have an official service with the mayor of the village. There had been no need at all for my haste. The proceedings take almost an hour. To think, I could have put in an another hour's work in *le jardin*. Finally, the formalities are completed and I follow the gathered wedding guests round the corner, to the church. I meet up with Dominique and we find a place to stand at the back of our tiny church. Colleagues of the bride and groom, who were not in the church, have been waiting patiently in a cluster outside for the ceremony to conclude. They include members of the Brive-la-Gaillarde football team who the groom plays with. When the glowing couple finally emerge, they form an arch and toss a football to their just-married team member.

While inside, for what seems to us to be an interminable ritual, Dominique and I try repeatedly to catch Françoise's eye, in the choir at the front, to no avail. The ceremony is so long that we sink onto two cold stone steps tucked at the back of the church. We watch with amusement as a young woman, who arrives very late, tries to slip in unobtrusively. It is impossible on the slippery-smooth stone floor of the ancient church. She teeters precariously on impossibly high heels and her thin legs bend like a young giraffe's. Dominique and I whisper and giggle conspiratorially like school girls. I try my best to be more reverent and my gaze lingers on the tribute in front of me. It is a memorial to the men of Cuzance who gave their lives in the First World War. Their names are inscribed in stone, and next to them, the name of the village where they were born. Most of them were from *petite* surrounding hamlets. Only one, Albert Barre, was born in Cuzance. It is a very long list for a village and surrounding *commune* as small as ours. Its presence adds a gravity to the proceedings and provides a solemn link to the past and the hopefulness and joy of the marriage taking place before us. It is always both strange and moving to be in the very country where a war was fought and not so far away at all from Cuzance. Whenever we travel on the *autoroute* to Brive, I think about the advancing march of German soldiers' boots and the fear that would have echoed in the hearts of the villagers. The despair of the farming families seems to reverberate through the years. Not just the loss of lives, but the farms that then languished, unable to be passed on to the next generation.

To pass the time, I whisper to Dominique and share stories of my own wedding in Istanbul, a far cry from this country wedding in Cuzance. I tell her about the ferocious thunderstorm that everyone assured us would bring tremendous luck. In a soft voice, I convey how I was fortunate to even get to the ceremony at all, as the taxi driver nearly crashed on the narrow streets of Besikatas, that were awash with the torrential deluge. In a low murmur, I describe the Nato battleships that were at anchor in the Bosphorous and featured in all our wedding photos. I tell her how I didn't understand a word of the Turkish celebrant and that my main memory is crying out at the end, 'The rings, the rings!' Somehow, we had forgotten to exchange them. And yet, here we are now, with a *petite maison* in France. It would seem that the prophecy about thunderstorms and luck may well have indeed been true. In return, Dominique shares with me the astonishing fact that they have been married for an extraordinary forty-five years.

At long last the ceremony is over. We are not however, prepared for the collection plate that is passed round. We don't have a single *euro* between us, so we slip quietly out the door into the bright sunshine and the patient throng awaiting the bride and groom. Jean-Claude makes his way through the groups of gathered neighbours and friends, to go up to the tower so that the bells ring in rejoicement. As we wait to meet up with Françoise and the church empties, Dominique and I, in the way of women throughout the world, chat about what everyone is wearing. A young woman in a too-tight, too-short skirt that is not flattering by any stretch of the imagination, emerges. Dominique murmurs a single word to me, 'McDonalds'. And who said French women don't get fat?

The four of us retreat across from the church for *apéritifs*, in the welcome shade of the huge pine tree on Jean-Claude's and Françoise's upper terrace. Hours after I had rapidly shed my work clothes for wedding attire, I make my way home to inspect Stuart's progress cleaning up *la grange*. The evening ends as I am sitting at our dining table writing in my notebook and Dominique taps on the window as she and Gérard slowly wend their way home after their evening *promenade*. There is a tinge of apricot pinkness on the horizon as they wish us '*Bonne nuit*'. The wafting aroma from the pig farm firmly reminds us that we are in the country as we close the door on the night after another memorable Cuzance day. The only sound is the plaintive bray of a lonely donkey that drifts across the fields.

Summer Sunday Afternoons

The summer Sunday afternoon tranquillity is quite unlike any other day. Families throughout France gather and settle for long, leisurely lunches. The shops are shut, the roads are quiet. This Sunday starts for us with the *vide-grenier* of all *vide-greniers* — Gignac. Even for the French who never venture to one and to whom a *vide-grenier* is *passé*, for weeks beforehand there is speculation about the rich treasure trove that is Gignac. The farmer's huge field is already half-full when we arrive — and we are not late by any means; certainly not on a market Sunday. The stalls stretch endlessly, overflowing with possible delights, the rows of enormous walnut trees creating a natural delineation for the stallholders to have set up their tables in long rows. Though there are always dozens of people milling about — sifting, searching, scrutinizing — there is a solemn expectant hush hovering over the walnut grove. The pursuit of treasure is too serious a business to be disturbed by idle chat. While many others make their way to village churches on Sundays, for those here, the canopy of walnut leaves creates a cathedral and the reverence is reserved for the worship of all things old — and the possibility of nirvana in the form of a true antique that may be stumbled upon.

There is a definite strategy to Gignac. One quick pass, up and down each row, scanning eagerly for the esteemed finds of the day, those that leap out and clamour to be bought. A short break for a *café* and *croissant*, then fortified, off for a more leisurely stroll, to pause, to linger, to discuss and share and choose. The *petite maison* is already full to the brim — it is *petite* after all — and after only a few years, we have to exercise caution and care in our selections. There are only so many old straw baskets and glasses and pieces of ancient cutlery that you can possibly have, tempting as they all are. We have already learnt to be far more discerning, though there are items that linger long in the mind afterwards and fall into the category of regrets.

Today there is another market to head to, so we head off to Estival. We have not been to it in previous years and we don't have high hopes at all, for, unlike Gignac's repute, we have not heard a word about it. It proves to be utterly charming. There is a cluster of pretty houses in the shadow of the solidly built church. The stalls are set up in a radius that spreads out from the looming church and down the tiny village lanes. Stuart is pleased to meet up with our roofer from last year, and even more pleased that he remembers his name straight away, '*Bonjour Jean-Luc, ça va?*' Jean-Luc asks if we are working as hard as last year on our *maison* and *jardin*. Stuart assures him we are not.

The first stall we encounter is crammed with an abundance of old linen. Two old women, who I think are sisters, stand behind their array of old handmade wares. I think that they have spent a lifetime sewing and hemming and embroidering the faultless pieces, for they are as old as their linen. White-hair caught up in matching buns, stooped from sitting in matching armchairs late in to the evening next to a blazing winter fire, heads bent with fastidious precision over their sewing; each piece on their stall reflects the story of their life. As always, my imagination is fired by the romance of it all. I imagine they have lived their whole life in Estival, sharing each day together in a picture-perfect cottage, surrounded by *fleurs*, perhaps meant to marry but their loss recorded on the village war memorial that they pass each day when they step out to buy their daily *pain*.

Estival proves unexpectedly to be more fruitful than Gignac. Stuart spies the prize of the day. It is a 1950s Peugeot ceramic coffee grinder. As we leave, the narrow country road is choked with *dîner* time traffic, slowed to a standstill at times. The *voitures* creep along, forced frequently to edge cautiously to the side, to allow another one to pass, so narrow is the one road in and out of Estival. The edges drop away sharply, so there is quite a skill involved in the art of French country driving.

We drive through Martel on the way home to Pied de la Croix and notice the big banners strung across the main street advertising the international sheep shearing competition. We are sure there would be Australians taking part and make plans to watch it next year.

Today our basket is piled high. When we arrive home, we make a ceremony of laying out each find on the dining table. There is often a dilemma for me about what to keep in our *petite maison*, what to take home as gifts and what to put aside for our house at the sea. I am excited to have found exquisite French summer frocks for Emmi and Macy, the two little girls of our friends Healey and Souni, who live in Sydney, as well as linen galore for presents. I especially love unearthing old tea-towels and pillowcases, though today there was a funny moment when I reached to the back of a stall to examine a pile. As I was deliberating over my choices, I caused much amusement when the stallholder grabbed the tea-towels back. He explained they were to later wrap his *déjeuner* in and were not for sale. Another special find is two tiny original watercolours of Corsica. They will be taken home to add a touch of this exotic landscape to our bedroom walls. As usual, we leave everything displayed to show Gérard and Dominique. Sunday afternoons we can definitely count on them to drop in for we have an unspoken competition about who finds the best bargains of the day. Invariably, I win!

We break our Sunday rule of taking the whole day off; there is just always too much to do. It is perhaps not quite true after all when Stuart told Jean-Luc that this year is more of a *vacances*. He gets stuck in to plastering the spare *chambre*. Next, he has to measure for new skirting boards as the old ones have simply crumbled to dust. We know only too well what old wood and little mounds of dust signify. We hope that it is not a sign of ominous activity in the open space under the floor where the floorboards too have rotted away. We pull a piece of old lino over the hole, cross our fingers and hope, as is our tendency, that the problem simply goes away.

My next task is to sand the front door where the varnish has peeled and faded with the extreme weather conditions that batter the little house, from the searing summer heat to the icy blasts of winter snow. My new sander works like a dream as it glides efficiently across the breadth of the door. As I climb the stepladder to sand the arch over the door, I discover stencilled in to the wood — 1989. Like the window frames, the door is quite a recent one, for this year, our *petite maison* is 130 years old. New varnish will help to ward off the icy tentacles of winter when it may well drop to minus eighteen again. The only thing that will ever lure us to a white French *Noël* is if we do one day renovate *la grange* and it is fully insulated and heated. Pied de la Croix's thick stone walls provide welcome coolness on hot summer days but winter in Cuzance is an altogether different matter. I have absolutely no desire to ever stay in a house where the freezing nights can only be kept at bay by stuffing huge wads of newspaper in to every crack and crevice. I have removed the tell-tale evidence and I don't intend to ever replace the pieces of *La Figaro*. Let our *petite maison* slumber through the depths of winter; I intend to never cross its doorstep, slippery with ice. Christmas in the country can remain a romantic notion.

As the temperature soars steadily, the grass browns and becomes crisp and crunchy underfoot. At the same time, the weeds continue to flourish — the curse of country life in Cuzance. Swallows fill the evening sky and swoop in graceful curves. The hay is all cut for the season and tractors have mown the fields in both straight and rounded rows of pale gold. As the heat intensifies with the passing days, even the birdsong chorus becomes more subdued.

A Cuzance Working Week

On Mondays, we dance to the dictates of our own demands. Our fourth week sees us fully resume our old *rénovation* habits. Up early, pull on our work clothes, a hasty *petit déjeuner*, then it's off to the spare *chambre* for me. It is not quite like last year when the very morning of Liz's arrival, this was the project I started on, yet it is very similar, for Lydia and Eric are due to stay in just two days.

The tin of paint is like rich molten chocolate as I dip my brush in. It glides on to the thirsty skirting boards as smoothly as silk. Unlike most renovating projects, I'm finished ahead of my self-imposed schedule, so I move on to varnishing the front door to bring it back to life. Next, I manage to paint the front grill that overlays the door, in a glossy black shine. And then, the gravel arrives — all twenty-five tonnes of it. This is when a new word is about to permanently enter my vocabulary; one that will be indelibly stamped into my memory: *castine*. This is not a word in vocabulary lists in guide books for a *vacances* in France. I abandon my brush, grab my camera to record this momentous moment, and dash outside to watch the proceedings in a state of high anxiety.

The truck is massive. After considerable manoeuvring, it literally just manages to squeeze in past our two stone pillars. I then clutch the purple hibiscus near the pillars, close to my chest to protect it, as the truck lumbers past, down the stretch of grass that leads to the orchard. Stuart races along next to the truck to direct it. The placement of the gravel is critical. We have to move all twenty-five tonnes of gravel by wheelbarrow and then spread it out around *la piscine*. A few feet in the wrong direction will make all the difference in the world to the number of loads we have to move. There is a heart-stopping moment when the truck tentatively approaches the far side of the pool, the one with the slope that dips towards the edge of it. My heart is in my mouth. It seems an inevitable collision course is unavoidable; gravity alone can surely not prevent the truck tipping on its side and losing its load straight into *la piscine,* with the truck tumbling after it. This is a moment I cannot capture on my camera. Truth be told, I can barely even watch.

Next, there is an enormous roar as the tilt tray swings up and a colossal mound of gravel flies out in a mountainous pile at the rear of *la grange*. There is a choking cloud of white gravel dust. The dust flies in billowing plumes across the garden. This performance is repeated half an hour later. One truck load wasn't enough for the mammoth task that awaits us. It now resembles an instant quarry site next to *la piscine*. I look at the mountains of gravel and feel utterly daunted. Stuart looks at the mountains of gravel and feels the exhilaration of an exciting new challenge. And therein, the difference lies.

And so, as the burning sun spills over the pool, we move wheelbarrow after wheelbarrow after wheelbarrow, ad infinitum. We work into the late evening, day after day. We rise early to start before the heat saps our strength. The sight of *castine*, the thought of it, discussing the width and length of where to place it round the pool; is the sole focus of our life. It would seem that the old days of relentless renovating toil are certainly back. Did I miss them? I think not.

Yes, back with a vengeance. For more days than I care to remember, we fall out of bed, and resume moving the piles of gravel that seem to barely diminish in size. The sheer size of the gravel pile is overwhelming. If I let myself think about it too carefully, I will simply not be able to go on. Just the mere thought of the magnitude of our task is exhausting in itself. So, I don't allow myself to think about it. I pick up the shovel, throw a pile in the wheelbarrow, and repeat the action, again and again.

We've been told that a heatwave is about to hit the south of France. The perfect definition of irony. A pool that we can't even use. It's like being in a desert with a mirage of water. We work from sun up to sun down. There is simply no respite. Now, just like the last two years of *rénovation* in our *petite maison*, we also need to finish painting the spare *chambre* as well as Lydia and Eric are due to arrive — now in just one day. And this is a holiday, is the one constant thought that reverberates through my mind that is as numb as my work-weary, aching limbs. What we seem to have also overlooked in the frantic flurry of work, is that the paint fumes will still be lingering in the spare room. Why does this always seem to happen when friends are due to stay?

By now, the summer sun scorches like a searing Australian summer. The masses of bright, white *castine* are blinding in the sharp, bright light. The walnut tree beckons, but it is not possible to retreat to its enticing shade. Instead, Stuart's excitement is complete to have two deliveries two days in a row. This is his idea of nirvana. Once again, it is not quite mine. Another massive truck manoeuvres gingerly through our precious stone pillars. It too misses them by a mere fraction. This one carries a cargo of Bavarian stone, crazy paving that will in the end drive us crazy with frustration. It is no coincidence that it is so named. The truck is also bearing bags of cement and another mountain to be painstakingly moved; this time one of sand. The truck has a hydraulic system that, despite its precarious consignment, levers the six pallets in six fluid movements.

As the heat soars, we start to get up at five — though it still only gives us a few hours before the sizzling sun forces us to seek sanctuary in the coolness of the house. And there, we do not rest. No, instead we paint. When we eventually return outside, raking the gravel does not quite have the Zen quality of meditatively raking smooth white pebbles in a Japanese garden.

Tourist Season — Not on Our Agenda

By the end of July, the tourist season is in full swing. In Martel, there is a discernible difference. There are both French tourists and visitors from a spectrum of other countries. If we get to the markets late after working, it is shoulder to shoulder at the stalls. At our favourite stall for aubergine, courgette and *tomates*, the middle-aged jolly couple now have their son working with them. He serves me and, despite the long queue and frenetic pace, Madame still has a moment to extend a warm '*Bonjour*,' to me. It is moments like these that I feel I belong. Later in our personal *rénovation* season, Stuart is simply working too hard laying the paving to even come to the markets with me. It simply doesn't seem right that he has to miss sharing one of our favourite things to do while we are living our other life. It is times like these that I yet again have occasion to wonder, are we doing the right thing? My doubts crowd in and cloud my grand, glorious visions.

The tourist season means that my longed-for weekend in Lyon with Françoise is postponed until the following year. Bénédicte, their youngest daughter, points out that all the shops will be shut for the hottest month of summer, when virtually all of France goes on *vacances*. As shopping was high on our agenda of planned activities, there seems little point in going. I am bitterly disappointed. How I longed for a break and the sights of Lyon, for the sight of *castine* is one I never want to see again. Once again too, I also muse about how everyone at home simply thinks we are having an absolutely marvellous holiday in France at our own little house. Well, parts of it certainly are but I'm not sure what fraction of the whole constitutes a *vacances* in anyone's mind.

Gérard and Dominique are about to leave for *la plage* for a month. To say I am envious at the thought of relaxing at the beach for a month is the understatement of the year. How I long to run away and join them. We are invited to a farewell *dîner*. Last year when we joined them for an evening meal in their home, it was always a very formal affair. *Apéritifs* were served in their *salon* and the *amuse-bouche* were always laid out ready on arrival. Unlike when we invite our *amis* for the *apéritif hour*, there was no casual sitting outside sipping our drinks and enjoying appetising snacks. Instead, there was always a formal sense of ritual and occasion, in what seems to us to be the rather formal French way.

We are touched and delighted upon arrival — always sure to be precisely punctual, as the church bell strikes the hour, for this too is part of the protocol — to be told that this time it will be a family *dîner*. Once again, all the rules we have read about the formality of the French and the virtual impossibility of being accepted into their friendship circle, are broken. After *apéritifs*, Gérard serves our favourite meal of *canard* in their cosy *cuisine*. Just like Stuart, he too is the family chef. We bid fond farewells and make plans for *l'année prochaine*. Making such friends in such a short time is something we never expected, let alone *amis* to make plans with for the following year. Suddenly, life seems ever so much brighter. The *castine* pile will diminish with time; we will make time to spend under the walnut tree and we will be able to one day soon revel in the luxury of our *piscine*.

The following week passes in a haze of heat. My mind drifts to Dominique, soon to be relaxing at *la plage*. Now the alarm is not only set for *vide-grenier* days. We are simply so exhausted we can no longer rely on waking early to set to work. And so, we set the alarm for every single day. *Castine* waits for no man, or indeed, woman. The sun has become so fierce and intense, that by now we are forced to stop by nine thirty every morning. On a normal *vacances*, this is the sort of time most people would wander out to start their day. Yet nothing is ever what I would deem to be normal about our days in Cuzance. In just four days, we have trundled countless wheelbarrow loads of *castine* and raked and raked it out over the rough ground to form a smooth base for the paving. Singlehanded, I have also unloaded three enormous crates of jagged-edged crazy paving. Each piece is tremendously heavy, especially as I reach the bottom of each pallet. Once again, I lift and stretch and heave and lug. The only way I can manage to manoeuvre each piece of heavy stone is to balance each one on my leg as I unpack it from the crate before I lay each one out on the grass around *la piscine*. It will be Stuart's job to then choose each piece to assemble our giant-size, outside jigsaw puzzle.

It becomes more and more difficult to balance each paving stone on my leg as I haul them out the crate. This becomes harder and harder the more I unpack and the lower the level gets in the crate. Balancing crazy paving against your leg is not to be recommended. They slip out of your grasp as you struggle with the sheer size and weight. I have the corresponding, jagged-edged scars on my legs as an indelible reminder of my latest French summer.

The relentless pace is broken by the arrival of our Belgian *amis*. They arrive just in time too, before my spirits are broken — not to mention my back. Once again, I wonder how I possibly manage the unrelenting physical work. For two days as the heat hovers at forty, we picnic on the banks of the Dordogne and relax in the shade of the pine trees that border its edge. The distinctive towering limestone cliffs form an impressive backdrop to the smoothly gliding river, full of holiday makers kayaking. To my delight, there are groups of children kayaking, adorned with colourful Indian feather headdresses. The afternoons are spent luxuriating at Jean-Claude and Françoise's *la piscine*; a special place in the world for me; a place where the beauty and tranquilly never cease to seep into me. After a month, our stolen picnic days seem less normal than our *rénovation* routine.

Eleni, at sixteen, is poised on the page that is turning from late adolescence to blossoming into a stunning young woman. One moment shy and awkward, the next, glimmers of future sophistication. First-year-at-university Jorn is serious and reserved. He quietly watches and listens to everything. I catch expressions on his face that reveal how he truly thinks; that we are amusing simply for the very fact that we are Australian. He is clearly bemused by the fact that we have chosen to renovate on the other side of the world in just a few short weeks every year. Like us, Lydia and Eric have wandered reluctantly into middle-age. The bond of long-ago days, travelling together in Turkey, binds us all tightly together.

We eat late *dîners* at Pied de la Croix, the six of us gathered in *le jardin* under the lowering shadows. The sun slowly sinks in a blaze on the horizon and then a quarter slice of moon hangs in the clear country sky behind the pine trees.

On our last evening with Lydia and Eric, we eat our final *dîner* with them, a baked salmon that they have prepared for us all. We sit outside relaxing with our *apéritifs* and are waited on by Jorn and Eleni; it is like being in our own *jardin* restaurant. Just as we savour our last delicious mouthful, a storm rolls in — the thunder roars ceremoniously and the rain pours in heavy sheets. We frantically grab everything from the table and race inside for dessert. The freshness of the air is like the sweetest perfume imaginable. The scorched, baked earth exudes an invigorating freshness. We scoop up morsels of *mousse au chocolat* and watch the transformation of our little world. The smell flows in through the open windows. It is a smell that is like no other and one that city life never yields. It is a heady combination of dry earth that is rapidly revived, overlaid with the pungency of freshly mown hay, an undertone of farm yard manure and freshly awakened dry, crackling leaves that unfurl with new life.

Castine Days Continue

Despite friends staying, the *castine* still calls to me. I wake early and creep out of the slumbering house. The metallic tines of the rake, ting, ting, ting against the gravel. I develop a slow, steady rhythm. Rake the gravel out smoothly three times, lift the rake, repeat the process — over and over. The rain that has tumbled down overnight, as if on cue, has tamped down the gravel for us. It is perfect preparation for hiring a compacter.

Hiring a compacter is yet another French exercise that proves to be both fascinating and frustrating; not in equal parts however. The frustration factor far outweighs the fascination of hiring equipment in a foreign land. Stuart sets off to Souillac on Saturday morning as soon as our friends leave on the long trip home to Belgium. He is headed for the machinery hire business that Jean-Claude has found for him in the local phone book. It is closed. An old woman pops out from the house next door just as he is leaving. She indicates to Stuart that there is a phone number on the shop window and after discovering that he is not French, goes back inside to ring the owner for him. *Voilà* — all is arranged for the hire the following week. He returns home, we resume work.

While clearing the land — *jardin* still remaining very much a euphemistic word — we decide that, just like people, there are good weeds and bad weeds. The tall fronds of delicate Queen Anne's Lace add a meadow-like touch yet the brambles spread their tentacles ever further. They mock us and tear ferociously at our clothes and skin as we hack and attack.

Just after Lydia and Eric leave, the week-long fever pitch starts in readiness for our very own *vide-grenier*. We have flown home before it the previous two years so we are elated to be here this year to take part in it. Every *commune* takes great pride in showcasing its villages in their annual market glory and all the associated events. Just like in previous years, a tractor appears with three men on its tip-tray to attach a banner of fluttering flags to the roof of our *petite maison*. The other end is tied to a large *prunier* tree in *le jardin* across the road. Throughout the following week, the *commune* van makes its rounds each early evening, the megaphone loudly announcing the forthcoming festivities. In the afternoon, Paulette from the Hotel Arnal, makes a point of dropping in with two notices about village celebrations. I can translate some of it, such as the Friday night disco, but I need Stuart to also interpret what else we can possibly attend. I understand enough to know that I will certainly not be going to the disco.

When Jean-Claude visits later with Henriette, on one of his many daily *promenades* through the village with her, he tells us that we missed the *vide-grenier* at Strenquels as it was on today, Saturday, not Sunday as we had thought. I literally stamp my foot in petulant annoyance. Perhaps the presence of two teenagers for several days in our *petite maison* has affected my behaviour. Jean-Claude finds my outrage so entertaining that he asks me to repeat my childish performance. Like a teenager, I refuse. We are dismayed that we confused the dates, for after all, our *vide-grenier* outings are the jewel in the crown of our weeks. He leaves, still laughing about my amusing antics.

Next to drop in, just before their departure for their *la plage vacances,* is Gérard and Dominique. We show them the Cuzance pamphlets for a more accurate insight in to the village activities. One offers the opportunity to learn dry stone walling. I ask Stuart if he interested in learning this traditional skill. He gives me a look that succeeds in fully conveying he thinks I am quite simply mad. While words are not needed to elaborate upon his expression, to ensure that I fully grasp the foolishness of my suggestion, he points out that he actually has quite enough dry stone walling of his own to do, or words to that effect. The other notice is a free reading about the history of the omelette and famous black truffles of le Lot. How fascinating we think. Who knew that omelettes even had a history? Dominique tells us however, that even she would not be able to fully understand the talk as the regional patois would be so thick. It says, in part: *Nous vous conterons l'histoire de l'omelette et celle des origins du diamante noir.* I do know that this will also be an account of the famous black truffles for which our region is renown. Once again, I wish Henriette would unearth some of this black gold, as it is known, on one of her visits. That would ensure the transformation of *la grange*.

Talk of truffles leads to two other stories. The first Gérard shares with us is the annual Cuzance *grand dîner,* held every November in a marquee. Five hundred people attend from the *commune* for the event is famous both for its truffles and value. Truffles are served with every course, even dessert, and there is endless champagne. The cost is only fifty *euro* a head. While this is expensive for many villagers and local farmers, he explains that elsewhere it would cost five hundred *euro*, a truly staggering amount of money. At the *dîner* just the year before, the soon-to-be President of France even attended as he was originally from the region. To think that our simple little rural village was graced by François Hollande. It is yet another insight that we would simply never have discovered without the stories shared by our French *amis*.

This is followed by another truffle tale, an exceptionally *magnifique dîner* at the restaurant of the famous chef, Alain Ducasse, in Provence. It is a restaurant that is so famous and exclusive that guests even fly in by helicopter simply to spend an evening dining there in sublime luxury. Gérard was invited there on one memorable occasion by his uncle. However, at the end of the exquisite meal, it is Gérard who is chosen to have *l'addition* presented to him. He tells us that he nearly choked with shock. The bill was, *très, très cher*. The cost was seven hundred *euro* for each person — and there were ten seated around the exclusive table. Fortunately for Gérard there had been an error in giving him *l'addition*. His rich uncle paid for everyone. *Oh là là*, we all think.

The Spirit of Cuzance

We love the sense of community spirit in Cuzance. It is both a celebration of life in the village today and an honouring of days long ago. Loud music emanates every now and then to remind the village of our much-anticipated *vide-grenier*. The festivities cater for everyone of every age and we discover too that the *commune* of Cuzance gathers in the outlying scattered hamlets of Baladou, Rignac and Lagarrigue.

On the Sunday afternoon in the lead-up week to the most significant event in Cuzance's annual calendar, a group of *lycée* students visit every *maison*. They are all wearing white T-shirts with *j'aime* Cuzance emblazoned in red. The attractive, lively students are selling Tombola tickets for two *euro* each. The first prize is: '*1 Voyage de 4 jours pour de personnes de Espagne*'. How exciting. Even I know that it means a trip for two to Spain for four days. The second prize is: '*2 assiettes gourmande a la ferme de la Truffe*'. Once again I am pleased that I know exactly what the prize is, a dinner for two at the local gourmet farm restaurant that specialises in truffles. No one we know has ever been there for it is far too *très cher*.

When we buy our tickets, we are also given a bright pink brochure — Cuzance *Fête Votive* 2012. The weekend will be truly celebrated in style. Friday night starts with a *Soirée* — *entrée gratuite* — a Rock Festival, followed by *concourse de Petanque* — a game of *boules* on Saturday afternoon with a *Bal Disco Vinyl* in the evening. Sunday of course is the culmination of the *commune* celebrations, with the finale on Sunday afternoon of a traditional dance display. The *vide-grenier* is also a *Marche de produits regionaux*, so there will be local produce for sale. *Déjeuner* will be available and served in Marinette's walnut orchard. Truly, a weekend to look forward to.

Sunday afternoons are meant to be sacred. We have made a vow not to work, to enjoy a time of leisure like the rest of France. As I head to the walnut tree after *déjeuner*, book in hand, Stuart has not been able to resist the lure of *la grange*. It is his idea of an afternoon's recreation. I pause as I pass by, hesitate; torn by my desire to relax under my beloved tree and the desire to join in — sorting, cleaning, tidying; paring away the debris to discover the bones beneath. It is not a long battle. The lure of *la grange* wins.

We work side by side for a full afternoon. I replace raking *castine* with raking old, dry cow manure and the flotsam and jetsam of a working barn. We ferry out wheelbarrow after wheelbarrow of dirt, manure and rubbish. We sort through the discarded farm implements, deciding what is treasure we will keep and what we will discard. Part of an old bellows and a large rectangular sieve for sifting grain are prized finds to be displayed on the walls, in the far-distant, future life of *la grange*. We unearth more enormous flagstones that one day will have to be carefully dug up and moved to the spacious, grand entrance. The dreams are taking shape.

We stretch and reach ever higher with our discarded barn brooms to bring down skeins of ancient cobwebs. The more we work, the more *la grange* yields in return. While cavernous, it is not a void. The space lends itself precisely to the placement of the rooms we imagine creating in the future. While enormous, it is not a cold, damp space. Just like restoring our *petite maison*, it too exudes a sense of warmth and lives happily lived in the past. There is an old wooden hook on the wall, smooth with age, that seems as if once long ago, a farmer's battered *chapeau* would have hung upon it. He would have placed his hat there as he bent to stoop over his twice-daily task of milking his cows. The straw is still strewn on the floor and in the cow mangers, and the ancient ghost of Monsieur de la Croix is a lingering, warm presence.

Most exciting to me of all our activities, is whisking the broom over the limestone wash on the walls and beams. As I sweep the broom rhythmically backwards and forwards, it crumbles and flakes, revealing a silky smooth finish. Once again I muse that the faded white wash is every designer's dream. It has a practical not decorative purpose however, in *la grange*, for it was used to repel *les mouches*. This makes perfect sense in a barn that was once used to milk cows.

It seems that like most of our other major life decisions, the conversion of *la grange* will be a fait accompli. Everything huge that we ever undertake seems to take on a life of its own. Our first significant car after a few years of marriage was meant to be on our dream list for a very long time. There are not many people I know who go to the fruit markets to buy bird seed for the parrots in their garden and return home with a classic (read old) BMW. And so it is that the decision to one day convert our barn seems to have been made when Stuart announces one morning, after inspecting his *castine*, that our new *la cuisine* in *la grange* will one day have a wonderful view of *la piscine* and the orchard. It will indeed be the *piece de résistance* of all our *rénovation* years. Meanwhile, the hard work does not seem to be yielding the same results as in past renovating efforts, to balance the consumption of *pain*, rich *mousse au chocolat* and delectable pastries.

Castine Consumes our Days

The weeks start to fly in a haze of heat and hard work, broken by languorous moments in *le jardin*. The punishing hours of working in the pervasive heat are punctuated by *café* breaks and a daily parade of pastries. When the heat wave of late July passes, the summer light softens in the early evening and dances in gentle waves across the grass in the orchard. The tap, tap, tap of a woodpecker, impossible to glimpse, joins the chorus of the donkey braying in a nearby field.

In the large *jardin* opposite, where a young boy has played alone for weeks with his Border collie, a young girl joins him for the summer *vacances*. They clamber up the *prunier* tree, wheel recklessly along the lanes on their bikes and race in a happy-go-lucky way across the land. Her plaits fly out behind her as they live a summer childhood of carefree abandon.

Most villages too have at least one eccentric old woman and Jean-Claude tells us about ours in Cuzance. She has been caught in the night stealing people's pots of vivid geraniums. Gérard and Dominique have the misfortune to live opposite her and her wild, barking *chien*. Whenever we visit, she peers out from behind her tall, straggling hedge. She spies furtively on all their comings and goings. Even from where we live, we hear her loud calls frequently echo through the village. Jean-Claude embellishes on the story in an email when we return home.

To bring water to your mill, I shall tell you about the story (or the part I know) of Thérèse Delpech who lives in front of the Murats. Once there was a problem with flower pots and I learnt through Mme Dal that

Thérèse stole her flower pots and had been caught red-handed in the dead of night by a farmer who complained to Jean-Luc, the mayor, who in turn summoned Thérèse to the Mairie ... and the following night, the geranium pots were back in place!

As you know, if you've been past the Murats' place, you are attacked, across the fence by two mad dogs belonging to Thérèse and, one day, the Murats got tired of it, and seeing Thérèse exciting the dogs against strangers ... so that, from their bedroom window, they started barking back, to Thérèse's fury, who in turn, shouted back insults. Now, every time Gérard sees her, he repeats them, mimicking her voice, which does nothing to ensure peaceful surroundings in their part of the village! That is why you may have heard me welcoming the Murats in a growl, 'Ah les connards!', for their greatest pleasure, since it is a standing joke between us and Gérard is quite a clown!

For once, this story is not sad (well in fact it is, if you consider how lowly human nature can be), unlike other stories I share with you.

Combined with the pig farm next door to them and the ever-present pungent aroma, despite their lovely sweeping views we know which end of the village we prefer to live. No wonder Gérard and Dominique have told us that as they drive round the countryside, they are looking for a farmer with a barn who they can approach and offer to buy it, so they can move and escape their mad neighbour. So, at least one obligatory eccentric old woman in Cuzance. Who knows what other secrets the village holds? Well, there are other tales Jean-Claude has shared but he has made us promise not to tell them. I make it my secret mission to try to discover more.

After a few weeks, we finally find time to wind our way across country, along the narrowest of roads and the sharpest of hairpins, to have lunch at our favourite restaurant from the previous year, Bonne Famille. There is a large group of workmen seated round a long table inside, their plates piled high. The tantalising aroma follows us as we sink into our seats on the terrace with pleasure and anticipation. The *menu du jour* does not disappoint — stuffed *tomates* followed by fragrant rice and *poulet*, chicken that simply melts as the first succulent mouthful is savoured. It is followed by my second favourite dessert in the whole world, *crème caramel*. We raise our glasses of *rosé* in a toast to summer days in France. On the way home, we drop in to a nursery to buy packets of meadow *fleurs* that Jean-Claude will scatter for us in spring.

Then the day of the compacter at long last arrives, a far cry from our vision of a meadow of spring flowers. In direct proportion to the building of the heat, so too do our stress levels escalate. Well, mine at least. Stuart, as always, simply takes it all in his stride. After a huge delay in the arrival of the compacter, when Stuart is finally able to collect it, it doesn't work. The hire equipment business has not called us on our *portable* as promised. We have lost precious days in our ebbing schedule and have been simply marking time. The mountain of *castine* is by now mocking us in its looming presence. Rather than waiting in vain for the promised call to collect the compacter, Stuart has finally given up and gone back to simply see if one is now available. It is and we are more than ready for the next critical stage.

As with most significant moments, Jean-Claude is on hand for the noteworthy — and much delayed moment — of starting the compacter. It doesn't start. While it has been demonstrated to Stuart when he collected it, now it simply refuses to fire up. Needless, to say, tempers are fired up instead. It is by now late afternoon, the sun is at its searing peak, the engine shudders, stalls, starts, shudders, stalls. It takes a whole two hours to start it properly. Finally, Stuart has it running and sets off with the shuddering machine across the *castine*. Progress is not smooth, not smooth at all. The *castine* is not evenly flattened. No, the tiny gravel stones spray everywhere and leave gaping channels behind. Clearly, there is something seriously wrong with the compacter. It judders to a halt. This time it completely refuses to start. By now Jean-Claude has discreetly exited stage centre left; that is, slipped quietly away around the side of *la grange*. We are left alone to grapple with the baffling complexities of compacters.

The compacter proves to not in fact be a fully functioning one. It now completely refuses to fire into life. I amaze myself by suggesting that maybe the spark plugs need cleaning. It is inexplicable, for it started the very first time when Stuart collected it. I am despatched to ask for Monsieur Chanteur's help. I know that his workshop will run to a simple spanner. Armed with my dictionary, I am intent on making my mission clear. I have already written out my three essential words: *bougie* — spark plugs, *prise* — socket, *outil* — tool. Once again, these are certainly not words you will encounter in any holiday language guide that I know. Monsieur Chanteur indicates that they will finish their *café* in their customary shady place under the walnut tree and then find what I need.

Monsieur Chanteur inspects the recalcitrant compacter. He gestures that Stuart should accompany him to his workshop to find the right tool. To say we are astonished is an understatement, for rather than walking the short distance back along the road, as nimbly as a goat, Monsieur Chanteur jumps over our adjoining stone wall. For a man of eighty-eight, it is a truly remarkable feat.

Spark plugs cleaned, it seems that at long last we can make up for lost time. It is not to be. More problems beset us. The starter cord breaks. A hasty repair takes place. It is now early evening — and still the compacter won't spring into life. By now, there are more than a few *merdes* flying through the air.

There is no choice but to return it to Brive — an hour-round trip.

Success at seven. And so it means, that just like last year, we work late in to the night. I move wheelbarrow after wheelbarrow of *castine* and rake and rake before Stuart is able to then compact it all. We labour long and hard until the fading light forces us to stop. Finally we throw ourselves in quick succession under the shower and head off to Martel for an exceptionally late *dîner*.

We need a hearty meal to set ourselves up for a full day of compacting. We are looking forward to another significant day in the history of Pied de la Croix that we are in the process of creating — the day we will start to lay the paving. At last, there would be progress in the surrounds of *la piscine*. After our late return from *dîner*, the huge ugly toad that lives in the cellar, crosses my path in the gloomy light as I stumble inside with exhaustion. It seems to be a fitting end to a day of utter frustration.

The summer idyll is truly over. We at last have a fully functioning compacter. We spray water to prepare the surface to compact correctly; it evaporates immediately in the heat. Stuart compacts, I spray. I trundle another wheelbarrow of *castine* and add another layer. The *castine* mountain does not however, seem to ever diminish. It seems to have become a permanent fixture in the rugged landscape of our *jardin*. The compacting continues for several days. Round and round *la piscine*, up and down the sides, round and round. It is a never-ending blur of slow motion. I heave and haul interminable wheelbarrow loads of *castine*; the tiny pieces have by now taken over my life.

As I drift off to sleep each evening, I surprise myself with both my thoughts and attention to detail. I think about such things as the construction of the concrete stairs in the barn and the critical consideration of their precise placement. I move rooms around in my mind. Where exactly will the *salle de bain* go upstairs? I know from past renovating that it's essential to run the plumbing for the bathroom in line with the existing plumbing to reduce costs. While I have other more pressing matters to consider, like the very real renovation in hand, rather than an imagined one of the future, these thoughts are nevertheless a world away from the daily routine of life and work at home.

Le Jardin — Strike *Trois*

In the early morning light breaking at the bottom of the orchard, huge bunnies bound, seeking new pastures where no one will disturb them. Last year, I was a naive fool in my single-handed onslaught. I used the only thing to hand in the spraying of the voracious brambles — a domestic-sized spray bottle. Now I am far better equipped with my industrial spray container with a sturdy strap that I sling over my shoulder. This time, I tell myself, I have a far better chance of success in the battle of *les herbes*. The sibilant sound of the wind stirring the towering pine trees in the neighbouring *jardin*, spreads a soft whisper across the garden as I resolutely continue my battle.

Working in *le jardin* continues to still be a very generous interpretation of the term 'gardening'. Day after day I continue to tussle, tug, heave and wrench at all the weeds that never quake or tremble when attacked. French weeds are like no other I have ever known, and weeds; indeed, I have known a few. The invasive bamboo in our garden when we lived at Austinmer, when we first escaped from city life, consumed our days in our never-ending battle to quell it forever. Now, in our Wombarra home, Stuart has chosen bamboo wooden flooring as an ironic homage to it.

As for French weeds, they fight back with ferocity. A measure of their phenomenal resilience is that they are already stealthily creeping back along the edges of the weed matting that has only been in place a mere matter of weeks. They seem to shout at me in triumph, as if declaring that foolish foreigners cannot simply descend and in a few short weeks, even be presumptuous enough to think that they can possibly imprint themselves upon the wild rural landscape.

There are long thin white ones that have a subterranean life all of their own, deep below the rocky surface. As I claw ferociously to dig them out, they are like dead fingers coming back to life, reaching up to me as I struggle in vain to chop off their heads. Shades of the old nursery rhyme drift in and out of my head.

As with everything French, we watch and learn. On our evening *promenades*, we note in other gardens, that the only way to win the battle of *les herbes,* is to first place the weed matting, then cut a very precise hole exactly where the plant will then be dug in. This was our first mistake. We had thought we could just lay the weed mat, next dig a hole, then bed down a plant. It would seem not. And so, we start all over again…This includes moving the copious rocks that we have carefully placed on top to prevent the weed mat from blowing away.

As I labour long and hard, I divert myself by searching my mind for various appropriate sayings. The expression, 'Rome wasn't built in a day', springs very readily to mind. As I pace myself against the chiming of the bell that signals that in another hour, the heat will be so intense I will have no choice but to reluctantly down tools, I watch *le chat* slink around the edge of *le jardin*. Though we have carefully searched all the outbuildings and at times we can hear the faint meow of the four French kittens, we simply cannot find where she has moved them to. We are just glad that at least she has moved them out of *la grange*.

It is the perfect touch of irony, that the books I have chosen to read in my rare moments relaxing in *le jardin*, are all about glorious landscaped gardens, complete with water features and sculptures. Nothing could be further than my gardening reality.

I do however, have to constantly remind myself, that only two years ago, when we first arrived at Pied de la Croix, while the garden may still be wild, nevertheless it is already hard to believe that on our first visit, it was so rampant that I left that first year without even seeing the orchard properly or even knowing the full extent of our garden. So, I do need to remember that in fact we have already come a long way. It just may not always feel like that.

As I claw the clambering weeds back, to rescue three baby oaks that have self-seeded, I wonder about future generations who will see them at their full height. It takes around 150 years for an oak to reach middle-age. It is unlikely that those who live one day in Pied de la Croix, will ever know about the Australians who once lived another life in Cuzance.

We discover one day over *apéritifs* under the walnut tree with Jean-Claude, that our middle outbuilding would have been used to hang out corn to dry and then feed to the cows during the long winter months. That accounts for the odd piles of dried corn husks lying in the barn. Another piece of the jigsaw to add to the layers of history of our *petite maison*. I had also discovered that the most recent concreting of some of the gaps in the limestone in the walls of the barn, was inscribed La Croix, 1977.

As we wander down the meandering lanes in the late twilight, the full moon hangs in the fading blue sky on one side, while on the other, the sinking red sun illuminates our rural stroll. The fields dip away, the hills roll into infinity, the brindle cows graze and Brigitte Dal passes with her *chien* on her nocturnal *promenade*. We fling the windows open on our return to let the cool, hay-scented night air fill our *petite maison*; the classical music flows out softy into the stillness of a tranquil Cuzance country night. The full moon peeps in our *chambre* window — the picture is complete.

The Unfolding Weeks

The days roll out in a haze with nothing to differentiate them except market days and the variables in the weather. Puffy clouds scud swiftly across the sky one moment and draw a dark curtain down. The next, the sun bursts through again in blaze of unexpected heat. It frequently looks like a storm is imminent yet Jean-Claude assures us they will be headed for the Masiff Central *département*. The darkness lifts and the pale wispy clouds seem like they have been painted on the sky with a thin artist's brush.

We find out that Wednesdays are a public access day to the *gendarme*. It means that they are available to answer any questions you may have relating to the intricacies of the law. As we drive home through Martel after our visit to the markets, I see a cluster of *gendarme* at the roundabout. As I peer curiously out the *voiture* window, I glimpse our neighbour, Monsieur Chanteur in his distinctive cream waistcoat. He is deep in an earnest discussion with them. Jean-Claude later confirms that he was indeed seeking their advice on family matters. It is on these matters that he has insisted that my lips are sealed. In my respect for our acceptance into our other life in Cuzance, I will never breathe a word of what I have been told.

For weeks, I again avoid driving alone. When I finally do, it's because circumstances foist themselves upon me. This time it is because of Stuart's new relationship with the compacter for he cannot leave its side. As long as I repeat my personal mantra learnt from Liz, 'Stay on the right, stay on the right', I will be alright. It all comes back to me and I am fine. Soon the *petite* Renault Scenic is zipping along the country roads. I am armed with a long list. Oh yes, the lists are still a dominant presence in our lives. Today: *Bank Populaire, la pharmacie, la boulangerie* to order a *gâteau*, the beautician to make an appointment, and *le bricolage* for wasp spray as wasps are invading *la piscine*. As always in France, the list is an eclectic one.

My first encounter on my solo voyage, is an interesting one. I park with success and walk along the narrow lane, bordered by medieval houses with bright containers of *fleurs*, to the main square in Martel. There is a *voiture* crawling slowly through the narrow space. An American pops his head out the window to ask directions. I direct him to my 'secret' parking space and wish him *'Bonne journée.'* In reply, the American, says, 'Have a beautiful life.' And so, I swing my basket over my arm, smiling to myself at his words and the encounter, as I trip along the ancient cobblestones.

Once again, what is commonplace at home assumes a different resonance while in France. As I queue to buy my *pêche blanche* — the prized white peaches — and warmed-by-the-*soleil,* Quercy melons, I watch the bent old man in front of me. He ends his buying by handing over his battered leather coin purse to the stallholder. Obviously used to his weekly practise, she patiently counts out his coins and hands back his worn purse. It is the simplicity of such acts that speak of many untold stories.

As always, a visit to the *boulangerie* is full of potential delight. It has been made even more so after discovering that the baker is an award-wining one. Fifteen years ago, Jacques et-Fabrice Bottero won the prestigious Best Baker in France Award. No wonder my tastebuds always tingle in anticipation every single time I set foot in the *boulangerie* and breathe in the tantalising aroma. It is always a difficult decision; to stick with tried and true favourites or branch out into tempting new choices.

Perhaps today I will buy for our afternoon *café, petite* strawberry tarts, glistening in their glossy glaze or *choux* pastry *éclairs*, gleaming with their shiny *chocolat* icing.

The mown fields of hay shine like burnished gold in the glowing light of late afternoon. We are just a few minutes off the *autoroute* to Paris and yet in Cuzance, we are in the depths of the countryside. It's like a landscape lost in time. The farmers work to the rhythm of the sun and the seasons. Each tight turn in the narrow lanes leads to a new perspective of the rural landscape. A swaying field of verdant corn, a grove of ancient walnuts, a *petite* hamlet of stone *maisons*, with shutters in shades of chestnut brown, moss green, crimson and white. A Border collie darts energetically across the road, herding a flock of reluctant sheep from one pasture to another. The leaves — yellow from the heat — twirl and dance and fall upon the fields to decorate them in a crisp carpet.

As we *promenade* through the village at the close of another day, the quintessential sound of shutters creaking closed, signals that the day is over for all in Cuzance. The sunset streaks crimson splashes across the fading sky. The full moon tugs a dark-grey velvet blanket over the village. The new day will start again with the drawn-out chiming of the church bell at seven.

History Lessons and Stories

Jean-Claude is an endless source of all that is both fascinating and informative. He provides a window into French life that I would not otherwise have a chance to glimpse through. On a rare luxurious afternoon relaxing at their *piscine*, Françoise plies me with *espresso* and homemade *crème glacée*. It is my idea of heaven. As the three of us chat, Jean-Claude tells me that after the Revolution, *maisons* were taxed on the number of windows that they had. So it is to his regret that a number of windows in their *magnifique maison* were filled in with stone. We glance upwards at the towering levels of their house and sure enough, there are the imprints of old windows, distinguished by the stone that stands out in slight relief from the surrounding stonework. He goes on to tell me that next it was the turn of the piano to be taxed, for just like windows, pianos were the province of the *bourgeoisie*. Later, with the advent of technology, televisions became the source of additional revenue. And so, aerials were hidden in attics.

When I arrived for my afternoon of freedom, Françoise was in the garden, polishing a long wooden cross for the church. After she is *fin*, I carry it across the road to the church for her. Once inside, under her instructions, I place it against the wall. She tells me it is used for *fêtes* — celebrations. We have had our own as I carried the big old cross and Françoise carried Henriette. Françoise is devoted to the church. Next, she is about to go and collect *fleurs* for the High Mass on Sunday. She asks if I would like to go with her and then help arrange them. I decline both offers. I have declared it to be a self-proclaimed holiday after shovelling *castine* until very late the previous evening.

Church duties complete, we return to Françoise's *petite cuisine*. The three of us squeeze into the tiny space as she squeezes us fresh juice with oranges from Portugal. Jean-Claude announces that it is the fiftieth anniversary of Marilyn Monroe's death. He starts to sing *Happy Birthday Mr President* and Françoise joins in the duet. Later, as I relax next to *la piscine* I flick through a copy of *le journal, Mademoiselle*. There is a captivating black and white photo of a young Mick Jagger, taken in front of an Aston Martin in 1962. Jean-Claude shares yet another fascinating fact with me. He tells me that President Sarkozy apparently refused to buy an apartment in Paris as it was too near Mick Jagger's apartment. I was very surprised to hear that he and Carla Bruni had once been in a relationship in her heyday as a young model. Now as the recent President's wife, Jean-Claude declares she is the picture of decorum, indeed, she has even had lunch with the Queen. I wonder if President Sarkozy would have bought the apartment if it had been near Freddy Mercury's?

Whenever I descend the stairs to their *piscine and* lower, park-like *jardin*, I always pause under the stone archway, wreathed in mauve wisteria. I breathe in the beauty. I let the tranquillity seep into me. A visit to their garden never fails to restore me. I let the peace wash over me. Momentarily, until my *rénovation* resumes again, I am replenished.

When we return home to the other side of the world, Jean-Claude keeps the spirit of Cuzance alive for me, by frequently sharing stories with me. I never cease to be astonished by the full extent of human drama that is contained within one *petite* village. Indeed, it would seem that Cuzance is a microcosm of the world's stage; all its richness, drama, sadness and amusing incidents.

One day after school, this tale is in my Inbox.

Thirty years ago when we arrived in Cuzance we were astonished

Our House is Certainly Not in Paris 193

to see a file of three people going east every morning and afternoon and we learnt that it was the Delpech tribe who was mourning the father's death. First, invariably came the mother, then the daughter (Thérèse) and then her younger brother who was mentally challenged (like the Dédé Mabit you already know) ... and we discovered in the churchyard, by the entrance, a tomb covered with mementoes and artificial flowers. The mother died a few years after but it was possible to communicate with the son (better than with Dédé), whose godfather is Paulo, my neighbour, and who was sent by Thérèse on errands like buying her cigars. Then we saw this man becoming paler and paler; he had got leukaemia and died of it after two years ... and I learnt through Paulo that he complained to him that he was beaten by his irate sister, in spite of the fact that his invalid pension went to her.

Another day, Jean-Claude reveals that:

Of course this story is about Bernadette, just as the other sad story I will tell you one day is about Pascal; and you can use all these stories by changing names — that is no problem. (Which I have duly done.) *As for getting a new char, wait until we are in Cuzance! But it will be hard since Bernadette was introduced to us by a woman from Cressensac, who did the char for us for three weeks to our greatest satisfaction, two years ago ... but then broke her ankle by falling from an apple tree she was picking from on her farm — she still limps and anyway, confided recently to Françoise that she found our house difficult because of its age and numerous storeys!*

I now remember I had promised to you other publishable (but sad) stories: here is the one about our charwoman who had found happiness with a man in Cressensac. After divorcing her husband; they had a house built, the garden organised and the house painted ... but not the same colour as they had notified the authorities: blue instead of beige ... and the authorities protested and declared they would have to re-paint the house and the woman, who had occasional bouts of depression, went out of her mind since she had insisted on that colour! And now, she has disappeared, refusing any further contact with her live-in. It is all terribly sad.

It would seem that when I reflected that I would miss our neighbours, Madame and Monsieur Chanteur, that my thoughts had an eerie prescience, for it was only a matter of months later, that I received the following from Jean-Claude.

You will be sad to learn that Christiane Chanteur died this week and has been buried in Paris. This morning I received a kind letter from her husband Roland. I must say the sad news is not totally unexpected on my part, as I saw that her state of health and mind was definitely deteriorating this summer in Cuzance. I am now going to send a letter of condolence to Roland ... and I wonder if we shall see him again in Cuzance since he had come there essentially to allow his wife to see her daughter and her grandchildren.

Please don't hurry to follow the same road...

I certainly don't intend to.

Jean-Claude replies to my response and lets me know that: *I did send a word of sympathy from us (and you) to Mr Chanteur, but I doubt we shall see him again since he sounded quite satisfied about his flat in La Rochelle and carefully pointed out that he was in Cuzance for the sake of his wife (and considering the poor level of attention devoted by his children in Cuzance, I would certainly understand that he no longer comes).*

I had not realised though when I mused about the future and the fact that one summer we would return and the Chanteurs would no longer be there, just quite how soon this would actually happen. The sad news reiterates that I will miss terribly, my fond observations from afar, of the loving old French couple.

There are amusing tales and other sad ones.

Taking advantage of a moment of freedom, I shall tell you about the sad fate of Pascal, the son of a deceased farmer friend of ours. He built, by himself, a house in Lagarrigue. Then, fate struck a first time by attacking his wife with cancer; it lasted through years of unsuccessful treatment in Bordeaux. When she finally died (leaving a nice little girl), Pascal then decided to change jobs. Instead of eking out a meagre salary from his old father on the family farm, he decided to work driving lorries for the agricultural cooperative which is present in Martel and Souillac, while also attending to the farm in the evening and on weekends. Then fate struck a second time during the reaping of tobacco leaves: they are conveyed on a moving mechanical belt lined with metal hooks: one of the hooks (no bigger than a fishing hook) broke and flew in the air ... into one of his eyes that started leaking intra-ocular liquid. His friends immediately called SAMU (emergency medical help), which sent a helicopter on the spot. After long stays in Limoges and Toulouse, he finally lost vision in this eye. Of course he could not drive professionally but the cooperative took him on nevertheless as an assistant in their shops and walnut factories. He drives his own car and hunts ... and now lives with the girl who sells fresh vegetables in Malastrège, on the road that goes from Cressensac to Martel!

There are also utterly fascinating tales that wing their way across the time zones and oceans and miles.

I have a book that tells of a gangster murder in Cressensac ... and also (I think) of the very dangerous former camping site in Cressensac which was famous all over Europe for its homosexual possibilities. It was closed when they opened up the motorway!

It is extraordinary too to discover such events and places are on the very doorstep of Cuzance.

And another day.

Going back in history, I do not remember if I told you about the Cuzance treasure (some coins are on display in Musée Binche in Brive) but most of it is in another museum in Paris. That is why on the Cuzance escutcheon appears a gold doubloon!

Truly, there seems to be no end to the fame of our *petite* village, even though it is buried in the depths of rural France.

In my Inbox on yet another occasion, to balance the pathos.

After sad stories concerning Cuzance, I must tell you about one that made people in Cuzance hilarious last year. Across the lane southward from your house, a young couple had a maison built a few years ago. The young woman tried to have activities so she claimed to give watercolour lessons (in fact she should have been paying for the lessons) and then she was offered a job looking after school kids before and after school hours. After one year she disappeared and I asked what had happened to her ... Well, people told me, she had separated from her husband and was living with somebody else in the village where the Bonne Famille restaurant is; but she had separated from her husband on such good terms, that before leaving, she had taken the trouble to find a replacement to keep her husband happy and had introduced her to him. Last year, she was back in Cuzance looking after the kids ... but I don't think she is back in her home yet! Funny? Sad? Contemporary anyway!

During the long, cold winter months in Lyon, there is more time for Jean-Claude to write and share his stories of Cuzance. He has embraced my desire to soak up his stories from afar and this, his last, sums up all that is extraordinary, alarming and heart-warming in our *petite* village.

Let me tell you a very sad story that is unfolding in Cuzance these days. Do you remember the Pech, that is, the hill that is crowned by the stadium (and now the Maison de la Truffe)? When you go up the hill, on the right, there is a low-slung one-storey bungalow; twenty years ago it was quite solitary on the hill except for the old house on the left of the road. The inhabitants were a jolly fat woman who we mainly saw in her Volkswagen Polo and her live-in, who went about riding a bicycle (he was later killed on it on his way back from Souillac — he was not overprotected as are Tour de France cyclists!).

My contacts with this woman then deteriorated because I was attacked by her dog every time I went past her house. (Rest easy, when I say deteriorated, I mean that I ignored her as far as possible) ... However, her next dog — a Pekinese — did not, and had a strange bias against me whenever I walked past her house or past Madame Dal's house where the dog took refuge all day since she was mostly absent.

Well time went by; she had another live-in (an ex-circus, odd-job man) ... and they built three council houses just below her house. In one of them lives my friend Michel Bournat, so that I saw quite a lot of her place, in fact. Her place deteriorated and I heard rumours about her being a danger on the road since she drove carelessly and at excessive speeds. Then, one day, there were two dustbins overturned on the road between her house and my friend's, and plenty of litter on the road. I enquired about it from my friend and he told me it was the woman who had become quite mad at him for no reason at all. (You know the dapper little man he is and how clean his wife is.) Sometime later, I was surprised to see that Michel's gate was locked and he told me that the woman had taken a fancy to pouring garbage into his garden! Later, I was apprised that she attacked the children of another house further up the hill.

Then one day I saw that her roof was quite ruined ... and this was the start of a story that made me quite proud of the Cuzance citizens, because when we arrived in the next spring, I remarked to Michel that the woman's roof had been repaired. He explained that her roof had been ruined by a storm, as a consequence of the lady being swindled by Irish gypsies, who told her they would clean and renovate her roof but replaced her tiles with worthless used-up ones. So, that when a storm struck, the roof blew down. And, this is where I fall in love with the villagers: they worked on her roof for free so that she should have something over her head.

Time elapsed until one day, Michel stopped by our place, quite agitated and full of nervous tics. Apparently, the woman had attempted to kill him and his wife with a knife. Another neighbour saw the scene, photographed it, called the Maire who in turn called the gendarmes, who had the woman sent to a psychiatric hospital in the vicinity. The next day she was back, mouthing horrors and threats against the whole world ... and especially against Michel and his wife!

And so the problem goes on since the woman refuses to take her medicine, she suffers from violent bouts of aggression ... and the gendarme are called ... and the rigmarole goes on. I even heard she hurt a gendarme once, but nothing can be done to (or against?) her. If you go by her house, you will notice it because of the weeds and abandoned look (all her shutters are closed and she goes out only at night); sometimes (rarely) her children come and tidy up the garden ... and the situation deteriorates slowly until ... drama strikes?

Sad is it not? A portrait of our civilization!

And that indeed sums it perfectly. There is simply nothing else I can possibly add to Jean-Claude's history lessons and stories.

Crazy Paving, Never-ending

Is it the paving that is crazy or the people laying it? This is a question that is full of imponderables. Stuart comments that it could certainly drive people crazy — and very quickly too. As a prelude to laying it the following day, after an *apéritif*, we start playing around with the pieces, laying them out in various configurations round *la piscine*. The permutations are endless. Not only are the sizes any number of variables, so too the thickness of the stone varies. It's definitely going to be an alarm clock morning to get the paving underway. Once again, the task ahead is a daunting one.

My job is to unpack the paving, then sort the pieces and start laying them out. It is soon rapidly apparent that the appellation 'crazy paving' is not a misnomer. Meanwhile Stuart has to come to terms with his industrial cement mixer and the different proportions of sand and cement to mix. Unlike *artisans* we have heard of, he will not abandon a batch of fresh cement if the church bells strikes twelve, signalling *déjeuner*. No, we will work on regardless, especially as Sunday is absolutely a day of rest — our very own village *vide-grenier* day. We are hoping Cuzance defies the odds of the weather forecast and the predicted storm does not strike at lunchtime. If the storm does hit, the annual lunch will have to be abandoned for the third year in a row. The only satisfied customers were the pigs as they were the happy recipients of all the food.

After just a short time, it is quite evident that I am simply never going to grasp the intricacies of how to lay crazy paving. The novice assumes that the very random nature of it, means that it will just literally all fall into place in a pleasing pattern. This is not the case at all. Far from it. Its placement requires logistics and mathematical precision. These are not skills I have. They are not skills I am going to acquire. So, now this task is down to Stuart as well.

What I am left with? It would seem that labouring is my forte. This is an odd division of labour, for I am not the physically strong one in our team of two. It means that one of my main jobs now is to continue to unpack the crates of crazy paving — all six of them. Not only does Stuart have to now mix the concrete and then apply it, he also has to first put all the paving into place. I labour. I lay out all the paving in ever-widening rows so we can see at a glance which piece may possibly fit into which place. I fetch and carry and move and appraise. I move them again.

Laying the concrete between the pavers does not proceed smoothly either. The concrete goes 'off' far too quickly. Apparently this is the correct term when the mix is far too dry. Similarly, there is an unexpected art form to filling the spaces between the pavers and using the tool to smooth it off. This task too was meant to be one of my designated jobs. I just can't get the hang of it at all. There are many times in our other life in Cuzance when it is not all one of beer and skittles. Or should that be, *pastis* and *boules*? There remains a yawning chasm to pave round *la piscine* that seems far beyond our reach in the time frame we have. Yet again, the phrase rings prominently in my mind, 'When will the *vacances* become a true holiday?' It's time for a drastic reassessment.

While it's all well and good to bond so firmly with Pied de la Croix through our sheer hard work, it rapidly gets to the point with the paving that it simply consumes our lives. I have cause again to question the reasoning behind buying our *petite maison*, rather than having a

French *vacances* each year in a quintessential French farmhouse. What has happened to the anticipated outings, the exploratory drives, the leisurely lunches? Time seems to have rapidly evaporated.

When we renovate, we are not used to not reaching our targets. Once we set a *rénovation* goal, we work resolutely towards it. Not this time it would seem. We moderate our plans; they were just too ambitious. The paving project may now have to be completed next year. As for the bathroom plans? They too will have to be postponed for the year after. Surely then the annual French *vacances* will begin in earnest?

Our Cuzance *Vide-grenier*

Fête en Cuzance is in full swing. As we work away on Saturday afternoon, there is a *boules* tournament outside the *Maires'* office. Do we have time to go and watch? *Non*. Preparations for the *vide-grenier* have been going on for days. From our little porch, we can see the red tape in Marinette's walnut orchard marking out places for the stalls to be set up on Sunday. The first village dance went until 4 am on Friday night. A set of keys was found as they were tidying up. It was thought they are ours. I am profoundly grateful there was not a knock at the door at that time to find out if they were indeed ours, keys clutched in the *Maire's* hand. I am not sure though why it is that they think the keys may have belonged to us.

The outside disco, held in a marquee on Saturday night, does not start until darkness falls at 10 pm. Another huge day spent with the compacter, ends with *dîner* al fresco, accompanied by the discordant, surreal sound of the annual Cuzance disco beating loudly across the fields with an overtone of wafting pig aroma. Our gaze settles on the huge holes that *lapin* have started digging in the grass in front of our *petite maison*. Rabbits look altogether different bounding happily through the fields. Ah, life in the country.

We watch groups of young people drift in excited clusters past our *petite maison*. We wonder where on earth they are the rest of the time and what they all do. Until tonight and the evening a group of *lycée* students came to sell us raffle tickets, we had always thought the population of Cuzance consisted of mainly much older inhabitants. It's quite a mystery. Wherever the young members of our village may be the rest of the year, it is wonderful to see all ages and generations come together to celebrate life in their village.

There is nothing quite as exciting as opening your shutters to see your own village *vide-grenier* unfolding right outside your *petite maison*. Cars are parked tightly, end to end, either side of our stone pillars and clear-out-the-attic stalls stretch out from the nearby curve in the road, leading down to the Hotel Arnal and beyond. As I eat my *petit déjeuner*, I watch Stuart from the window as he sets off on his second reconnoitre. He was up so early in anticipation that it was still dark and on his first foray, the stallholders were still setting up in the dim breaking light.

It is quite an experience to set off from our *très jolie* steps, basket as always slung over my arm — ever hopeful of filling it to the brim with treasure — and *voilà*, we are immersed in our own Cuzance *vide-grenier*. This year we were so determined not to miss it, that we have booked our return flights after the *grand* event. Our hopes are not disappointed at what we hope will be the first of many times at our own village annual market. My first — and what proves to be my best — purchase is a sweet, black *chapeau*. The woman tells me it was her grandmother's gardening hat. Who she was and where she gardened, I will never know. My elation knows no bounds when I wear it immediately and am told I look like Audrey Hepburn — my style icon. It makes an enormous change to feel stylish rather than in my usual dishevelled daily state.

For the first time in three years, the weather stays fine for lunch on trestle tables laid out under the walnut trees in Marinette's orchard. There are hundreds of people gathered from the outlying hamlets, and as the matriarch of the village, Marinette stands on the terrace outside her *maison* and gazes down with a sense of proprietary pride. The Cuzance band plays vigorous tunes and *La Marseillaise* is particularly fervent and stirring.

We settle with Françoise to enjoy our *déjeuner* in the walnut tree shade and as always, I turn to Françoise with our latest request; not a tablecloth or a hose or wire cutters this time. No, Stuart has actually agreed that we need help with the paving. This for me is the surprise of the century. Stuart absolutely never outsources anything. It is a huge concession on his part. I ask Françoise if she knows of anyone at all in the village who may be able to help. *Voilà*; their neighbour, a sculptor, is looking for extra work. As always, they swing into action on our behalf. By early Monday morning, Jean-Claude has spoken to Jean-Louis' *maman* and found out that he is due to return home from *vacances* that very evening. By seven Monday evening, Jean-Louis comes to visit us to talk about the concreting. He even gives Stuart extra tips — we need to get a waterproof additive for the concrete as well as a water repellent finish for the pavers. He will start on Friday morning. I am elated. Help is at hand at long last in the unexpected form of a shy, silent sculptor.

By now our work clothes are beyond grimy. They are layered with sweat stains and encrusted with dirt. My socks are so dirty they could walk by themselves. After a cooler period for a week, the heat once again surges. By Friday, the very day we finally have someone to help us find our way in our world of crazy paving, it is thirty-five degrees. I push and push myself each day beyond the borders of weariness. My obsessiveness with the ebbing of the weeks leaps the boundaries of exhaustion.

In the most surreal of coincidences, in my stolen moments under my precious walnut tree, each new book I choose to read is about gardens. Not just any old *jardins*, but splendid, magnificent ones. The first, *Capability's Eden* by Diana Saville, centres on a reproduction on a sweeping scale of the garden of Eden. The next, *The Savage Garden* by Mark Mills is a monumental tribute to Italianate style. And my favourite book of my French summer, *The Thirteenth Tale* by Diane Setterfield, also has an exquisite garden as a central motif. What all the books have in common is that the gardens are grand and elegant. I keep wondering if there is a subliminal message.

By the middle of August, the morning light is already perceptibly softer. The evenings draw to a close more rapidly. The sun sinks earlier and subsides more swiftly on the horizon beyond the fields. The *jardin* remains thoroughly *rustique.*

Crazy Days of Crazy Paving

Our driving force, both against the heat and time, is to now lay all the paving before we leave. Surely our soon-to-be team of *trois*, will make all the difference in the world? As with restoring the *jardin* in previous years, by now I have a far greater degree of familiarity with the size and shape of the pavers in the six crates than Stuart does. This is because not only have I unloaded them all, but by now I have arrayed them all in rows, virtually single-handed. Since I have failed miserably at applying concrete, as with everything, we have to continue to divide our skill sets. Once again, mine remains unskilled labour.

Stuart too proves to have a better eye for their intricate layout. You could lay crazy paving a thousand times and each time the configuration would be different. In yet another piece of irony, it falls to me to pass the huge slabs to Stuart so he can mix and match them and fit them all together in our enormous, outside jigsaw puzzle. As some of them weigh about a third of my body weight, this is no mean feat.

There are literally thousands of pavers on the six pallets. After a week of laying *castine,* we have now sifted and sorted through them all, trying to find perfect sizes and shapes. Each has a completely different identity, as if each one has its own DNA. Just in time, we find the perfect ones for the sweeping entrance at the back of *la forge's* enormous wooden doors. They are the thickest and heaviest. Even more special is their imprints of *petite* fossils — leaves, ferns and perhaps even tiny creatures from the Palaeolithic era.

As well as unpacking the six huge crates, I have also used four pallets to sort and divide shapes and pieces of about the same size. I am now able to readily identify the categories that I have devised: very large, large, medium and medium-to-small. I am not entirely sure that my crazy paving sorting skills will ever come in to play in any other part of my life.

I start to feel like a trader at a horse auction. As I bring the pavers out one by one from their pallets in the barn, I call out the size, shape and pedigree of each paver, to present to Stuart for his larger-than-life jigsaw. It is not lost on me how me how my actions would appear to Martians, peering down, examining our earth-based activities.

We start laying the pavers at the back of *la grange* on a blistering August afternoon. Our hopes though are as high as the temperature. Indeed, our expectations are well-founded. While the sides of *la piscine* are yet to be *finis*, we have reserved the best and biggest pavers for the back of the barn. As they are enormous, we are hoping it will give us a great sense of progress to see them go into place quickly. And indeed, they do look *magnifique*. The golden colour of many is a perfect match to *la grange* while the reddish hue of others complement the natural ochre pointing between the limestone blocks of stone in the barn walls. Finally, the *castine* pile starts to diminish as we move more and more into place as a solid base under the pavers.

After a mere hour, we have to take a break, not simply because the sun sears us. It becomes altogether too confusing trying to merge and marry the intricacies of each individual piece of paving. Once again, the term 'crazy' is not lost on us. It is clear that we need to return to its intricacies later, with fresh eyes.

The job is never-ending. And this time, we don't reach our target. The job is not *finis* when we leave by any means. I greedily count the remaining weeks like beads on an abacus.

Return to the *Mairie*

Towards the end of our stay, one day when Jean-Claude drops in, he informs us that we have been summoned to see the *Maire*. We are full of trepidation. 'We are the slaves of administration,' Jean-Claude declares emphatically.

Our *maison* and *jardin* remain in full view of the *Mairie's* office. I urge the new plantings to hurry up and vigorously flourish. Every single thing we do can be clearly observed from the upper windows of their office and all our *rénovation* is subject to scrutiny. Our fear is that we will be subsumed by piles of perplexing paperwork and will need to get approval for our paving before it can continue. Like the mountain of *castine*, it is unlikely to simply disappear. Shades of our roof the previous year and the imperative paperwork resurface. Although work had already started on *la grange* roof, it too had seemed as if it would grind to a halt. However, through some guiding intervention, the source of which was completely unknown to us, it all smoothly unfolded and fell in to place and work was able to seamlessly proceed.

We are faced with two choices. Simply ignore the summons, or face the music. It is not without some degree of apprehension that Stuart nervously sets off the few short paces to the *Mairie's* office. We have hastily constructed several possible scenarios and sequence of plausible responses, depending on the outcome of his visit. All feasible responses are to be of course conducted and conveyed with the utmost compliance and courtesy. One — to plead ignorance of the bureaucratic process required; coupled with secondly, ignorance of the French required to engage in the conversation — feigned if necessary.

I await in a state of anxious anticipation of the outcome of the visit. Will work have to grind to a shuddering stop? How long will the possible paperwork take? Will it be completed before we have to leave? Will there be a *très cher* fine for contravening some unknown *rénovation* requirement? The possible outcomes — none of them good — seem to be endless.

Within just a few minutes, Stuart returns with a palpable air of relief. Yes, paperwork was indeed required — but, it was for last year's work on the roof and *la piscine*. It is now all signed and in order. Let the paving continue!

Soaring Summer Days

An unlikely hero has appeared to save the day, in the form of a steadfast sculptor. He arrives fully prepared; he even has tools and equipment for the job that we have quite overlooked, like a huge sponge to wipe the concrete off the paving after each piece is laid. Jean-Louis works methodically and patiently. Just like the roofers the previous year, he works for four hours straight, only downing his tools when the church bell strikes the *déjeuner* hour.

By now, drowsiness hangs in every particle of heavy summer air. At least the weight of our overwhelming workload is alleviated by the fortuitous appearance of Jean-Louis in our lives. We discover through their fragmented conversations, for Jean-Louis does not speak English, as Stuart and he work side by side, some fascinating insights into his life. To supplement his meagre income as a sculptor, both Jean-Louis and his wife work at the factory near Martel that produces Chanel perfume bottles. Perhaps that is where the intact perfume bottle came from that I unearthed one day in the garden? It would seem that original owners of our little house were highly successful in their truffle searches, for Chanel perfume is esteemed the world over and not a find I would usually associate with the farmers who once lived in Pied de la Croix.

The more I work in *le jardin* and disturb the earth, the more relics from the past rise to the surface. I remember my first forays into our garden, when I was overcome by the wonder and surprise of my archaeological discoveries. Each and every one, I carefully placed aside. In just a few years, these discoveries, while still delightful, have become almost — but not quite — *passé*. Another ancient glass bottle, another twisted old spoon, another bent fork. After only three years, I no longer hoard them so scrupulously. The shards of shattered pottery, do however, make it to my cache to be kept. Somehow, they tell another story, of *dîners* long past; of a family who once long ago lived within the walls of Pied de la Croix.

My drive to bring the garden back to life, means that I start to clear the rampant growth along the stone boundary wall. My exertions allow me to rescue more *petite* oak trees that are being smothered by blackberries. Encouraged by such finds, I continue to wrench back the smothering weeds and brambles, heedless of the trailing branches of ferocious thorns that whip me in the face. I spray ferociously — secateurs in one hand, industrial spray bottle in the other. I have recently improved my process of eradication for I've taken to decimating them at their source in the dry, stony ground. My constant incantation is: 'Chop off their heads, chop off their heads'. The lines from the old children's nursery rhyme *Oranges and Lemons*, once again reverberate in my mind:

> '*Here comes a candle to light you to bed,*
> *Here comes a chopper to chop off your head.*
>
> *Chop chop chop chop*
> *The last man's dead!*'

I am more determined than ever to halt the progress of their grasping, greedy tentacles as they march invasively across *le jardin*. It is always a fortunate thing that my vision sustains me. If it didn't , it would be oh so easy to simply give up; for after all, as I have been told countless times, it is a *rustique jardin*.

I 'garden' at times in the most ungraceful and unorthodox of ways. I sit in the dirt. It is simply the only way I can summon sufficient strength to wrench out the wretched weeds. I also clamber on the high stone wall, struggle with the ivy, and throw down discarded old farm rubbish.

The Queen Anne's Lace forms a floating sea of delicate white heads under the heavily laden branches of the orchard trees. The weight of the fruit now pulls the boughs down to fully meet the scorched ground. The *petite* apples are drying into brown wizened forms before my very eyes. I place cairns of rocks to mark the places for new trees, two *mûrier-platanes t*hat will grow straight and tall, to form an umbrella arch of shady leaves. One day, my walnut tree will no longer be with us and I will miss it like a much-loved friend. It is with this in mind, that I plan for future days. The black cat slinks past on her mysterious meanderings. The days draws to a close with a final flurry of swallows swooping while a last surge of gold from the setting sun infuses the evening in a soft glow.

Crazy Paving Calculations

In the course of a day, Stuart moves from mathematical calculations for the laying of the paving, to scientific measurements for the salt and chlorine in *la piscine*. Meanwhile, when I went to the market in Martel, I also remembered to go to in to *Bank Populaire* for a statement. What I forgot, however, is that two statements are necessary for a French bank account. One for a current account and one for the savings account. The 'current' account shows the daily comings and goings of *euros* in and out, while the savings account automatically 'tops' it up. The complexities of it all remain a baffling mystery for me. What I can grasp is that the *euros* are flowing out rapidly. What I can also manage to very clearly understand is that there is not a source to top up the account. The mathematical calculations for the paving clearly need to also be applied to our bank account.

After days of paving, we know that another day will certainly send us crazy; it will tip us over the edge. We decide to take a break and be tourists for a day. However, to avoid the tourist influx of one of the most visited towns in France, we still get up early. We have also been told that Collonges-la-Rouge is best seen in the early morning light, when the red stone for which the town is named, will be glowing in the breaking dawn.

It is absolutely true that the country drives in France are always as much a part of the journey as the destination. Each curve, each stretch ahead brings a new vista, a renewal of wonder at the timeless beauty of the rural landscape.

Collonges-la-Rouge is one of the most beautiful villages in France. All the houses have been built from the local sandstone, which is striking and unusual because of the red stone. This is in fact how it got its name and its unique in that there is no other village that I know of built from this stone. As too are many of the other villages with the accolade, 'one of the most beautiful villages in France', it is a delightful place to wander round, for each winding pathway and alley leads to another red turreted *maison*.

After a morning happily spent wandering the quiet streets and taking abundant photos, like true tourists, we make our way back to Martel to continue our day of luxury away from the work site. We have driven past the Auberge des 7 Tours restaurant just off the roundabout in Martel many times, and been attracted by its *menu du jour*, as well as its terrace with a view. There has simply never been time to stop, but today we finally do. As we walk along the gravel driveway past the vivid orange bougainvillea and pots of bright petunias, a *chic* older couple are driving out in their equally old Citroën. Both them and their cream and green *voiture* are straight out of a French film. They pause to spontaneously recommend the restaurant to us. It is an omen. So it is, that in the ebbing weeks, we find the perfect restaurant and it rapidly becomes our favourite haunt for both *déjeuner* and *dîner*. As with many things in life, it has literally been right on our doorstep all along.

On our first visit, we sigh with relief as we sink into our chairs on the shady terrace under the *mûrier-platanes*, the ferocious sun still beating a steady rhythm on our backs. Every element of the unfolding tapestry of dishes is a taste of perfection. The setting — the view of the rolling green hills of Martel, the exquisite *fleur* beds, the symphony of tastes and textures — all add up to what is hoped for in the French lunch of dreams. A light, tangy tuna salad, tender pork and ratatouille, plum tart, a *petite* carafe of icy *rosé*, two *espresso* — all accompanied by the low murmur of French people on *vacances*. This is why we are in France.

The weeks have been greedily gobbled up. We continue to work more long hours of daylight than are conceivable. With our departure looming we are torn between our desire to do even more and push on and finish the paving, or soak up the essence of our French summer. As it has been in past years, it is a dilemma. The more we do now, the less there is to do in future years when we return. In the past few years, we have pushed and pushed ourselves, beyond the boundaries of any conceivable *vacances*. It has paid off, yet the catchcry remains — namely from me — 'When does the holiday start?'

Dust and French Linen

While Stuart and Jean-Louis work steadily as a new team at Pied de la Croix, my days are now engulfed by vigorous hoeing. I use the ancient, long-handled wooden hoe that Erick gave us. I am preparing a channel at the front of *la grange* that will be filled with *castine* to form a border between the grass and stone walls of the barn. It is yet another attempt to stem the tide of weeds. Each laborious drag of the hoe through the stony soil yields even more rocks that I place in ever-increasing piles. My hard work means that I have increasing respect for the creation of the immaculate vegetable *jardins* that most French people have in the country. Not a weed or a rock is ever in sight. I have seen farmers as old as eighty, patiently tilling the soil. Their vigour and love of the land is what infuses their daily life.

I wonder about the farmer whose gnarled hands once gripped the wood of the hoe that is smooth from age. I see his wizened form, bent at an angle, as he stoops over his vegetable *jardin* and lovingly tends to his plants. I've seen such farmers at times in Martel. They favour sturdy thick blue overalls, often with a red checked shirt underneath and they are always wearing a battered *chapeau*. I imagine too that they still cook their daily meals on wood fuel stoves like the one in Pied de la Croix that was the entire kitchen. Time seems to have entirely passed such farmers by.

It is not long before I am enveloped in clouds of choking dust and soaked in rivulets of sweat. It is not a good day to have chosen to wash the linen, flapping nonchalantly just near where I toil. My billowing cloud of white French sheets and pillowcases is soon engulfed in dust from the dirt and stones. What a fool, I think to myself.

The next ten days are filled in a similar way. Hoe, pick out the stones, make a pile, move the pile, trundle another wheelbarrow of *castine* from the *derrière* of *la grange* to the front. Once again, my objective and driving force is to win my fight against *le herbes*. Mind you, *les herbes* has the ring of a Michelin chef's *cuisine* rather than the more prosaic word 'weeds'. In any language however, they remain the same, and they must be banished. The only saving grace is the two grapevines that loop gracefully against the golden stone of *la grange*.

Day after day too, Jean-Louis arrives punctually on the dot of eight. His shabby old *voiture*, parked in the front of the barn, tells me every story that cannot be shared in words. Not only do he and his wife work shifts at the perfume bottle factory, he has undertaken this arduous job to support his son at university in Limoges. It is an entree to another world beyond the village. Jean-Louis was born in Martel so his life has had a *petite* radius. His son's world, through his father's labour, will move far further than the tiny world of Cuzance.

After a restorative *déjeuner* break, Jean-Louis always returns promptly at two. There are days we try to convey that as it is *le chaud*, it is simply too hot to continue in the burning afternoon heat. He indicates that he has his *chapeau*, so with a shrug and hat on his head, he steadfastly sets to work for another four hours under a blazing Cuzance sun. Not a ripple of air stirs the land and I finally concede defeat to the heat and retreat inside. The thick old stone walls means that it is blissfully cool. The end of our week is a glorious one, for real progress is at long last being made.

As another Cuzance day ends, the *noir chat* slips through the shadows on her secret night-time adventures. The sun hugs the horizon and the melodic birdsong hushes as darkness falls across the now fallow fields.

Over *dîner*, in another parody of the seasons, we discuss the complexities of heating *la grange*. Yet again, our dreams fuel us. We are toying with the idea of a year in Cuzance one day. Right now, on a day that soared to forty, it is inconceivable to imagine the minus eighteen of the past hostile winter.

Trench Weed-fare

I continue to conduct my own daily Cuzance assault. In shades of previous years, I fall out of bed, pull on my work clothes, consume a hasty *petit déjeuner* — and it's back to the trench for me. When I resume my trench weed-fare, I adopt an even more ignominious *jardin* style. I now crouch in the trench with my spade to scoop and shovel the dirt and stones in a sideways motion. It saves my back from constantly stooping over and most importantly, it works. I seem to have stumbled upon a very efficient rock-moving, dirt-moving, method. At other times, I seem to find myself balancing — one leg stretched out to the side, ballet-style. At least I have sufficiently maintained my sense of humour to be able to observe myself and laugh. One thing I do know, is that I will not soon be auditioning for *Swan Lake*.

As we pause for our morning *café* on our *petite* porch, we hear an unusual cry. I race to the side of our *maison*, to see to my horror, that Madame Chanteur has fallen on the road. My instinct kicks in and I run to help her. I pat her back and use soothing words that I know she won't understand but my calm tone is universal. A *voiture* rounds the corner. Instinctively, I put up my hand in the stop gesture. Fortunately it is Monsieur Dal and he was not careering wildly. Just the other day, two teenage boys, with high holiday spirits racing in their veins, nearly pushed us down a steep embankment on their fast-moving tractor as we crept around a country corner.

While not in sight when I arrive at Madame Chanteur's side, within seconds, Monsieur Chanteur appears in response to her frail yet frantic cry. He moves her gently off the road and tenderly admonishes her for wandering. Monsieur Dal conveys to me that Monsieur Chanteur is far too old himself to have such consuming, enormous care and responsibility for his wife. It is simply heartbreaking to see every day how rapidly she is declining. I am not sure his devotion is sufficient to sustain them both.

It must be a mirror in the eyes of the many older village inhabitants of what life may hold in store for them. I am full of sadness, for I know Monsieur Chanteur cannot continue to care indefinitely for his wife. What makes me even sadder, is that they moved to Cuzance to be close to their family in a nearby village. Yet, not once, have I heard the joyous cry of *petite* grandchildren ring in the *jardin*, to fill their hearts with happiness.

At the end of each Cuzance day, the closing of all the heavy wooden shutters, never fails to have a sense of symbolism. The closing out of the night, that after even the street lamps go to sleep at eleven, means that the heavy blanket of country darkness is only broken by the stars peeping through the scudding clouds. And then, each morning, the pattern is repeated, when the open shutters welcome a new, bright day. I know inevitably that the day is close when I will never again glimpse from our *chambre* window, Monsieur and Madame Chanteur, hand in hand in their *jardin*. And I will miss them.

Relentless Toil

Where my force and drive and energy come from, I simply don't know. I work feverishly, like a possessed person. The urge to do more, to press on, is all-consuming. A solid morning's work is translated by the corresponding pile of rocks and stones. As I work at the front of *la forge*, I watch the endless parade of tourist cars and caravans. I wonder about their destinations and how it is that such a procession can be constantly moving through such a *petite* village. I wonder too, if they ever think about me as they glance ever so fleetingly in my direction. Do they think I am French in my own homeland or are they able to deduce that I am a possessed foreigner? In a flash, they disappear round the bend, off on *vacances*. As I dig and hoe and wrench and heave, my trench is my sole focus. The demanding, backbreaking task is my whole world. Sometimes, I wish I could run away with the tourists.

In a feat of magic, after another relentless day of interminable toil, we transform ourselves for a marvellous evening in Martel. We park in the overflowing main street and gaze at the medieval market place and surrounding restaurants, all transformed at night by soft lights that glow upon the ancient golden stone. The towering church spire stands solidly against the soft dusk sky.

After just a few visits to Auberge des 7 Tours, it pleases us enormously to be greeted by the friendly *maître d'*. We sigh with pleasure and relief, as we slowly savour melon and prosciutto, followed by two of our favourites dishes, local duck and then walnut tart. On the outside terrace, under the trees festooned with twinkling lights, it is an enchanting place to be on a balmy summer night.

Darkness descends earlier each evening, edging towards autumn. The autumnal tones start to appear and the yellow and red leaves tumble and dance. Crunchy carpets of gold decorate the fields. Summer is closing its door on the countryside. As we go on a late walk, replete after a splendid *dîner*, the gloaming gathers around us. Silence envelops the village. We walk along the empty, silent roads on the knife-edge between light and the all-consuming darkness. The sky is streaked with banners of mauve and adorned with ethereal clouds.

Dog Days

By day however, huge white fluffy clouds hang suspended in the sky like fairy floss. The heat soars yet again. It is the fourth time it has surged unbearably in our Cuzance summer. The mercury remains at forty for more days in succession than we can keep count of. We are told by our *amis* that the French call these 'dog days'. For us, it is definitely not a dog's life, lying in the shade and panting, though truth be told that's all I long to do. The only time it is a true dog day is when we see Henriette on her daily *promenade*. Then our tails wag figuratively too.

Our new plantings of lavender and laurier droop with fatigue in the relentless heat. Their leaves curl up in brown protest. As we trudge across *le jardin* with our heavy watering cans, I fervently whisper to them to survive the extremes of the elements in our absence. I find it hard to comprehend that the temperature has a span of sixty degrees in our *petite* village.

Almost overnight there is a sudden change in the evening light. An utterly golden radiance suffuses the village and all the stone *maisons*. An otherworldly quality seeps across the twilight fields. Meanwhile, throughout each day, my relationship with the paving continues to be a close one. Too intimate at times, for when I am especially weary — read always — it sometimes slips out of my grasp and leaves gashes down my legs. When the heat becomes simply too unbearable, I slip away for stolen time at Jean-Claude and Françoise's *piscine*. The respite is pure paradise. Despite the blanket of suffocating heat, Stuart and Jean-Louis continue their paving crusade. Like being given a prize for his endless sweat, quite literally, we are rewarded with an impromptu *dîner* invitation, a simple supper of omelette, salad and the most delicious mushrooms we have ever tasted. Françoise tells us that the *cèpes* were picked and preserved by her friend Elizabette. We have long known about the revered *cèpes* and their secret places, buried deep in the woods; so secret that one French person will never reveal the source of their precious mushrooms to another.

The fifteenth of August is a national religious holiday, the Assumption of Mary to Heaven. We too take the opportunity to have a holiday and head to St Chapelle Aux Saints to a mid-week *vide-grenier*, one positively brimming with treasure. I rummage through piles of long-abandoned finery and my persistence once again pays off when I unearth scarves adorned with designer labels and the magical word 'Paris'. We eat *déjeuner* at a wooden trestle table, one of many laid out in rows, expectant of a huge holiday crowd. In front of us there is a stand of one hundred soldier-straight poplar trees and a farmer demonstrates the wood-moving skills of his cart horse. There is an entranced audience and the children in the crowd are invited to work beside the farmer and his horse. As I watch, I hope that it inspires one of the young children to follow in his footsteps so that the traditions of the land live on.

Our departure date looms ever closer, and as always, we have set our goals too high. We again moderate our aims and adjust our short list of what's critical to complete before we leave. Repairing the sagging, broken barn doors is high on the list. We have no desire the following summer to find another litter of French kittens has taken up residence in *la grange*. Meanwhile, plans are already being made for our return. Françoise has suggested that after our stay in Paris with Patrick, we go on the train straight to Lyon to stay with them. She already knows us very well, for she realises once we are ensconced in Cuzance, it's hard to leave, even for the delights of big-city lights.

The changing light at least means that we have to slightly adjust our working hours. It means that we have *dîner* somewhat earlier rather than just before falling into bed, exhausted after another day's interminable toil.

We continue to work in temperatures that we would never contemplate working in at home. The days pass in a glimmer of a moment. It becomes more and more imperative to place some satisfying ticks on our final checklist. Progress is hindered when Jean-Louis cannot quite get the hang of how to correctly apply the concrete for the huge pavers or how to level them correctly. There is certainly more to laying paving than meets the eye, for these were tasks I simply couldn't grasp either. His methodical approach is perfect for fastidiously concreting the gaps between the pavers but it is becoming only too clear that we will certainly not be *fin* this summer.

I have a well-known propensity for tidying and cleaning. Sometimes it gets me in to trouble as I scoop things tidily away and out of sight. I realise just in time, that it may have been a bit more than a mere 'Where is my…?' that I have swept up a still-smouldering cigarette from the work site and put it in the rubbish, which consists of empty cement bags. And yes, cement bags are made of paper, and yes, to use the Australian summer cliché, it is tinder dry. The rubbish is piled up in the barn. I frantically — and surreptitiously — pour water over the flickering flames. I take care not to share this with Stuart. It has been a trying morning; the temperature is tipping forty; tempers are rising to match the mercury. All our dreams for *la grange* would have been literally up in smoke. It simply doesn't bear thinking of.

Scorching air is sweeping across Cuzance like an open oven door. The very air is hot to breathe. The washing dries virtually the moment I hang it out. Our energy levels are as frayed as the cuffs on my work shirt. There is no choice but to advance the *apéritif* hour. We eat sunshine-warm Quercy melon that gleams in golden crescents on our plates. The *glace* clinks in our antique glasses of pink-rose coloured *rosé*.

After *dîner,* Stuart browses through advertising catalogues. He shows me an astonishing *jardin* implement — *Dèsherbeur thermique* — a blowtorch to destroy weeds. If that's the sort of product available to fight garden weeds, no wonder my battle against *les herbes* is a losing one. Nevertheless, I prudently decide that it would not be wise if I was let loose with a blowtorch in *le jardin*.

We have long declared that Sunday is supposed to be sacrosanct, our one day of compete rest. In previous years, despite our perpetual exhaustion, we never failed to set the alarm clock for our *vide-grenier* quests. Now, our bodies are so in tune with getting up early to work, that even now on our second-last Sunday, we still tumble out of bed at the same time as squirrels start to scamper across the road in the fresh dawn light. We break our self-imposed rules and lay weed matting for several hours before heading to the stunning hilltop village of Turenne. It is a market we have visited in previous years and one we have come to love. The heat, almost but not quite, defeats our treasure hunt.

The find of the day — for there is usually one esteemed find that stands out from the crowd — is a large and *magnifique* hand-carved wooden bowl. Heads turn to look and admire it as Stuart carries it in his arms through the thronged market. We even hear admiring comments about our bowl, floating on the still air. Indeed, a true find, and worth traipsing through the enervating heat to discover.

By now, almost the end of August, the heat and weather seem to have a life of their own. It is the one constant dominating daily conversations and dictating what we do and when. We know that at home everyone would find it hard to believe that a French summer can match, indeed at times surpass, the hottest of Australian days. When rain finally cascades, the leaves unfurl greedily to lap up the rain drops. Soft yellow light washes the orchard and the sunset-sky is smudged in a palette of pale red and pink.

Rural Parisians

We are not the only ones to escape to the solitude of country life in Cuzance. Indeed, quite a few Parisians have found their way to this quiet corner of rural France. Nearby, a couple from Paris are living in what was once a chicken slaughterhouse. They in fact fulfil the reputation of Parisians, for they are haughty and aloof. At times however, they are more like mad dogs and Englishmen for they labour in the unbearable heat during the middle of the day. There is not a murmur or stir in the rest of the village for all are slumbering and seeking refuge from the sun that burns like a fully fuelled furnace. We watch askance as Monsieur Paris constructs a very strange lean-to structure, out of galvanised iron, at the rear of their *maison*. As for its purpose, we cannot possibly hazard a guess. Perhaps it is for more *poulet*. If so, we can only hope that it does not house a raucous rooster to disturb our serenity. The *maison* does not seem to have progressed much beyond its days as a *poulet* slaughterhouse, for outside is piled all manner of household flotsam and jetsam. As we walk past, we try to peep inside the ivy encased windows. We have been told that inside there is such a state of chaos that even the stuffing from the sofas is escaping, trying to join the *jardin* detritus.

Meanwhile as I muse on life in Paris, far away, I have progressed to sanding the doors and windows in readiness for a coat of thick varnish to ward off the icy tentacles of winter. No task is ever straightforward however. To sand and varnish the window over the original kitchen sink, I climb on the sink and precariously lean far out the window to sand the rickety old shutters. It proves to be yet another vantage point to watch the world go by. As always, I am only too aware that this type of *vacances* is not going to feature any time soon in a glossy holiday brochure.

Stuart is fond of saying when offering me another *apéritif* or *crème glacée*, that we are on holiday after all. I tend to look at him quizzically whenever he makes this statement. Certainly it is not the normal routine of home, but how it is normal in any sense of the word, to endlessly renovate on *vacances* is quite beyond me. I long for the day we will be *fin*. It is a day on a far distant horizon that I simply can't envisage. Roll on perpetual walnut-tree-days, I at times think mutinously.

An Enchanted Evening

There are moments when time itself stands still. Even as you're living it, savouring every moment, you already know that it is one of those rare enchanted evenings in your life that you will remember forever. At the height of the Cuzance summer, we have *dîner* next to Jean-Claude and Françoise's *piscine,* overlooking the *jardin* at the peak of its seasonal beauty. In many ways it is like sitting in a garden at home, for there are bright blue agapanthus and vivid red hibiscus. There is an old wooden table on which Françoise has placed two elegant silver candelabra. The atmosphere is magical, for the soft flickering candle light is the prelude to the darkness that will soon creep across the garden. We dip in the pool and then have icy glasses of chilled *rosé* followed by a simple salad, freshly prepared from their immaculate vegetable *jardin*. The dessert is a truly exquisite confection that Françoise has conjured up in her enviable Michelin style: poached *abricots,* melted warm *chocolat* and *vanille crème glacée.*

As darkness descends, *la piscine* lights are switched on and the lights from the village church opposite, flood the still, evening garden. There is not a whisper of wind or a murmur in the soft summer air. Henriette is now the focal point of all our gatherings, and after just a few short weeks, no one can imagine life without all the joy she brings us. The herbaceous border of lavender, the bright splashes of petunia and the burst of orange bougainvillea; the sweeping lawn, the towering walnuts — all floodlit by the lights around the pool; creates a scene yet again straight from the studio of *Canal+*. Yet, for now, we are the ones living this moment, rather than characters observed and envied, with a director's call to 'cut'. It is a tangible moment of pure pleasure, a distillation of time; the essence of which I try to consciously capture and preserve.

In just a few short hours though, I know that the shrill of the alarm will summon us to continue our relentless *rénovation*. For now, I savour it all, lean back in my striped director's chair, for in this brief moment, I am indeed the director of our own French vignette. I sip my wine, Henriette sound asleep at my feet.

Fin — Rénovation — **For Now**

In a decision that is unprecedented and a strangely uncharacteristic one for us, we decide to draw a line in the sand a week before leave. We have not reached our goal of finishing the paving yet unless we stop and have a proper break before returning home to work, we know that we'll still virtually have our tools in our hands when we are boarding the return flight. Enough is enough we declare in unison. This is a decision we make in complete harmony.

Some things never quite change though. Mmm, what few minor tasks will we 'just' fit in? The two grapevines arching gracefully on *la grange* have had vigorous growth spurts in the heat. We've noticed from looking at vines in other gardens, that they are at their most attractive when the main stem of the vine is the feature, forming a long bare length at the bottom, with the branches and tendrils then shooting sideways and upwards. So, this too is our aim.

It has long been Stuart's intention to do the pruning. But time 'waiting for no man', seems to be in full play in Cuzance. He is frantically still paving as much as possible, before the line is fully drawn. Wasn't it already? Perhaps the sand is wet and the line keeps disappearing. No, in fact, it is the concrete that needs to be kept damp, and the refrain is now, 'I'll just finish this bag of concrete before I stop.' I have heard these words before — or a variation upon them — many times over our many renovating years.

So, what can I possibly accomplish in the time remaining? I decide to try my hand at pruning, with the intention of creating the feature stem. This proves to be a little more specialised than my pruning in the orchard, which when all is said and done, is really only sheer hacking of old branches. It all goes terribly wrong. With one simple snip of the secateurs, I miscalculate where to cut. *Voilà*, all the splendid summer growth tumbles to the parched ground. In fact, not just the growth of summer, but, how many years old must it be judging from the thickness of the stem? Quite a few I'd say. And how many more years to re-establish itself? Again, suffice it to say, more than a few. The decimation is somehow sadly symbolic for me. Not only is it hard to leave Cuzance again but it is also hard to walk away when our project is not *fin*. Next year — next year is the echo for everything.

Weary beyond words and emotions running high, we set off to Martel for a much-needed *dîner* of steak and *frites*. Not only is the meal bitterly disappointing — the steak is dry and the potatoes are clearly left over from *déjeuner* — *l'addition* is also ridiculously *très cher*. Strike that restaurant off our list. A bad end to a bad day.

Petite Vacances

The reality of renovating is that *fin* is never really possible, it is never a finite actuality, particularly once a year in a short hot summer. We enthusiastically embrace our self-declared *petite vacances*.

The shadows start to lengthen ever earlier, creeping across the *jardin* as our days ebb too. Further hints of autumn yellow appear on the trees. Yet, there have been so many consecutive dog days that we can no longer keep count of them. I had thought it was a colloquial term used by our *amis* until Françoise told us that it is used in the weather reports on television. There is further confirmation that it is an official term when we return from shopping in Brive, and the overhead sign on the *autoroute* states: *Attention. Jours de canicule. Arrêtez-vous et réhydrater.* Stuart loses no time in translating it for me. 'Attention: Dog Days. Stop and Rehydrate.' Ah, the French will use any excuse for another *apéritif*.

All the days of our summer have blurred. The final days though when we declare a *petite vacances* at our *petite maison* are even more so. The walnut tree is definitely my new best friend. At least now it is an indolent, indulgent blur. Days of reading, daydreaming, afternoon *café* and *crème glacée*, icy gin and tonics in the evening. 'This is the life,' is another of Stuart's favourite expressions and this time it's true. We sigh with pleasure during our last lazy Cuzance summer days and the sweat, toil, and yes at times tears, recede and fade.

The church bells ring imperiously every hour, its chimes are always immediately repeated in case you did not grasp straight away, the marching hours of the day. At both seven in the morning and again at ten at night, the pealing is longer and more resonant to ensure that the villagers know that the working day has started and when it is *fin* at the end of another fleeting day. At midday, there is another clamouring cry from the bell. It commands that tools are downed and that the *dîner* hour — or two — is duly respected. You can measure life by the ringing of the sonorous bells.

I know that I am fully immersed in my French life when I take our *voiture* to the local Renault dealer for a service. I almost manage independently, though of course Jean-Claude is on stand-by as my back-up. It also gives me enormous pleasure each time I go to Martel, despite being the height of the tourist season, to be a recognised, regular customer by the women who work in *Le Bureau de Poste, la boulangerie* and *la pharmacie*. I never fail to take delight in the courteous exchange of *Bonjour* and *merci beaucoup*, and *au revoir* as you leave. I especially love the ring of '*Toute allure*' and all that it implies; full speed ahead, have a good day. The greetings on arrival and departure infuse the everyday transactions with a measure of French timelessness and tradition.

While Stuart's decision to not press on and *fin* the paving is not one I would have initially made, nevertheless as we indulge in our *petite vacances*, I have every reason to be grateful for such a sound decision and not finish it. The toil truly can wait until next year — and the one after, and indeed all the years to come in our *petite* corner of French provincial life. For a few days of utter indulgence, we enjoy outings for *déjeuner* and long, luxurious afternoons next to *la piscine*. For a short moment in time, the biggest decision of the day is what *la robe* to wear out to *dîner* and what choices to make from the *menu du jour*. The world with all its responsibilities and commitments is held at arm's length. Life is spectacular. A lone kite, wheeling high in the sky, cries plaintively, the sole sound to puncture the heavy summer silence.

Le Relais Sainte Anne

There are few things that I can imagine would be more wonderful than arriving for *déjeuner* when the entry is outside a high stone wall, so high that it is impossible to peep over. The moss-covered walls encircle an old convent, that in its most recent history — the start of the nineteenth century, was a school for girls. Now, in its latest incarnation, it is one of the most prestigious restaurants and hotels in Martel.

There are also few places that I have ever visited, that on arrival, I have paused to simply breathe in the complete charm and beauty. And so, an exquisite few hours unfold, in the company of Jean-Claude and Françoise, on this, our last Friday in France. It had been Françoise's suggestion to have *déjeuner* here, for although they have been a stone's throw away for twenty years, they had yet to visit it. It is our surprise to them that *l'addition* will be our way of saying *très merci beaucoup* for all they do for us.

The *jardin* is perfectly manicured and while Le Relais Sainte Anne is in the centre of Martel, a very popular tourist destination, now at its peak in August, there is a tranquil hush within the grounds. The lavish *menu du jour* is served on the spacious, flagstone terrace overlooking the chapel, which is flanked by a bed of bright yellow *fleurs*. The meal and company will be long-lodged in the memory bank of: 'Do you remember?' Indeed, it was by far our best meal in France, in the most delightful company in the most ideal of settings. And while the *cuisine* was sublime, *l'addition* was by no means extortionate, especially when *foie gras* was served in both the *entrée* and main course. We are fully aware of some people's ethical objections to the production of *foie gras*. What can I say? We are not in that camp.

The *entrée* is finely minced *canard,* the duck is encased in a golden brown pastry parcel. The main dish, *canard* again, a regional speciality, is served with a delicate *foie gras* sauce, while the dessert is a *magnifique* concoction of strawberries, *crème glacée* and paper-thin *fraise* wafers embedded on a layer of fine shortcrust pastry. Jean-Claude and Stuart have chosen an exotic creation of meringue and *chocolat,* served with hot *chocolat* sauce. We all sigh with utter pleasure.

A wander round the soothing *jardin* completes our outing. We all concur that a visit to Le Relais Sainte Anne will be an annual pilgrimage; a homage to all that is the well-deserved repute of fine French *cuisine*. Yes we may be far from Paris and the Michelin restaurants but we have found our piece of Paris buried in the country — and unlike the *grand* Parisian boulevards, it is not at all *très cher*.

On the short drive back to Cuzance, Jean-Claude takes us on a country lane not travelled by us before and through the *petite* hamlet of Remedy, a sign that has often caught my eye for all that its name conjures up. We are not five minutes from Martel, yet we are in the depths of the country, where copses of trees are now in full autumn flight, cloaked in a medley of rich colour. We drive past a half-finished *la grange*. Jean-Claude as always our own personal tour guide, a font of local knowledge, tells us that it was not completed at the end of World War I as the money went out of the truffle business, for which le Lot is renowned. It seems incomprehensible to me that no one has finished building the barn in all the intervening years.

My Idea of 'Fun'

On our very last Saturday in Cuzance, the autumn rain sets in steadily. Similarly, the leaves now fall in golden torrents, the onset of all the trees surrounding us, being stripped completely bare. *La piscine* and all final relaxation is abandoned. Our plans for a farewell onslaught on *les herbes* are thwarted by the downpours. Instead, we turn our attention to another outbuilding. It is attached to the *derrière* of *la grange* and our long-term dream envisages it as a *salle de bain* and laundry.

From the layout of the old wooden stalls and the remnants of hay piled up, we imagine it was a cow byre. Once again, we look around and try to utilise what is on hand. Stuart sets to work with the crowbar, pulling down the thick ancient wooden planks. He needs the wood to repair the rickety broken doors of *la grange* before we leave. I rake the hay into mounds and trundle wheelbarrow after wheelbarrow out to *le jardin*. I am ever mindful of what may be lurking in the long-abandoned hay. At least it is lighter than my previous countless loads of *castine*.

Next, I use one of the many old abandoned straw brooms that once saw another life. I stretch and reach to drag down the skeins of thick dark cobwebs. Now we are able to look through the *petite* apertures that have been left in the huge stone slabs that form the wall. We pause and gaze around at the magnificent space, overlooking the back garden. We pace the space; a bathroom with an orchard view. What could be better?

As I work away, I muse once again about my concept of fun, for fun indeed it is to clear out this long-neglected building and peel it back to its bones. I am filthy beyond description, dust flies in my face and

I am ever conscious of hidden mice, rats and even snakes. And yet, it remains strangely satisfying, despite the fact that the weather continues to thwart our *petite vacances* plans. We could certainly sight-see for there is plenty in our *département* to still explore but the connection with the past and the imprint we are creating, exerts a strong tug.

The *vacances* has been totally abandoned by now. There are even shades of prison camp moments, as Stuart informs me one cool damp afternoon when he has spent hours moving enormous rocks and attempting to dig holes for more trees to be planted. The ground is so stony, that he is forced to give up, defeated by the limestone rocks that lie in wait just below the surface. They prove impossible to move. Another plan thwarted...

We learn that the cool damp days in Cuzance are echoed at home. It would seem the weather gods are laughing right around the world. Ferocious claps of thunder reverberate in the weather gods' loud merriment.

Nature has truly reclaimed the land and exerted a strong hold on our *rustique jardin*. I continue my efforts trying to free trees on the boundary that are being choked by blackberries. They fling themselves rapaciously in my face and despite my thick gloves, the thorns are so sharp they pierce my hands with a rapier-like onslaught. I feel like a human pincushion.

By the time we stagger inside our *petite maison*, defeated by darkness, we both slump in utter weariness over our bowls of pasta, barely able to lift our forks to our mouths. The direction of the wind brings the sound of traffic speeding to Paris on the *autoroute*. Despite my consuming exhaustion, and despite my true love for it when I do visit Paris, I remain perpetually happy that our house is not in Paris. The quiet of a Cuzance evening is a balm.

Le Coiffure

Pure crisp light illuminates *le jardin* and there is now a distinctive chill in the early morning hours as the season perceptibly changes. It is time to face the reality of leaving and our return to the 'real' world. Appointments are duly made to be ready to return to work. As the weeks have passed, so too has my confidence grown. I set off to *le coiffure* in Martel, key words all carefully checked and written down prior, for fringe, colour and cut: *frange, couleur* and *couper.*

What I do lack is the French to explain, *désolé,* sorry I am late as I was held up behind a slow, trundling tractor on the narrow, winding road. French drivers are the most reckless that I have ever encountered. Double lines, blind corners — no problem. The foot goes down and off they race, frequently with no way at all of telling if there is an oncoming *voiture* beyond the narrow curve of the road. I wouldn't say that I am averse to putting my foot down at times but not on these roads and not when I am still schooling myself in the right way of driving on the wrong side. Eventually however, even the farmer turns his head round to check why I haven't bothered to overtake him.

When I arrive at *le coiffure*, it is a situation that I do not attempt to mime. Perhaps I will end up with a basin-cut if I do. Things are already looking a bit tricky, as the only word that I could find in the dictionary for 'fringe' is 'on the fringe of the forest'. Very fortunately for me, *frange* does turn out to be the right word.

There is only one other client in *la coiffure*. The hairdresser, Emilie, is young and attractive, and engages in a non-stop, impassioned conversation with the older woman. I am at a complete loss to follow, though I deduce that very possibly Emilie has had her heart broken, possibly betrayed by an *ami*, possibly both her ex-boyfriend and now ex-friend have left for Paris, where possibly he has joined the *gendarme*. Then again, I may well have possibly got all this quite wrong.

After her other client leaves, I notice she writes a cheque to pay. I always find it interesting that cheques are still used so frequently in France. You see people writing them everywhere; in the *supermarché*, in restaurants and *le bricolage*.

I return home and my last Monday ends with cutting back our lavender plants. It is surreal that in just a week I will have had my first day back at school. It is immensely satisfying meanwhile to do something so pleasurable in the garden; not something I ever imagined doing in my life; cutting my own lavender in my own French *jardin*. As my fingers brush against the stalks, the aroma wafts around me in a fragrant cloud. By the time I finish, my round, woven French market basket is full. I take it inside and the pungent freshness of summer fills our *petite maison*. I wonder if there will be any lingering remnants of it when we return in a year.

The rain-soaked windows echo our own emotions about leaving; hearts heavy at the thought of not seeing our *petite maison* for another year. Yet the sadness is balanced by the prospect of reunions — our beloved Henri, family, friends and my students, who always stay in a corner of my heart. I think of many of them while working in *le jardin*. I wonder if any of them will ever follow in my footsteps and one day find themselves in a *petite* village in rural France. Who knows? The seeds have been sown.

New *Amis*

On the eve of departure, we make new *amis* in our village. Jan and her little boy, Arthur stop on their daily *promenade* for a chat and she invites us for an *apéritif* the following evening. She tells us that when she was young, she was friends with Jean Pierre who lived in our house. I then find out that Pied de la Croix did not get a bathroom until the seventies.

Jan's *maison* is in the quiet lane behind our house. It is one we have admired. On one of our evening *promenades* we had seen the extended family, gathered round tables in *le jardin* for a summer reunion and *dîner*. At the time, I had thought once again, like many other vignettes, how much it too was just like a scene in a French film — and now, we too have been invited. I ask Jan to let her mother know that we had glimpsed the whole family gathered in *le jardin* one evening, when I peeped over the hedge and that I had already felt entranced by the generations, ensconced deep in the French countryside. Jan assures me that we will be part of those gatherings in future years. I feel profoundly touched.

Jan tells us she has been having summer holidays in Cuzance since she was a child in the seventies, when her mother first bought the house. While we are still deep in rural France, the last fifty years have seen significant changes. When she was a child, there was no water in the village. Everyone had to drive to Martel to collect their water. However, in those days, there were two shops in Cuzance. One, now Brigitte Dal's house, where the old scales for weighing are still in place, and the other, the room overlooking our village road, that Françoise now uses to iron. I learn from Jan that Françoise and Jean-Claude's *magnifique maison* is referred to by the locals as 'the castle'. I can well understand that, for I remember being awestruck when we first visited their fairytale home.

Apéritifs with Jan and her *mère,* Margot are served in their utterly secluded *jardin* that is surrounded by lauriers and susurrus pines. Unlike our house and barn, their *grange* was built first, followed by the *maison* in later years. Arthur swoops upon Stuart and parades his collection of toys for him to admire. The talk flows over *foie gras* and sweet white wine, served in delicate wine glasses that were Jan's great-grandmother's. Whenever we have *apéritifs or dîner* with friends, it is the same. The treasured family heirlooms are a part of everyday life, not *objets* to be locked away. Even *petite* Arthur has his orange juice in an exquisite old glass.

Jan tells us that we are 'famous' in the village. It is very flattering but quite a surprise to us. We did know however, that the inhabitants of Cuzance have long been intrigued about why we come from so far each year, to this little corner of France and then spend our days working endlessly. Nevertheless, it is pleasing to be told that everyone appreciates and admires our efforts.

What thrills me the most as we chat about life in the village, is to be told that in fact, our *petite maison* hid *Résistance* fighters. This has long been my dream that this was the case. To have it confirmed by Margot, who has been living between Paris and Cuzance for fifty years, creates a feeling that I can hardly describe. Perhaps in part it explains the warmth our little house exudes; that it played a small part in preserving freedom. I think about the long-abandoned cross hanging on a chain in the attic — a relic that I will never remove. I now wonder even more about it and to whom it belonged.

So the *la grange* of our new *amis* and our *petite maison* are linked, just as we are forging a new friendship, for we are also told that their barn was a repository for British bombs. I try hard to peer into the past to catch a glimpse of the valour of the brave men and women who fought stealthily to save Cuzance — and France.

The layers of history and intriguing insights shared over our *apéritifs,* extend far beyond Cuzance. I am particularly fascinated by Margot's stories, hinted at, but not fully revealed. I am assured that the gaps in between will be filled in for me when we all gather again in the summers to come. Most mysteriously there are allusions to an exotic childhood in Morocco and Algeria. All Margot will let slip is that her father was an American in the army. She and Jan exchange glances. My curiosity has now been fully fuelled.

The other piece of this French family puzzle that I am captivated by is when Margot tells us that long ago, she lived in London, where she worked as a French teacher and was friends with one of the last suffragettes, Josephine Butler. I asked her if she had met Emmiline Pankhurst and although she had not, Josephine was a close friend of hers. Who would have thought that I would ever learn such things in Cuzance? We may be far from Paris yet it makes me wonder even more about the older villagers who would also have more than their fair share of stories about the war, the *Résistance* and all the turbulent changes as a new century dawned. It saddens me that quite soon, all their stories will be lost forever.

For months after we return home, I think about whether our *la grange* or our *petite maison* housed British airmen or members of the *maquis,* French *Résistance* fighters. The seams of stories held in the stones are locked in the past. What I do know is that there are many barns and farmhouses like ours that bear witness to remarkable feats of bravery and courage. French farmers, and countless others like them, risked their lives and for the most part, their acts of selfless heroism are lost forever.

Spending time at Pied de la Croix for weeks on end, we create our own little world within the small world of the village. We work according to the weather — the heat, the rain, the damp days. We work according to what the land tells us to do. Clear brambles, move rocks and pick fruit when it is ripe. It is a life like no other I have known. It provides me with a glimpse into the past, some small insight into the life of famers then and now, and how all in a rural landscape adjust their daily pattern and rhythm according to the weather and the season. The days start to circle us like covered Indian wagons from long ago.

As we make our way home slowly through the village, after our final *promenade* for the summer, in the fading light after another endless hot summer's day, the few villagers not yet tucked up in bed, gently call out, '*Bonne nuit*' and '*Bonne soirée.*' The bell tolls at ten, the last peal drawn out to ensure that all know the day has ended; for us, it is the last evening chime of the church bell we will hear until next year. The silver sliver of a new quarter-moon hangs suspended from an invisible thread in the clear country Cuzance sky. It has been a three full-moon summer for us, a true marking of the measure of time immersed in our other life. The curtain closes on another chapter; another comforting day in the peace and quiet of our *petite* rural village — Cuzance.

Au Revoir Cuzance

Although there are discernible glimpses of autumn, August also sees the full surge of summer in Cuzance. The grass, crisp and brittle, crackles underfoot. Long loving letters arrive from home and my worlds again collide and merge. As I glide through the long summer grass in the cool early morning, I watch with delight the *lapin* bound through the orchard. I tell myself to hold on to these moments in the days of work and winter at home. If I had to recall the one strongest visual image to imprint on my memory, it would be the golden quality of the late evening light when our little world is suffused in a pale pink glow. And if there was only one sensory image to capture the essence of Cuzance, it would be the utter stillness of the country, overlaid by a soft chorus of birdsong.

By our third summer in Cuzance, our sense of belonging coalesces. Our rhythm and sense of familiarity with our French world brings endless joy. We are now well known in the string of shops we frequent in Martel — *la boulangerie, la pharmacie,* Le Bureau de Poste and our favourite *café*, Mespoulet, the one that the locals frequent. We now favour only two stallholders on our twice-weekly market visits — our jolly family of three and the man who only sells berries: raspberries, strawberries, and red currants, and just before we leave, blueberries come into season. The pungent aroma fills the centuries-old covered market place. When I ask for my favourite weekly punnet of *fraise*, the stallholder takes the time to suggest I also try the vivid blue-purple blueberries. I am not disappointed by the recommendation. I have high hopes of being greeted by all, as customers of long-standing, when we return for our fourth summer.

My only sadness is knowing that, as the years pass, so too will some of the older inhabitants of Cuzance. Though my encounters with them are brief, the fleeting moments and short exchanges, bring a layer of richness through the sense of times past that their eyes have seen — the impact of the war, the rapid changes in the world and daily life of the village — and yet an air of timelessness pervades their unhurried pace. The days and seasons seem to ebb and flow around them; Monsieur and Madame's Chanteur's daily meals under their walnut tree, Madame Dal's daily *promenades* with her beloved *chien*, Monsieur Arnal's customary seat outside his hotel, watching our *petite* village go by; Jean-Claude's strolls with Henriette, tugging at her lead, impatient to explore her new world.

The very land and buildings seem to hold history within their hands, offered as a gift if you peer inside the old carved stone doorways, beyond the pots of scarlet geraniums and aromatic lavender. It is a strange paradox, a summer in Cuzance. The days slip through your fingers like a rapidly unravelling ball of wool, yet time also stands still. There is an almost tangible thread woven through the village, that connects the past and stretches to the future.

A Night in Paris

There was a ferocious thunderstorm, complete with icy bullets of hail on our last morning. It was a portent of the swiftly changing season. It would also transpire to be an omen for our last day in France.

A night in Paris was not quite like our morning in Paris. Far from it. It was not planned, it was not on the itinerary. A night in Paris probably most exemplifies the differences between us; Stuart's casual nonchalant approach to life and mine — often the diametric opposite.

We packed up the house and put it under wraps for another year, with literally just seconds to spare before Jean-Claude, Françoise and of course Henriette picked us up. First step of the always long and arduous return journey, Brive-la-Gaillarde station for the four-hour trip to Paris. Just prior to our departure, Monsieur and Madame Chanteur came to farewell us with a gift of *prunier* from their tree, for our journey. I had no inkling that it was the last time we would ever see them together.

After parking, in one of those split-second accidental timings, just as I reached for my suitcase, Jean-Claude closed the boot. It connected directly with my nose as I was bending down. There was no hint, bad enough as it was, that there was infinitely more stress, calamity and drama about to unfold.

Our timing was quite fine as it was. A mere three hours to get a taxi from Gare d'Austerlitz to Charles de Gaulle airport, with the mandatory two hours — minimum — check-in time for our flight. This is Stuart's relaxed travel style, not mine. I already knew that the tight timeline did not allow for any unanticipated events. I was anxious already. What in fact happened was beyond prediction in any scenario of unforeseen circumstances. It was the sort of event that you cannot possibly make up, let alone imagine.

French trains travel fast, very fast — about 198 miles per hour. The Société Nationale des Chemins de fer Français is renowned for its swift, efficient service. If a train is running two minutes late, it is a cause for considerable consternation. I was sitting next to the window, unusual in itself for Stuart usually has the window seat. I was bidding France farewell, watching the rich green countryside, villages and farms flash past.

Out of nowhere, a heavy shower of enormous rocks flew up against the entire width of the window in a deafening roar. The thunder of the impact echoed around the carriage. Large, star-shaped imprints were left in the thick glass. I grabbed Stuart's hands, and in utter silence, looked at him in fear and incredulity. It is astonishing what the mind can process in a matter of a few, sharply delineated seconds. I was convinced the train was going to roll. I thought that the end was near. Much later, when chatting to others in our three-hour state of entrapment, I discovered it was precisely what others thought too. I believed our train crash was going to be a leading item on the evening news.

The train jolted to a shuddering, clanging halt. Each and every passenger gasped aloud. We all looked at each other in shock and disbelief. There was then an eerie calm and quietness. Despite the alarming circumstances, there was no sense of panic at all

The first of many SNCF announcements followed shortly. A delightful 16-year-old French school boy, Leo, travelling with his younger sister, Claudette, was sitting near us and became our self-appointed interpreter. First, 'The train will be delayed.' Next, 'The train will be delayed indefinitely.' And then, infinitely more alarming, 'The train has been sabotaged.' The very use of the word 'sabotaged' sent a chill of horror through the carriage. All I could think was that it was a very grave word to use — the implications were endless.

We all waited — for an interminable three hours. What struck me most was the extraordinary calm and degree of patience of those around us; the young, elderly, women with babies and *petite enfants*. As the electricity had failed, the air conditioning did not work. The temperature rose steadily while we were told that negotiations were underway to resolve the situation. Stuart walked through to the next carriage to investigate. It was at precisely this point that the two adjoining carriages were disconnected. I jumped out of my seat to see where he was. We could see each other through the glass doors at the end of each carriage. Later, he told me that he thought the carriage he was in was going to be shunted off and we would be separated for who knows how long and with no means of communicating.

Once again too, as with many major and critical times in our lives, our *portable* let us down. This seems to be a recurring dilemma for any hugely significant juncture in our lives. Initially it did work for our first contact to our helpline in Cuzance. We had just enough charge left to place a panicked call to Françoise to explain our predicament. *Oui, oui,* she immediately grasped our dilemma and arranged to call the airline. We felt confident that in her capable hands, all would be sorted. *Portable* charge ebbing, we soon called her again, highly anxious to know that it was all organised. Yes, she had contacted the airline; yes, all should be fine to transfer our tickets. All we needed to do was call the airline by 10pm to confirm that we had to change our flight to the following day. Françoise could no longer communicate with us either for our phone was now dead.

Next, the source of the sabotage was identified. The hydraulics for the brakes were located in a section underneath the train. The brakes had failed. Steel rods had been placed on the tracks to stop the train and cause damage. It did not help matters for our future travel plans by train in France to be told by Leo, that this was apparently a frequent occurrence while travelling on SNCF. Whether he meant trains breaking down or actual sabotage, I did not enquire further.

Finally, a replacement train arrived. We were all moved off, carriage by carriage — eight in all — in a very orderly manner. Previously, while Stuart was trapped, the train driver had nevertheless been able to walk through each carriage, explaining to everyone what had happened and what would eventuate. I was struck too by how calm and contained and capable he seemed. I was also astonished that I stood out as the only foreigner in our carriage and that, despite his huge degree of responsibility and inordinate stress he must have been under, the train driver paused to explain the situation to me personally.

Yet again, it was like a scene from a movie. This time, however, one I would not have chosen to be in. However, this time we were in it. We had to hand our luggage down and then gingerly descend the steep steps, supported at the bottom by an SNCF person on each side to help us jump down. Despite the arms that gripped me firmly, it was still quite a jolt landing on the tracks. I wondered how the many elderly passengers coped, for it was quite a long way down to the tracks. On the replacement train, there was another SNCF worker, who grabbed each of us by our arms to haul us up.

Finally, we sped in to Paris — there was only about forty minutes left of the journey. It passed quickly as we were all given a cardboard box with water and packets of food in it. We needed it by then, for it was almost midnight in Paris when at long last we pulled into Gare d'Austerlitz — an entirely different world to the bustling daytime hours when the station is full of travellers setting off across to the four corners of Europe.

Thirty of us then waited for another two, very long hours. At first,

SNCF seemed to be very organised, taking everyone's name and a note of our destinations. Our initial high hopes of the situation being sorted soon rapidly faded. Another hour elapsed and by this point, passengers returned to the counter, impatient for results. By now, the organisation at the outset, seemed to have disintegrated. There was much consulting of lists and scurrying back and forth to an office with a closed door. Some passengers simply gave up, and walked off in to the Paris night.

Then at last, we were given a taxi voucher and told we had been booked into an airport hotel, 'All Seasons'. Another SNCF employee took us to the taxi rank and twelve hours after leaving our little house, we were on our way for a few hours' sleep. Now I don't have a good sense of direction at the best of times, but on the virtually empty roads of Paris, in the pre-dawn hours, even I knew the taxi driver was going round in circles, back and forth past the same myriad of airport hotels. The French to tell the taxi driver this was absolutely beyond either of us at this point in our convoluted and dramatic return home. The Ibis Hotel turned out in fact to be our destination; it was actually one and the same as 'All Seasons' though there was not a sign in sight to indicate this. However, our ordeal was not quite over.

The taxi driver was clearly annoyed and frustrated by this turn of events. He helped us into the hotel with our luggage, eager to be paid and off into the early morning. As we checked in at the counter, it transpired that he did not accept SNCF taxi vouchers. Apparently only blue taxis take them. His taxi was not blue.

We simply slumped in weary resignation against the reception counter. We had run out of energy to deal with another obstacle. The taxi driver's infuriation was growing by the second. To our enormous relief, the night manager called SNCF and got a fax sent that he presented to the taxi driver. He was to then take it to SNCF to be paid. He walked off into the night without a backward glance — still furious. We booked a wake-up call for only a matter of hours away. We needed to get to the airport as early as possible to sort our flight out. Rumbling snores that heavily penetrated the paper-thin walls of our hotel room, were the concluding note to our protracted journey, still in France when we should have been in Abu Dhabi.

We may well have been in Paris for our last evening but in reality we were in a cultural wasteland, a sea of bland, identical airport hotels. There were no smoky, late night jazz bars, no enticing bistros, there was nothing, nothing at all. It was not quite the last night in Paris that dreams are made of.

Apéritifs at Three in the Morning

After the stressful, exhausting chain of events, and despite the improbably late hour, a drink was called for. While we are not mini-bar people, this was a mini-bar occasion. The basic airport hotel room did not run to one. We returned to reception and in imploring tones, we asked the hotel night staff on the front desk, 'Do you have a bar?'

'*Non*,' was the sombre response.

Were they serious? Absolutely everyone drinks absolutely everywhere in France. And now it would seem, we were booked into the only hotel in France without a bar. We were in a hotel airport wilderness. Not a bar in sight. Could this truly be Paris, the city of dreams?

'Where can we get a drink then?' we gasped out. It was now 3 am. At the Hotel Western across the road, we were told. We staggered out into the cold dark night, not a vestige of Paris in the air. We staggered into the hotel as four *gendarme* walk briskly out onto the desolate streets. The staff on the desk were the only other people around. We repeated our question, 'Is your bar still open?'

'*Non*,' we were told.

Back to the empty cold streets, up to our room for the one *petite* bottle of wine we had left over from our disastrous train journey, out to the street again. We collapse on a bench to be approached by the only other person possibly awake in the whole of Paris: a derelict who tried to engage us in conversation. None of this could possibly be happening. We politely dispatched him; a shared *apéritif*, albeit warm, never tasted so good.

Bon Voyage — At Last

And so, to the airport. The queue for our flight already stretched in such a way that we knew it would be foolish to simply join it, and naively assume that the transfer organised by Françoise had all been smoothly put in place. There are some lessons you do learn in life that stand true the world over; not to trust the mechanisms of bureaucracy. How true this proved.

We did not join the check-in queue. Instead we prudently found an enquiry counter. There was of course just one person on the counter where we needed to check if we were on the flight, due to leave shortly — very shortly. And of course too, the queue was long, very long. At the best of times, patience is not one of my virtues; this was not the best of times by a long shot. Time was flying — and it did not seem as if we would be. It was time to act.

I left Stuart in the queue, the one which was not moving at all. I was on a desperate quest for an information counter and, hopefully, help. I presented my urgent case and was able to use their phone to, ironically, call the airline at the airport where we were. It seemed to be the only course of action. I needed to talk to someone directly — and now. Naturally, the airline representative I got through to was cast in a thoroughly bureaucratic mould. There was no hint of empathy, no vestige of sympathy for our plight. *Non, non,* I was crisply informed, we had not called by 10pm the previous night as we had been directed to do after Françoise explained our situation to the airline. No amount of explaining that we were trapped in a sabotaged train and that we had in fact called the office, to be met by a recorded message that simply told us officiously that the office was shut, elicited any hint of understanding. In the eyes of officialdom, we had failed to call and we would need to buy another ticket. No entreaty, no emotional pleading worked.

In tears of frustration and exhaustion, I ended the call. I returned to find Stuart had mercifully advanced to the head of the queue. In his calm, competent manner, he had sorted it. We were on the flight. Elated, with minutes to spare, we booked our luggage in and stumbled onto the plane.

This was not how we were meant to leave France, but leaving we were. Finally we arrived home within the last few hours of Stuart's birthday. Oddly enough, months later, Stuart seems to have glossed over the high level of drama we experienced, for he downloads the distinctive SNCF train announcement tune as his ringtone. Strangely, for both of us, whenever his mobile rings, the SNCF tune makes us both smile. (These chapters, courtesy of SNCF.)

Life at Home, Again

When we return home it always takes a while to adjust to the cadence and pace of our other life and work again. Yet eventually we pick up the rhythm of our life at home and immerse ourselves in all that is wonderful in our seaside village and satisfying in our working lives. In the two reflected halves of our lives, renovating continues at home which, I have to confess, I am by now quite weary of. Truth be told, my renovating days are really long over and yet we always buy homes, both here and in our *petite* corner of France, that seem to need a tremendous amount of work. I often wonder when it will end. Right now, the end is certainly not in sight.

Meanwhile too, there are still things in Cuzance to manage from afar. Fortunately no longer quite as challenging as buying a car by email or indeed installing a pool by email. But there is the matter of managing the *maçon* not to mention coordinating Jean-Louis' work in removing the tiles on our dilapidated outbuilding. This has to be done to tie in with the *maçon* as he will repair the roof after Jean-Louis has removed the tiles. Of course I cannot communicate with either of them directly as I lack the French to do so and they do not speak English. Jean-Claude's inordinate kindness leads him to again to be my intermediary. Since I have decided to hand over virtually all renovating responsibilities at home to Stuart, I enter once again into a flurry of emails with Jean-Claude to ensure all is in hand.

This time it is critical that as much is in place before Jean-Claude and Françoise close up Le Vieux Priory, which they do every year on November fifteenth.

Hello, I had put off answering you because I hoped to have something positive to tell you; but alas...

I met Jean-Louis in Martel on Saturday and he confessed he had not yet mailed you ... I think he's a bit afraid of computers but he assured me the roof would be attended to since he had already arranged it viva voce with Stuey!

Apparently, your maçon came to fetch the keys to la petite maison but although I was there, I did not perceive his ringing. Fortunately someone had witnessed his attempt and told me he would be back this evening (if again we can't make contact, I'll phone him).

I also have to tell you that the Hotel Arnal is going out of business since Chantal is retiring and fired her son earlier in the year and anyway their equipment is superannuated; they would like to set up a coffee-bar cum small shop for bread and other items. However, there is little hope, since they are still living on the premises...

The weather is freezing, with fog, but it will be sunny when we leave on Thursday for Lyon, which is a good thing, since I little appreciated the trip under snow three years ago!

Love to the three of you in warmer climes, JCC.

As I read this, I feel great jubilation that the Hotel Arnal is changing hands, for it has long been another cherished dream that a keen young chef from Paris may one day take over. Once again, as with so many elements of my life, I indulge in fanciful daydreams, that the hotel literally right on our doorstep, will become a gastronomical destination of note. Ah, I see it now; the enviable *menu du jour,* the hungry young chef, eager to impress and woo new clients. Failing this, a coffee-bar or small shop for *pain* is almost as enticing, for our daily source of bread is one of our big dilemmas. Oh, if only life was always so easy that it was reduced to the simple concern as to the procuring of our daily *pain*. This thought too is very appealing. A matter of a minute's stroll to a coffee shop where the locals linger convivially. The tempting thought too of fresh pastries a stone's throw away is highly alluring. It will be with enormous excitement that I wait for Jean-Claude's return to Cuzance the following March to keep me informed about such potentially promising developments.

And then there is more fascinating news.

I put off answering you again because I was waiting for your maçon (whom I'd phoned) to come and collect your keys; this being done, I am now free to write ... and thank you for your cheque which arrived yesterday — your mûrier-platanes have now lost all their leaves and stand tall on your grounds covered with white frost!

Concerning Arnal's replacement, the Rodez grocer (in the shed not far from us), objects to a general store being added as unwanted competition. However, the citizens of Cuzance will certainly do something to offset Baladou's own projects. By the way, concerning projects, when walking Henriette, I saw that the work on Maison de la Truffe is quite advanced and no doubt it will be finished when you arrive next year!

So across the miles, there is not only news of progress with the *maçon* collecting the keys to install my longed-for bathroom window, but news too of our newly planted trees. I thought too it was wonderful that when Jean-Claude emailed me previously that news of the *maçon's* visit in his absence had reached him via the close watch on all comings and goings in our village. Now, there is something else to follow up on that I am intrigued by, for I am not quite sure what the *Maison de la Truffe* is though I think it is the *très cher* truffle restaurant on the outskirts of Cuzance that we have not been to. In such a small village, there certainly always seems to be a lot going on. As for the nearby village of Baladou, what mysterious events are afoot there? More investigation on my part is required. I shall probe Jean-Claude when next we are in touch.

Thank goodness too for the new addition to their family of Henriette. Her numerous walks means that Jean-Claude is out and about even more frequently, with his sleuthing cap on, ready to investigate all new developments — and by default, convey it all to me on the other side of the world as it unfolds, piece by piece. It seems to me at times like my own personal viewing platform, perched on the other side of the world, and yet, through Jean-Claude's eyes, I never feel too far away. The daily intrigue and drama of village life could never be imagined. Who truly knew so much could ever possibly happen? The inhabitants may all verge on the side of very old and yet, they never seem to simply watch from the sidelines. Well, perhaps a twitching lace curtain or two at times, to fuel the otherwise slow pace of life in a *petite* village.

Email Friendships from Afar

Across the oceans and the seasons, emails keep our friendships alive from afar. They bring joyous news; they bring fascinating news. In early December we hear from Françoise that their daughter, Bénédicte, is going to have a baby. This has long been Françoise's dream, especially as Bénédicte has returned to Lyon to live with Maxim and it is where Jean-Claude and Françoise spend the long winter months. More splendidly for us, is that the baby is due when we arrive in Lyon to stay with them. It will be the first French baby I have ever known!

In his inimitable fashion, despite the fact that it is the eve of *Noël*, when the family gathers in Lyon from Berlin and Paris for Christmas, Jean-Claude has embarked on the ambitious project of installing a *rouge cuisine* in their Lyon apartment. In transcontinental links, as their news flows in so too the weekend paper has an article featuring Lyon. I plan where I will shop and eat and the sights we will see when we stay with them the following summer. To my amazement, the very street they live on is mentioned as a feature of Lyon — rue Victor Hugo. The very name has an altogether marvellous ring to it. Shortly after reading about the delights of Lyon, I hear again from Françoise to let me know that a vintage clothes shop has just opened on rue Victor Hugo. This is my idea of heaven. To simply saunter along the actual street where we will be staying and explore a shop brimming with vintage French clothes. And while we love Cuzance, the thought too of just slipping out in the early morning to the *boulangerie* on their doorstep, for *petit déjeuner* treats, is another source of enormous excitement. More accurately in fact, it means that Stuart will be despatched to buy the freshly-baked *baguette* and crisp *croissants*. I am sure that he will take *petite* Henriette to trot along by his side. If I buy him a beret, he will look like the quintessential Frenchman.

In our Australian summer, I picture the Chanel family gathered in Lyon for *Noël*. A Christmas far from our own, where we spend the day at the beach. Once again, my imagination takes flight and the vividness of it allows me to visualise them all quite clearly. I see the snow-covered streets decorated with festive lights, the snowflakes tumbling and twirling as if on cue to add to the Christmas spirit. I see the shops brightly decorated, the piles of fresh pine trees spilling out of them on to the icy pavement, ready to be whisked away by families eager to festoon them with decorations that are generations-old. I smell the cinnamon of freshly-baked *Noël* treats, I see the warmly-wrapped crowds gathered for carols. And while I simply loathe cold weather, my heart longs to be there, just once, to be in the folds of a French family for the festive season. Perhaps one day soon, when there will be a *petite enfant* to add to the joy of a French family Christmas, we will have a French *Noël*.

Just as Christmas is round the corner, Gérard and Dominique surprise us by sending photos of Cuzance adorned in snow and decorations. They again give us a glimpse into life in our village in a season that we will never know. The *Marie* is lit up brightly with *Noël* lights and they also adorn the black wrought iron street lamps. The snow blankets the fields in a pristine quilt of fresh crispness. They have also sent us photos of our *petite maison*. It is not bedecked with *Noël* lights or decorations. It looks abandoned and sad, sitting alone in its isolated wintery landscape.

Epilogue

The turmoil of such journeys does of course recede and now, once again, the future is a bright and shining road, full of French summer adventures and Cuzance delights. The arrival of Christmas and the imminence of another new year, marks our own personal calendar, for it signifies our countdown when our other life beckons on the horizon.

No matter how many times we return in future years, Cuzance will always remain in the subset of life's surreal experiences. Having a *petite maison* is not something ordinary people do. And yet, we have. It is for that reason, however frequently we fly away to France, that I will never cease to marvel at the sheer wonder of it all.

The last of the summer sunlight stains the orchard in a pink-gold tinge. The last of the season's swallows shoot like arrows across the deepening shadows on *la piscine*. The bucolic cluster of outbuildings cast off the day's heat and settle down to slumber peacefully. I think though that they miss the days when they sheltered squealing baby piglets that snuffled in the stone troughs, the only remnants now of their long-gone presence. The air in the country has a perpetual tinge of manure, farm animals and freshly mown hay. There is a palpable smell that I associate with Cuzance like nowhere else in the world. The late evening stillness is like a light summer eiderdown, thrown gently across the tapestry of the rural landscape.

When Jean-Claude and Françoise leave Cuzance each November to return to Lyon until the following March, without his stewardship our *petite maison* slumbers all alone through the long, cold, lonely winter. Now, even more so than usual, our little house lies in wait behind the heavy wooden shutters. Its warm beating heart will not fully awaken until we return each summer. Our love and laughter, and that of our friends and family, fills it instantly with warmth. It is only then its sleeping state is fully awakened once again. On our return visits each year, I feel that we are no longer just simply reaching for the stars; we're pulling them out of the sky.

To paraphrase Humphrey Bogart in *Casablanca*, 'We'll always have Cuzance.' And so the years will continue to unfold, and so the work will continue. Each return will bring a renewed celebration of friendship and celebration of all that we love about *vive la* France.

Driving on the *autoroute* to Brive, there is a sign to Paris. Every time I see it, it never fails to thrill me. However, what I also know, whenever I see the sign, is that Paris is 500 kilometres away. While I adore Paris above all other cities, it's true — our house is not in Paris. And for that, I am glad.

Fin

Acknowledgments

- My Mumma.
- Dave, who read *Our House is Not in Paris*, while we were in Cuzance, to 'be with us in spirit'.
- Ros and Kerry — colleagues, friends, my trusted first readers, *très merci beaucoup*.
- To Georgia, and the Hughes family, *très merci beaucoup* for taking care of *petite* Henri — and loving him.
- My 'library children' and their parents, both now and from the past — thank you all so much for your interest, support and encouragement with both my books.
- To our friends and family who have already shared our *petite* corner of France and those who will one day stay with us in Pied de la Croix.
- To all my readers, *merci beaucoup* for sharing our French adventure, some of you, for the second time. Thank you ever so much for your interest in our continuing journey on the other side of the world.
- Melbourne Books — for the opportunity to publish my second memoir.
- And of course most of all, Stuey, who doesn't just dream but makes dreams come true. (And all before turning fifty!) And of course, your superb proofread, the map and glossary. *Merci encore* — for simply everything.

- To Stuey:

'He said. Twenty years from now you will be more disappointed by the things you didn't do than by the ones you did do. So throw off the bowlines. Sail away from the safe harbour. Catch the trade winds in your sails. Explore. Dream. Discover.'
— Mark Twain

And you did. And you do. And you will.

Glossary of French words

A

abricot	apricot	**arrêtez-vous**	stop
amie	friend	**artisan**	tradesman
amuse-bouche	bite-sized hors d'œuvre	**assiettes**	plates
andouillette	tasty French sausage	**attention**	be careful
anniversaire	anniversary/birthday	**au revoir**	goodbye
apéritif	pre-dinner drink	**auberge**	inn
appétit	as in bon appetit	**autoroute**	motorway
armoire	wardrobe	**Avez-vous...?**	Do you have...?

B

baba au rhum	rum baba (tasty dessert)	**bonne soirée**	have a good evening
baguette	French stick	**bonsoir**	good evening
bain	bath	**bouche**	mouth
bal	honey	**bougie**	candle/spark plug
beaucoup	lots of/many	**boulangerie**	bakery
beurre	butter	**boules**	bowls
blanche	white	**bourg**	town
bon courage	good luck	**bricolage**	hardware shop
bon/bonne	good	**brioche**	brioche, sweet bun
bonjour	hello	**brocante**	antique shop
bonne nuit	goodnight	**bureau**	office or desk

C

café	coffee or cafe	**Carrefour**	a supermarket chain
campagne	the countryside	**carte**	card/map
canard	duck	**castine**	fine gravel
canicule	scorching heat	**cave**	cellar
caramélisé	caramelised	**cèpe**	tasty wild mushroom
caravane	procession	**cerise**	cherry

chaise	chair	combien	How much...?
chalet	chalet	commune	commune, district
chambre d'hôte	bed and breakfast	confit	food preserved in fat
chapeau	hat	confiture	jam
château	castle	connards	idiot
chaud	hot	coucou	colloquial hello
chic	stylish	couleur	colour
chien	dog	couper	to cut
chocolat	chocolate	couple	couple
chocolatier	chocolate maker	couture	dress making
chou	cabbage or sweetheart	crème brûlée	custard dessert
citron	lemon	crème glacée	ice cream
civilisation	civilisation	crêpe	crepe
clafoutis	clafouti, baked fruit dessert	croissant	tasty French pastry
coiffure	hairdresser	croix	religious cross
colon	settler	cuisine	kitchen

D

dégustation	tasting menu	deux	two
déjeuner	lunch	digestif	after dinner drink/liqueur
demi	half	dîner	dinner
département	French regional department	dinette	informal meal
derrière	behind	droit	right
désolé	sorry		

E

école	school	espadrilles	rope-soled sandal
enchante	pleasure to meet you	espresso	short black coffee
encore	again	Etam	department store
encroyable	incredible	euro	European currency
enfant	child	excusez-moi	excuse me
escargot	snail		

F

famille	family	flûte	long loaf
farine	flour	foie gras	duck or goose liver
ferme	shut/closed	forge	blacksmith's forge
fermier	farmer	fosse septique	septic tank
fête	celebration	fraise	strawberry
ficelle	string	frange	fringe (hair)
fin	the end	frites	chips
fleurs	flowers	fromage	cheese

G

gâteau	cake	glace	ice
gauche	left	grand(e)	big/large
gendarme	local police	grange	barn
girouette	weather vane	gratuite	free
gîte	B&B		

H

halles	covered market
herbes	weeds
hibou	owl

I

île flottante	meringue and custard dessert
Intermarché	a supermarket chain

J

j'aime	I like/I love	joli	pretty
jambon	ham	jour	day
jardin	garden	journal	newspaper
je	I	journée	day
Je m'appelle…	My name is…	jours	day (when counting)
je t'aime	I love you	jus	juice

L

l'histoire	history	lapin	rabbit
l'omelette	popular breakfast	le	the (masculine)
la	the (feminine)	les	the (plural)
La Dépêche	Regional newspaper	lettre	letter
l'addition	the bill at a café/restaurant	liqueur	liqueur
l'année	year	lycée	high school

M

macarons	macarons	marché	market
maçon	builder or stonemason	matériaux	materials (building)
madame	Mrs	méchoui	spit roast lamb
mademoiselle	Miss	melon	tasty French fruit
magnifique	magnificent	menu du jour	today's menu
Maire	Mayor	merci	thanks
mairie	town hall	merde	vulgar as exclamation
maison	house	mère	mother
maitre	ruler, master	moi	me
maman	mum	monsieur	Mister
maquis	French resistance	mouches	flies
marchands	shopkeeper, stallholder	mousse	mousse
marche	walk, march	musée	museum

N

noir	black
noix	walnut
non	no
nous	we
nouveau	new
nuit	night

O

objets	objects
oui	yes
outil	tool

P

pain	bread
pantalons	trousers
pastis	an alcoholic aniseed beverage
pâté	pate
pâtisserie	cake shop
pêche	peach or fishing
Périgord	an area in south-west France
personnes	people
petit(e)	small
pharmacie	chemist
pièce	piece
pied	foot
piscine	swimming pool
place	place
plage	beach
plat du jour	dish of the day
plombier	plumber
poisson	fish
pomme	apple
pompier	fireman
pont	bridge
portable	mobile phone
poste	post office
poulet	chicken
Préfecture	administrative area
prieuré	priory
problème	problem
prochaine	next
produits	products
projets	projects
promenade	to take a walk
prunier	plum tree

R

rapide	fast
refuses	to refuse
régionaux	regional
rénovation	renovation
rénover	renovate
résistance	the French resistance
rillettes	rustic pate
robe	dress

S

salle de bain	bathroom
salon	lounge
sanglier	wild boar
sapeurs-pompiers	fire brigade
sauvage	savage, uncivilized
seigle	rye
septique	septic tank
soirée	an evening function
solde	a sale
soufflet	bellows
sucrer	sugar
supermarché	supermarket

T

tabac	tobacconist's shop	toute	all
tarte	tart	très cher	very expensive
thermique	thermal	troc	second-hand shop
timbre	postage stamp	trois	three
toilette	toilet	truffe	truffle
tomate	tomato		

U

un chausson aux pommes — apple turnover

V

vacances	holidays	vive	long live
vanille	vanilla	voilà	there is…/there are…
vide-grenier	car-boot sale	voiture	car
vie	life	vous	you
vieux	old		
villages	villages		

The third book of the *Our House* series continues Susan and Stuart's renovation adventures in France. Read below for an extract from the first chapter of *Our House is Definitely Not in Paris*.

Packing for Paris

The first thing a woman usually thinks when she is heading for Paris is: 'What on earth will I wear?' After years of travelling — make that decades — I aim to finally get it just right.

First, the right bag. Now, while we had an embargo in our household on luggage-buying, I vetoed it — yes, again. And so the bright red Samonsite swivel case was bought. It is the travel bag of dreams. Next, the definitive backpack; must be smart, must be capacious. IKEA, of all places, provided the solution. It was Stuart's exultant find and he graciously gave it to me. The stylish zip-off day pack is truly the *pièce de résistance*.

Luggage sorted, it's on to the perfect travel wardrobe. This from the woman who trudged round Europe with the biggest portable wardrobe in the world on her back. Truth be told, I spend months planning the precise pieces for Paris. And yes, we've all read the articles — how to pack six items and create twenty-six outfits. These articles have been avidly devoured — and the advice subsequently ignored. But this time I am determined that, like my swivel case, heads will swivel to look at me. A lofty ambition indeed in the city of *chic* elegance.

There is no sight quite like it in the world, for a lover of fashion like myself, than to see a French woman strolling along the Champs-Élysées with such style and understated elegance. Their inimitable sense of *chic* is oh-so-casually contrived and yet oh-so-studiously studied. The Hermès scarf knotted ever so nonchalantly. The Christina Dior bag.

It is also to know and ruefully accept that no matter how hard I try, a lifetime would not be long enough to capture the incomparable *élan* of a French woman, and most definitely not one in Paris.

Months prior, I found a black and white Audrey Hepburn *chapeau* that had wire and would fold. Perfect. My Parisian wardrobe will consist entirely of clothes that can roll and unfurl into stylish ensembles, all black and white, of course. I declare jubilantly to Stuart that my new black jersey pants will take me anywhere, from a day of sightseeing and trips on the Seine to the quintessential Parisian bistro. A *noir* frock (or two), several white T-shirts, black turtleneck, black leggings, a long black tunic, black Birkenstocks for the daytime, silver slides for the evening, and just a dash of silver jewellery. A cute cardigan, and my oh-so-nonchalant Pierre Balmain scarf — a treasured find for a mere *euro* in a village *vide-grenier*. I'm set.

The first thing a man usually thinks when he is heading for Paris is: 'What will I eat?' Stuart's packing for Paris reflects his customary laid-back attitude to life. It is expressed in his nonchalant packing style: a couple of shirts, a few T-shirts, a pair of jeans and several pairs of shorts. I have to confess, however, that somehow his casual approach works. I am left wondering yet again about the profound difference in how I view life. How can he not have given the matter of what to wear in Paris endless deliberation? And yet, he effortlessly pulls off what I deem to be the desired look essential for a Parisian *sojourn*.

At the end of the day, though, I believe that I triumph in the Paris style stakes for, let's not forget, my esteemed vintage Guy Larouche trench coat, the ever-so-not-contrived *finissage* touch. Paris, I'm on my way!

www.ingramcontent.com/pod-product-compliance
Lightning Source LLC
Chambersburg PA
CBHW070529090426
42735CB00013B/2919